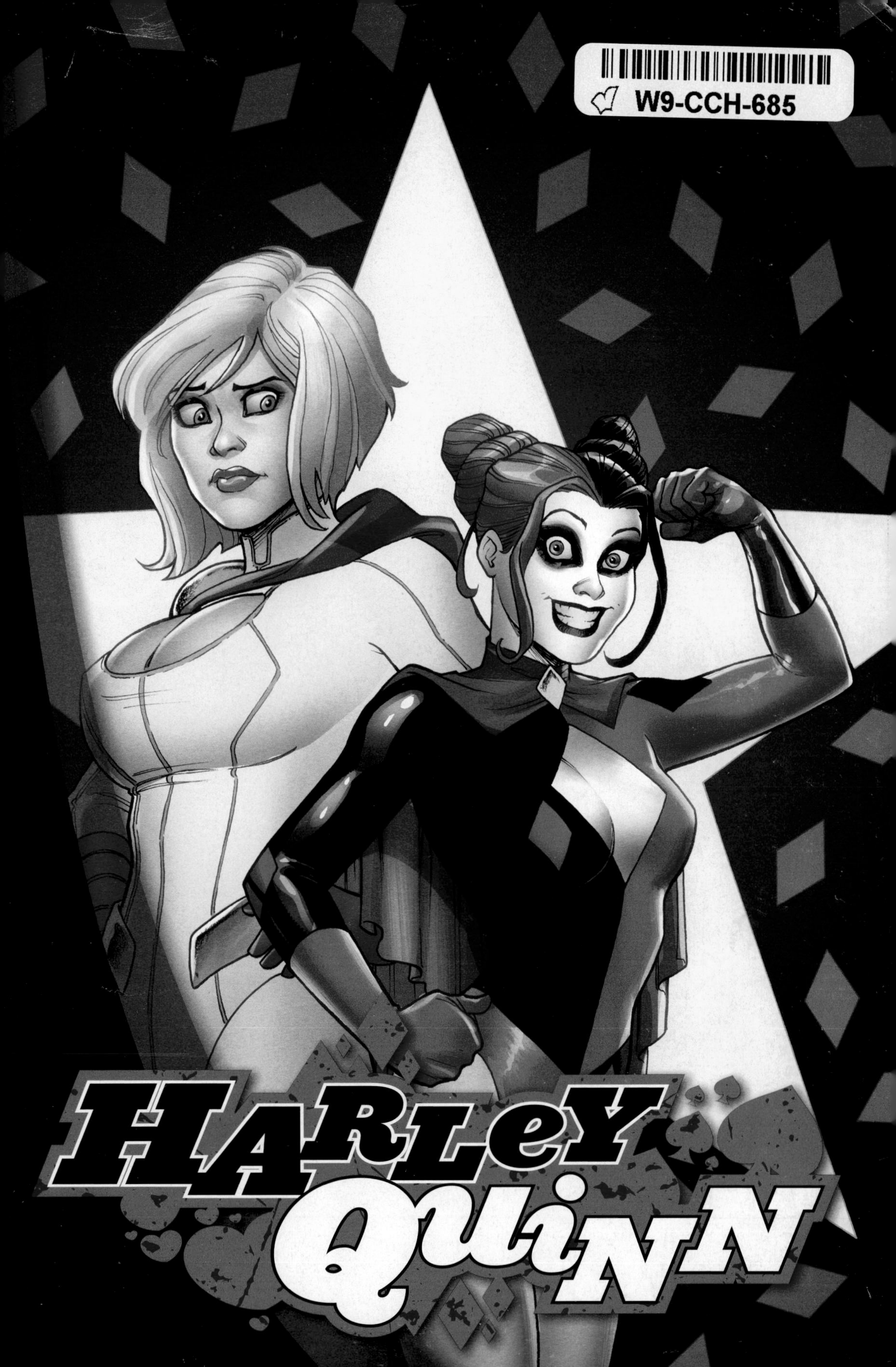

HARLEY QUINN

VOLUME 2 **POWER OUTAGE**

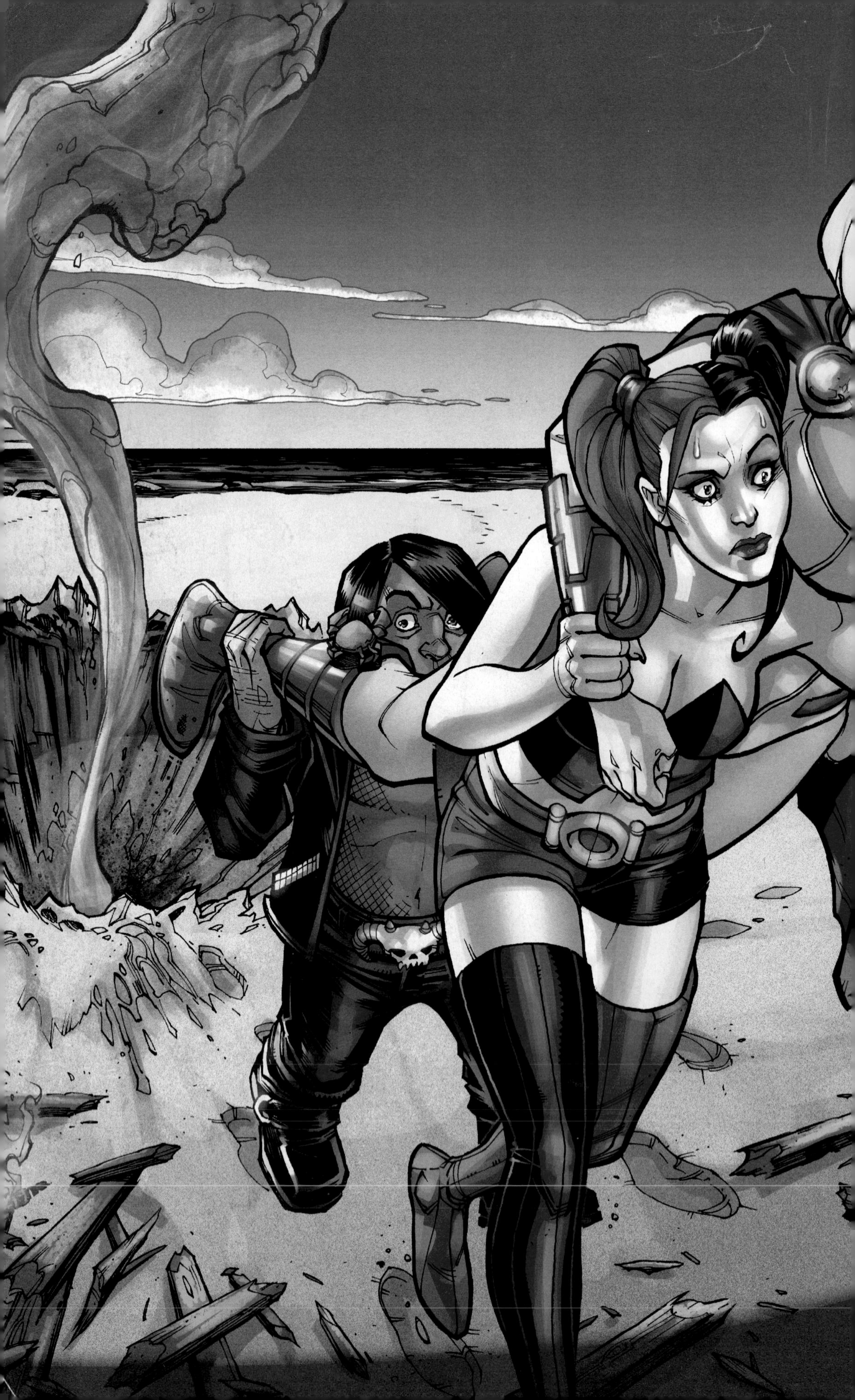

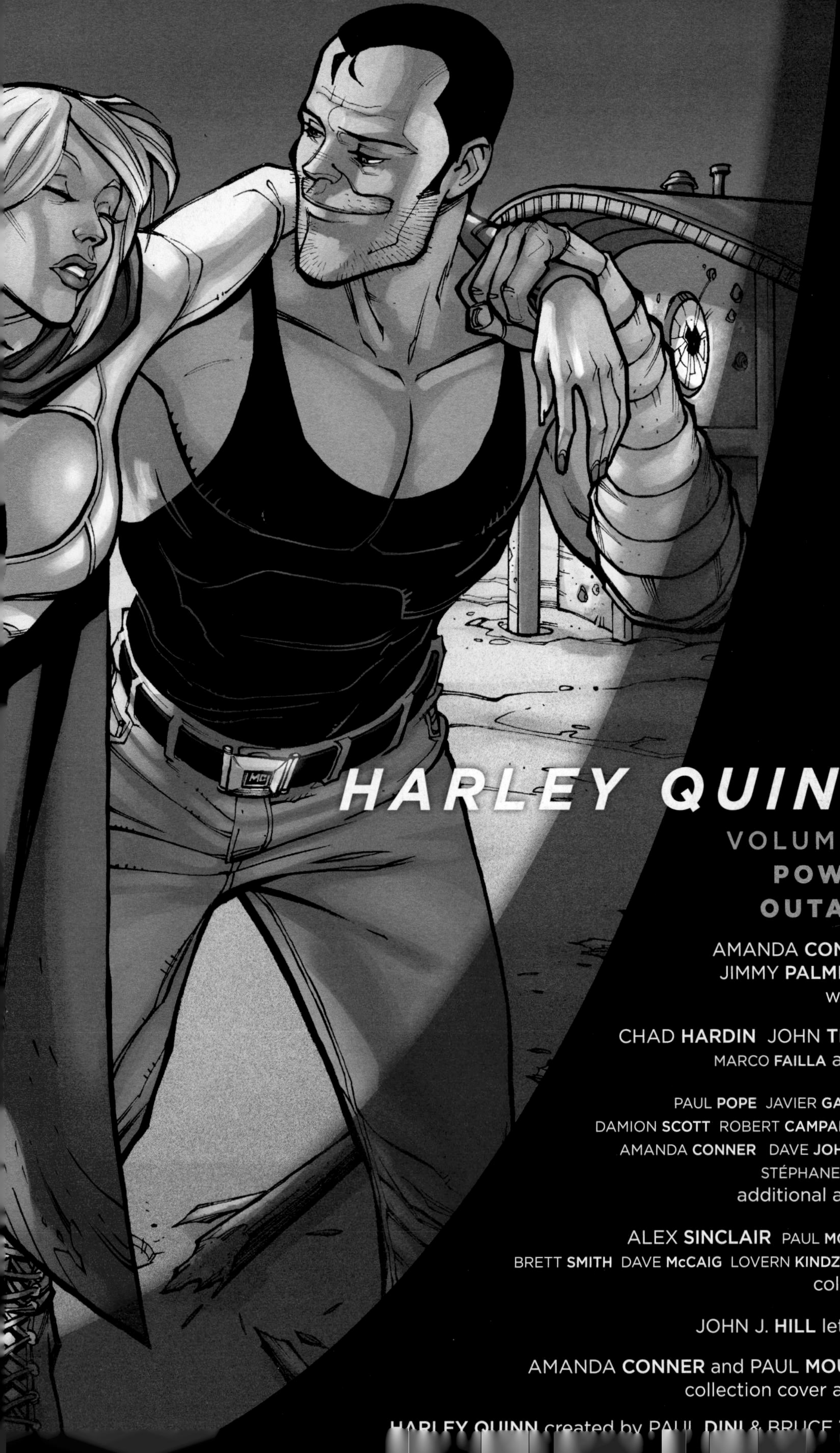

HARLEY QUINN

VOLUME 2
POWER OUTAGE

AMANDA **CONNER**
JIMMY **PALMIOTT**
writers

CHAD **HARDIN** JOHN **TIMMS**
MARCO **FAILLA** artists

PAUL **POPE** JAVIER **GARRÓN**
DAMION **SCOTT** ROBERT **CAMPANELLA**
AMANDA **CONNER** DAVE **JOHNSON**
STÉPHANE **ROUX**
additional artists

ALEX **SINCLAIR** PAUL **MOUNTS**
BRETT **SMITH** DAVE **McCAIG** LOVERN **KINDZIERSK**
colorists

JOHN J. **HILL** lettere

AMANDA **CONNER** and PAUL **MOUNTS**
collection cover artists

HARLEY QUINN created by PAUL **DINI** & BRUCE **TIMM**

CHRIS CONROY KATIE KUBERT Editors – Original Series DAVE WIELGOSZ MATT HUMPHREYS Assistant Editors – Original Series
JEB WOODARD Group Editor – Collected Editions ROBIN WILDMAN Editor – Collected Edition ROBBIE BIEDERMAN Publication Design

BOB HARRAS Senior VP – Editor-in-Chief, DC Comics

DIANE NELSON President DAN DIDIO and JIM LEE Co-Publishers GEOFF JOHNS Chief Creative Officer
AMIT DESAI Senior VP – Marketing & Global Franchise Management NAIRI GARDINER Senior VP – Finance
SAM ADES VP – Digital Marketing BOBBIE CHASE VP – Talent Development
MARK CHIARELLO Senior VP – Art, Design & Collected Editions JOHN CUNNINGHAM VP – Content Strategy
ANNE DEPIES VP – Strategy Planning & Reporting DON FALLETTI VP – Manufacturing Operations
LAWRENCE GANEM VP – Editorial Administration & Talent Relations ALISON GILL Senior VP – Manufacturing & Operations
HANK KANALZ Senior VP – Editorial Strategy & Administration JAY KOGAN VP – Legal Affairs
DEREK MADDALENA Senior VP – Sales & Business Development JACK MAHAN VP – Business Affairs
DAN MIRON VP – Sales Planning & Trade Development NICK NAPOLITANO VP – Manufacturing Administration
CAROL ROEDER VP – Marketing EDDIE SCANNELL VP – Mass Account & Digital Sales
COURTNEY SIMMONS Senior VP – Publicity & Communications JIM (SKI) SOKOLOWSKI VP – Comic Book Specialty & Newsstand Sales
SANDY YI Senior VP – Global Franchise Management

HARLEY QUINN VOLUME 2: POWER OUTAGE

DC Comics, 4000 Warner Blvd., Burbank, CA 91522
A Warner Bros. Entertainment Company.
Printed by RR Donnelley, Salem, VA, USA. 11/6/15. First Printing.
ISBN: 978-1-4012-5763-7

Library of Congress Cataloging-in-Publication Data

Palmiotti, Jimmy, author.
Harley Quinn. Volume 2, Power outage / Jimmy Palmiotti, Amanda Conner.
pages cm. — (The New 52!)
ISBN 978-1-4012-5763-7
1. Graphic novels. I. Conner, Amanda, illustrator. II. Title. III. Title: Power Outage.

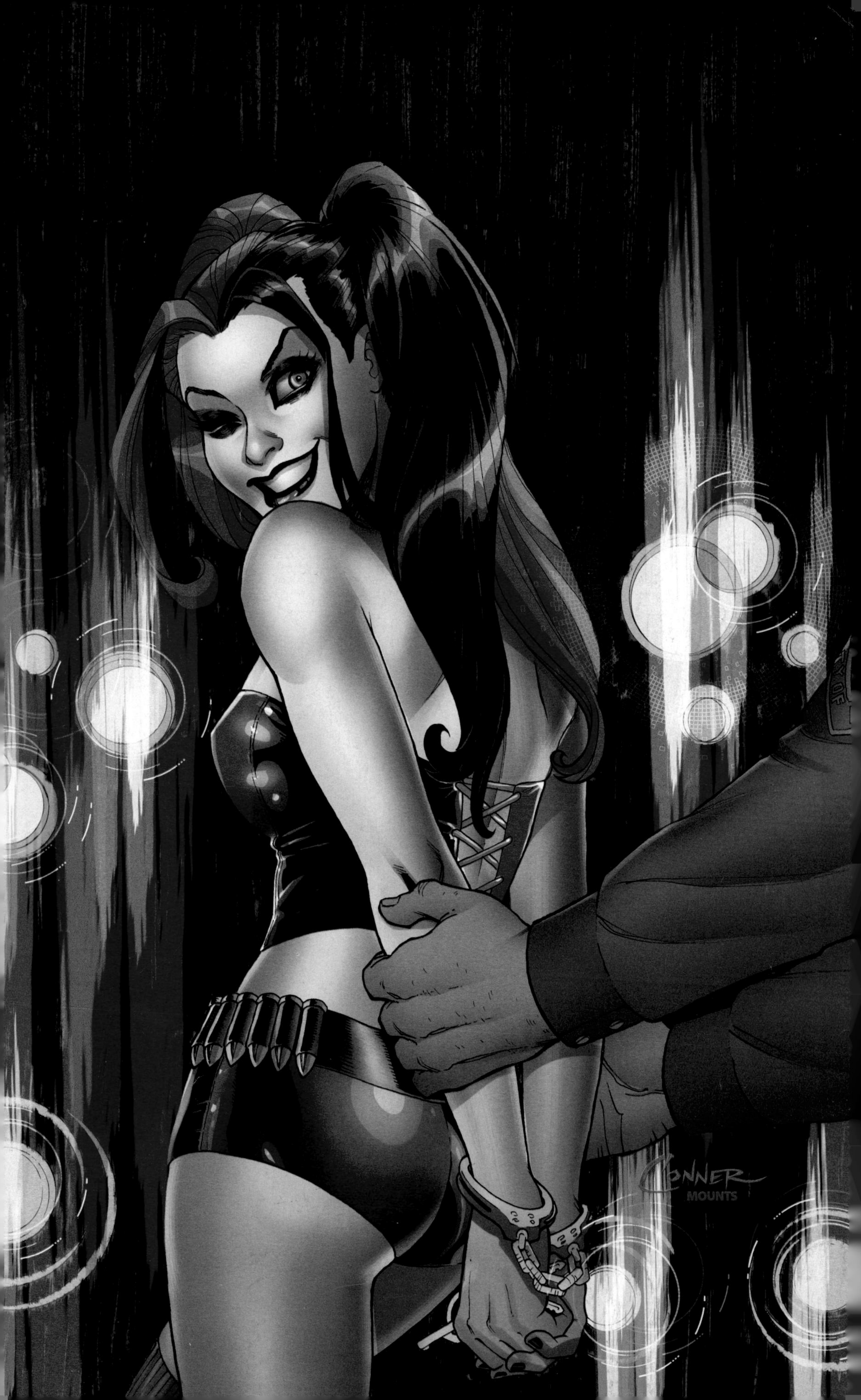
CONNER
MOUNTS

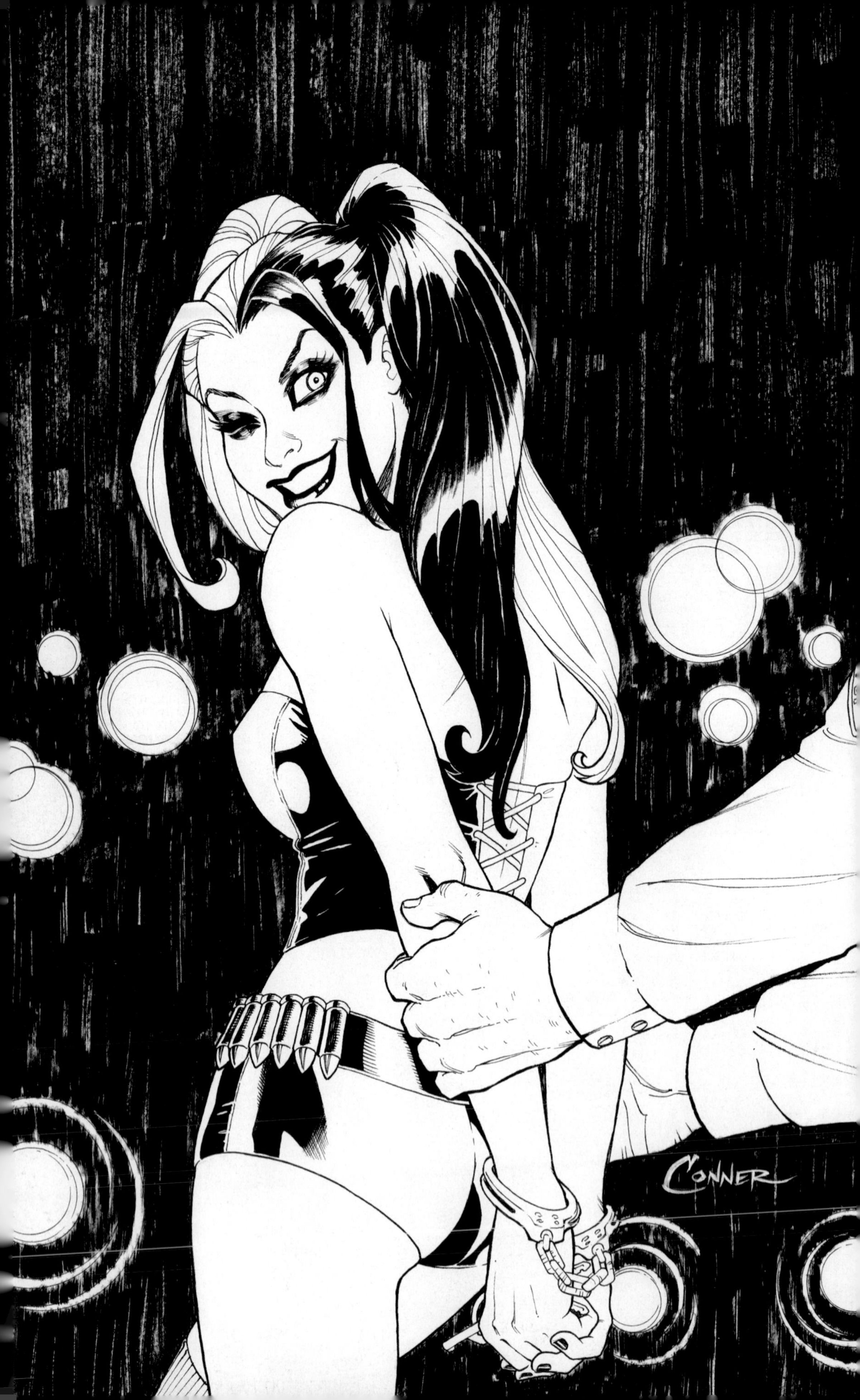
CONNER

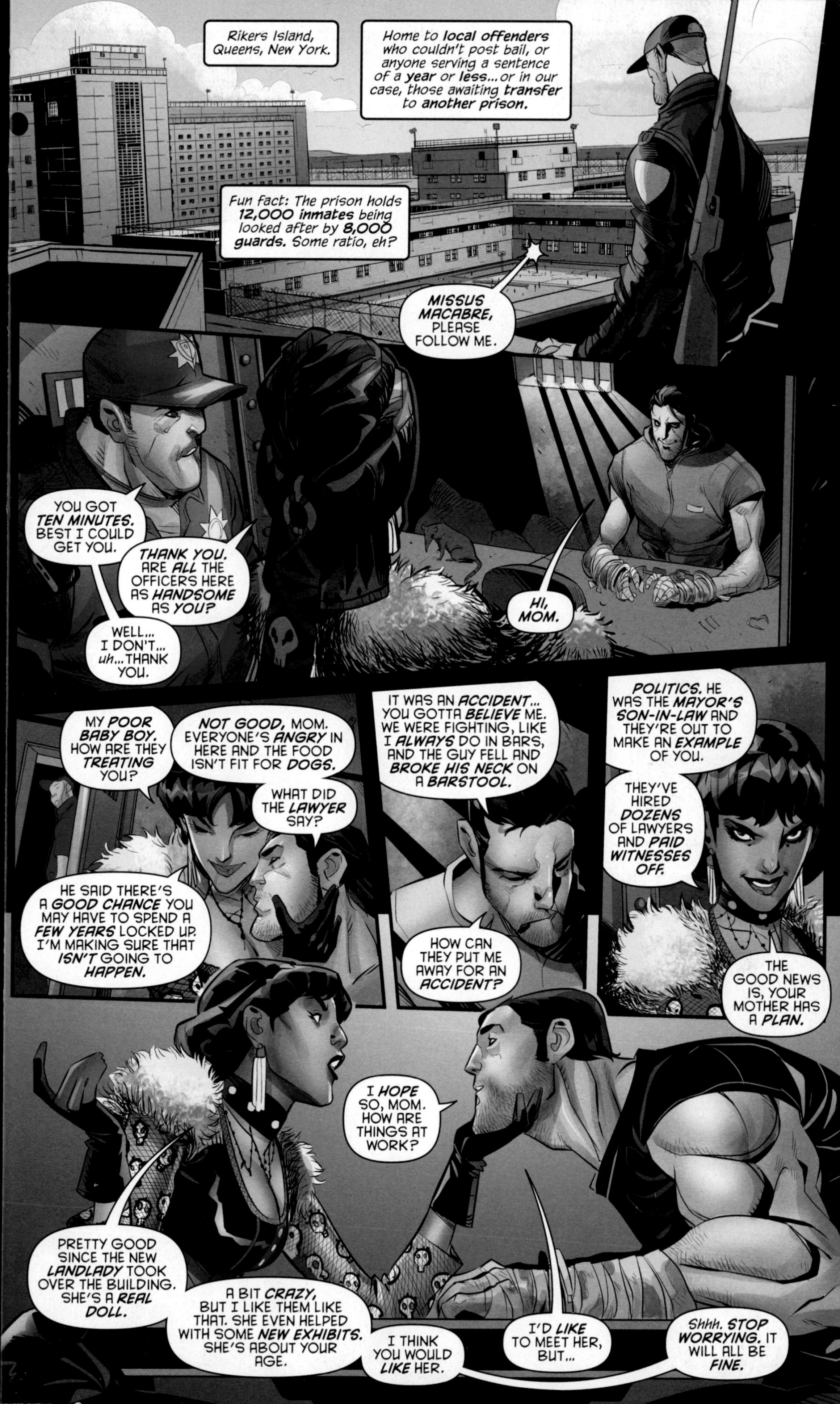
Rikers Island, Queens, New York.
Home to local offenders who couldn't post bail, or anyone serving a sentence of a year or less...or in our case, those awaiting transfer to another prison.
Fun fact: The prison holds 12,000 inmates being looked after by 8,000 guards. Some ratio, eh?
MISSUS MACABRE, PLEASE FOLLOW ME.
YOU GOT TEN MINUTES. BEST I COULD GET YOU.
THANK YOU. ARE ALL THE OFFICERS HERE AS HANDSOME AS YOU?
WELL... I DON'T... uh...THANK YOU.
HI, MOM.
MY POOR BABY BOY. HOW ARE THEY TREATING YOU?
NOT GOOD, MOM. EVERYONE'S ANGRY IN HERE AND THE FOOD ISN'T FIT FOR DOGS.
WHAT DID THE LAWYER SAY?
HE SAID THERE'S A GOOD CHANCE YOU MAY HAVE TO SPEND A FEW YEARS LOCKED UP. I'M MAKING SURE THAT ISN'T GOING TO HAPPEN.
IT WAS AN ACCIDENT... YOU GOTTA BELIEVE ME. WE WERE FIGHTING, LIKE I ALWAYS DO IN BARS, AND THE GUY FELL AND BROKE HIS NECK ON A BARSTOOL.
HOW CAN THEY PUT ME AWAY FOR AN ACCIDENT?
POLITICS. HE WAS THE MAYOR'S SON-IN-LAW AND THEY'RE OUT TO MAKE AN EXAMPLE OF YOU.
THEY'VE HIRED DOZENS OF LAWYERS AND PAID WITNESSES OFF.
THE GOOD NEWS IS, YOUR MOTHER HAS A PLAN.
I HOPE SO, MOM. HOW ARE THINGS AT WORK?
PRETTY GOOD SINCE THE NEW LANDLADY TOOK OVER THE BUILDING. SHE'S A REAL DOLL.
A BIT CRAZY, BUT I LIKE THEM LIKE THAT. SHE EVEN HELPED WITH SOME NEW EXHIBITS. SHE'S ABOUT YOUR AGE.
I THINK YOU WOULD LIKE HER.
I'D LIKE TO MEET HER, BUT...
Shhh. STOP WORRYING. IT WILL ALL BE FINE.

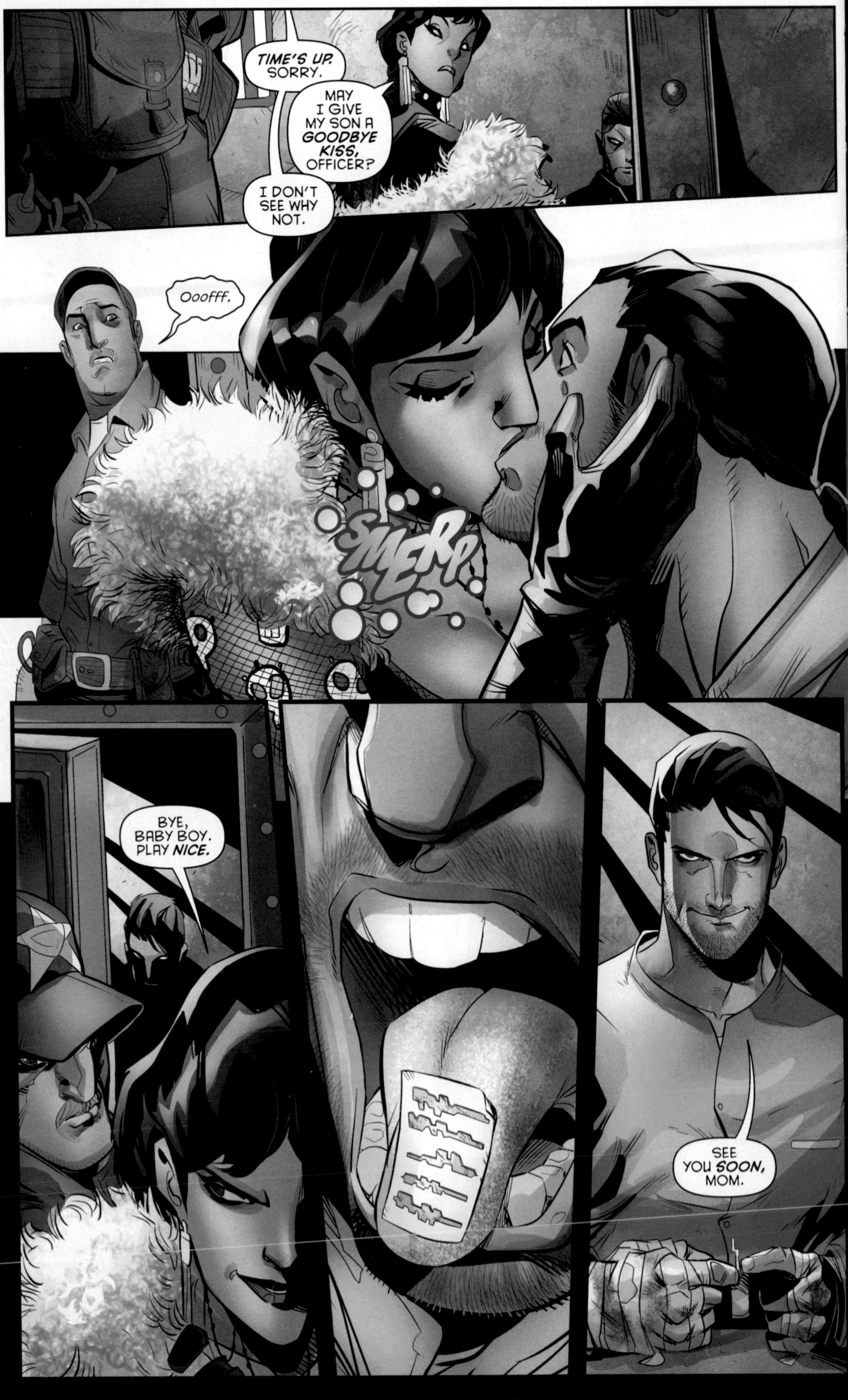
TIME'S UP. SORRY.
MAY I GIVE MY SON A GOODBYE KISS, OFFICER?
I DON'T SEE WHY NOT.
Ooofff.
SMERP
BYE, BABY BOY. PLAY NICE.
SEE YOU SOON, MOM.

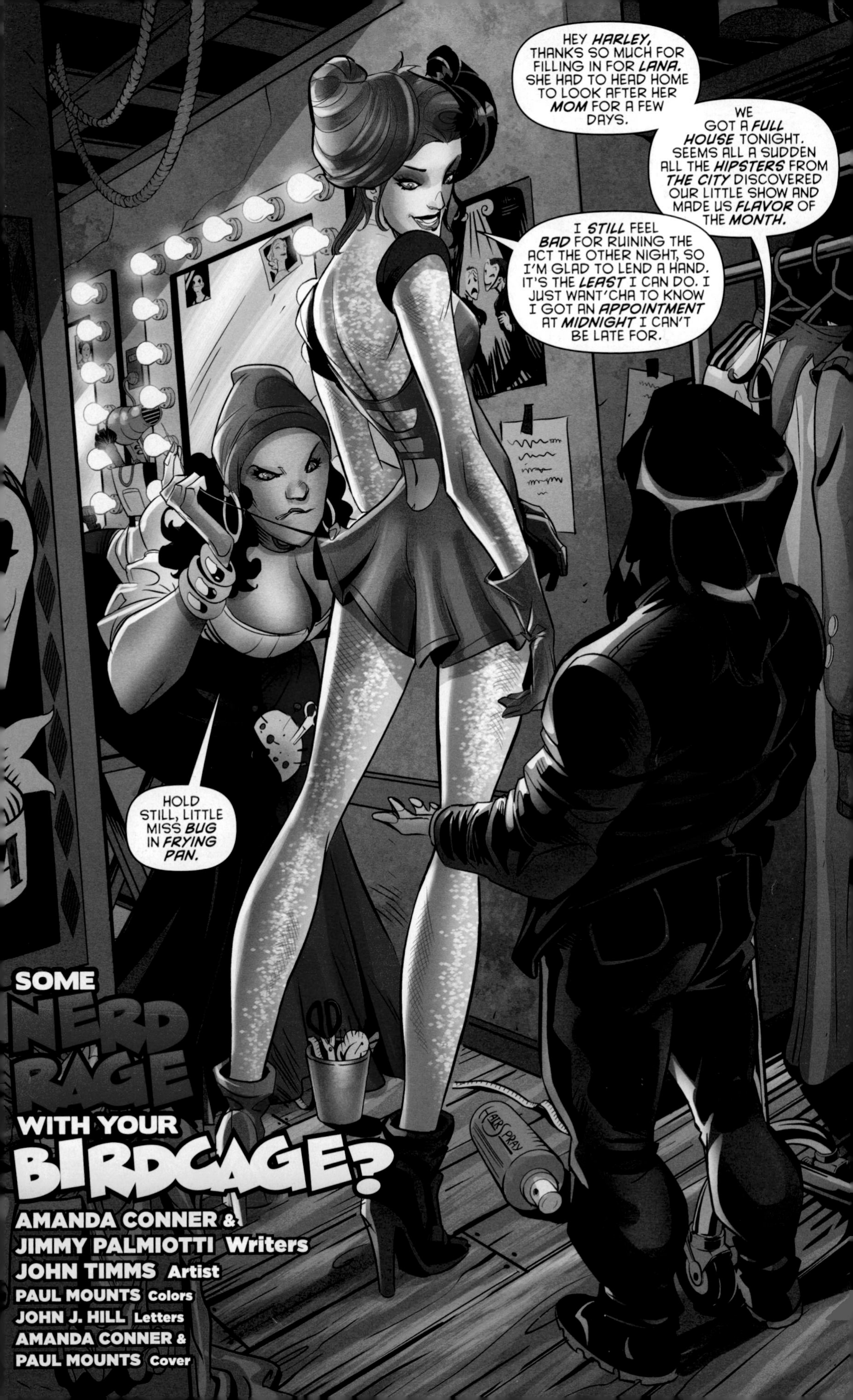

HEY HARLEY, THANKS SO MUCH FOR FILLING IN FOR LANA. SHE HAD TO HEAD HOME TO LOOK AFTER HER MOM FOR A FEW DAYS.
WE GOT A FULL HOUSE TONIGHT. SEEMS ALL A SUDDEN ALL THE HIPSTERS FROM THE CITY DISCOVERED OUR LITTLE SHOW AND MADE US FLAVOR OF THE MONTH.
I STILL FEEL BAD FOR RUINING THE ACT THE OTHER NIGHT, SO I'M GLAD TO LEND A HAND. IT'S THE LEAST I CAN DO. I JUST WANT'CHA TO KNOW I GOT AN APPOINTMENT AT MIDNIGHT I CAN'T BE LATE FOR.
HOLD STILL, LITTLE MISS BUG IN FRYING PAN.
HAIRSPRAY
SOME NERD RAGE WITH YOUR BIRDCAGE?
AMANDA CONNER & JIMMY PALMIOTTI Writers
JOHN TIMMS Artist
PAUL MOUNTS Colors
JOHN J. HILL Letters
AMANDA CONNER & PAUL MOUNTS Cover

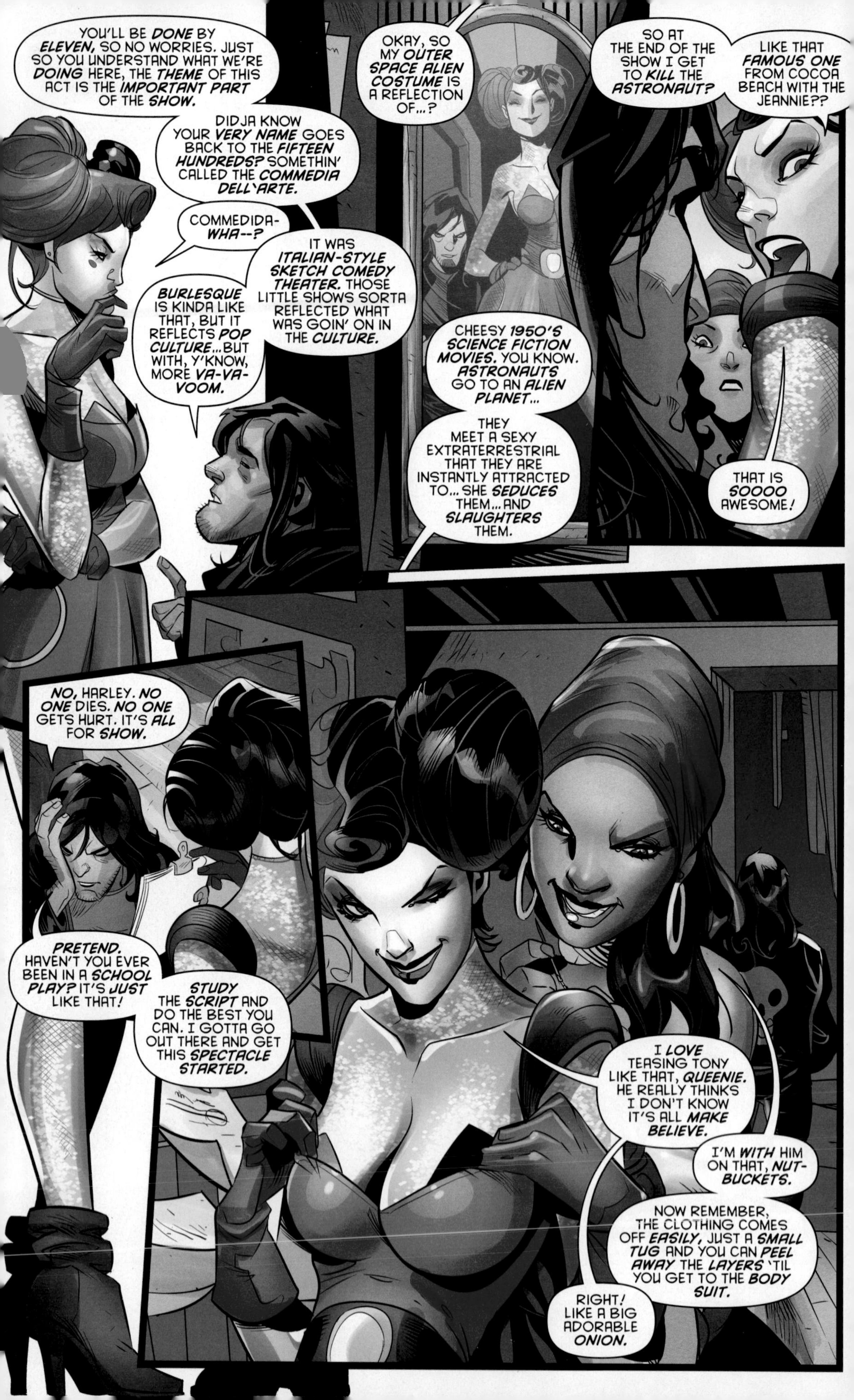

YOU'LL BE DONE BY ELEVEN, SO NO WORRIES. JUST SO YOU UNDERSTAND WHAT WE'RE DOING HERE, THE THEME OF THIS ACT IS THE IMPORTANT PART OF THE SHOW.
DIDJA KNOW YOUR VERY NAME GOES BACK TO THE FIFTEEN HUNDREDS? SOMETHIN' CALLED THE COMMEDIA DELL'ARTE.
COMMEDIDA-WHA--?
IT WAS ITALIAN-STYLE SKETCH COMEDY THEATER. THOSE LITTLE SHOWS SORTA REFLECTED WHAT WAS GOIN' ON IN THE CULTURE.
BURLESQUE IS KINDA LIKE THAT, BUT IT REFLECTS POP CULTURE...BUT WITH, Y'KNOW, MORE VA-VA-VOOM.
OKAY, SO MY OUTER SPACE ALIEN COSTUME IS A REFLECTION OF...?
CHEESY 1950'S SCIENCE FICTION MOVIES. YOU KNOW. ASTRONAUTS GO TO AN ALIEN PLANET...
THEY MEET A SEXY EXTRATERRESTRIAL THAT THEY ARE INSTANTLY ATTRACTED TO... SHE SEDUCES THEM... AND SLAUGHTERS THEM.
SO AT THE END OF THE SHOW I GET TO KILL THE ASTRONAUT?
LIKE THAT FAMOUS ONE FROM COCOA BEACH WITH THE JEANNIE??
THAT IS SOOOO AWESOME!
NO, HARLEY. NO ONE DIES. NO ONE GETS HURT. IT'S ALL FOR SHOW.
PRETEND. HAVEN'T YOU EVER BEEN IN A SCHOOL PLAY? IT'S JUST LIKE THAT!
STUDY THE SCRIPT AND DO THE BEST YOU CAN. I GOTTA GO OUT THERE AND GET THIS SPECTACLE STARTED.
I LOVE TEASING TONY LIKE THAT, QUEENIE. HE REALLY THINKS I DON'T KNOW IT'S ALL MAKE BELIEVE.
I'M WITH HIM ON THAT, NUT-BUCKETS.
NOW REMEMBER, THE CLOTHING COMES OFF EASILY, JUST A SMALL TUG AND YOU CAN PEEL AWAY THE LAYERS 'TIL YOU GET TO THE BODY SUIT.
RIGHT! LIKE A BIG ADORABLE ONION.

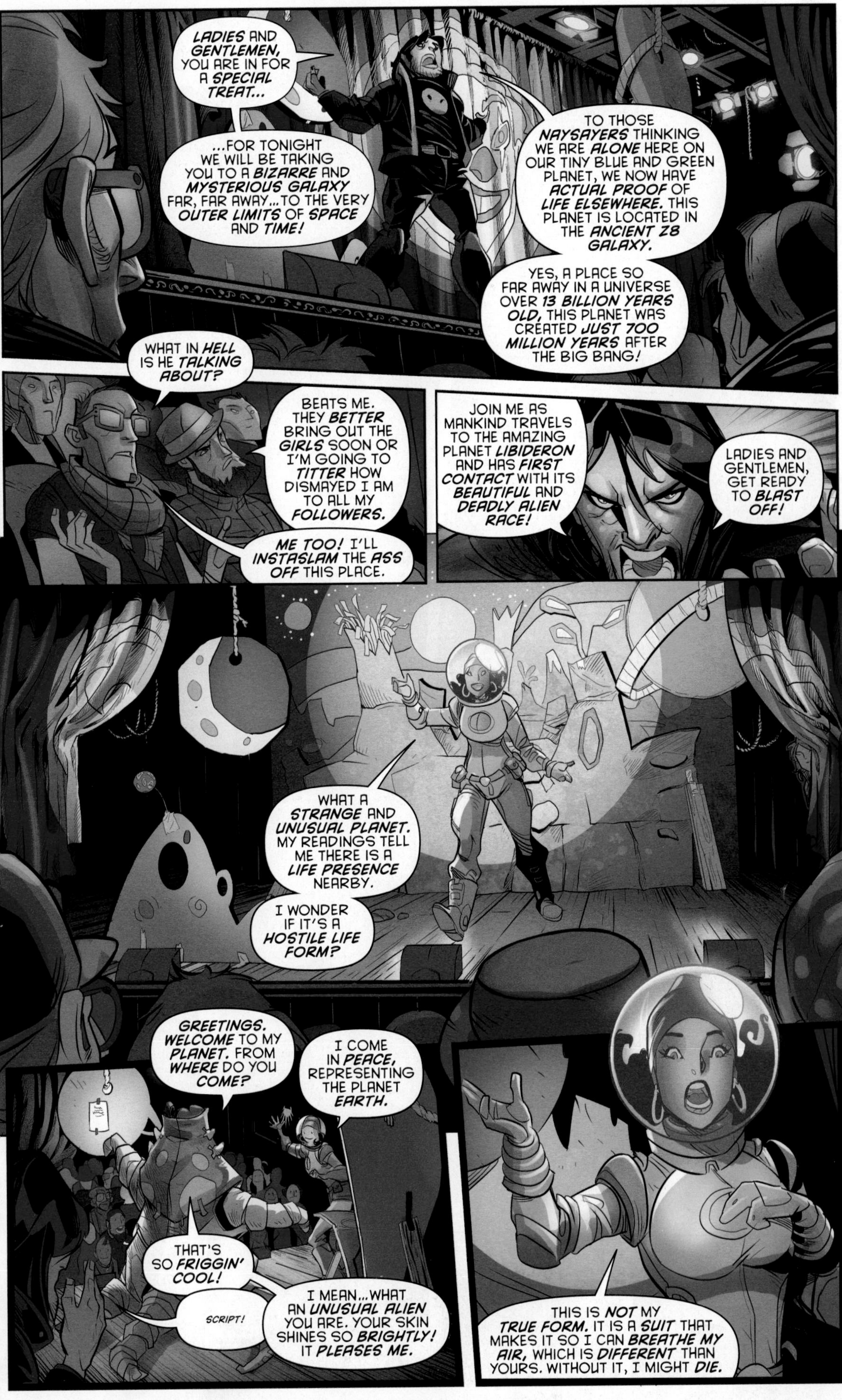
LADIES AND GENTLEMEN, YOU ARE IN FOR A SPECIAL TREAT...
...FOR TONIGHT WE WILL BE TAKING YOU TO A BIZARRE AND MYSTERIOUS GALAXY FAR, FAR AWAY...TO THE VERY OUTER LIMITS OF SPACE AND TIME!
TO THOSE NAYSAYERS THINKING WE ARE ALONE HERE ON OUR TINY BLUE AND GREEN PLANET, WE NOW HAVE ACTUAL PROOF OF LIFE ELSEWHERE. THIS PLANET IS LOCATED IN THE ANCIENT Z8 GALAXY.
YES, A PLACE SO FAR AWAY IN A UNIVERSE OVER 13 BILLION YEARS OLD, THIS PLANET WAS CREATED JUST 700 MILLION YEARS AFTER THE BIG BANG!
WHAT IN HELL IS HE TALKING ABOUT?
BEATS ME. THEY BETTER BRING OUT THE GIRLS SOON OR I'M GOING TO TITTER HOW DISMAYED I AM TO ALL MY FOLLOWERS.
ME TOO! I'LL INSTASLAM THE ASS OFF THIS PLACE.
JOIN ME AS MANKIND TRAVELS TO THE AMAZING PLANET LIBIDERON AND HAS FIRST CONTACT WITH ITS BEAUTIFUL AND DEADLY ALIEN RACE!
LADIES AND GENTLEMEN, GET READY TO BLAST OFF!
WHAT A STRANGE AND UNUSUAL PLANET. MY READINGS TELL ME THERE IS A LIFE PRESENCE NEARBY.
I WONDER IF IT'S A HOSTILE LIFE FORM?
GREETINGS. WELCOME TO MY PLANET. FROM WHERE DO YOU COME?
I COME IN PEACE, REPRESENTING THE PLANET EARTH.
THAT'S SO FRIGGIN' COOL!
SCRIPT!
I MEAN...WHAT AN UNUSUAL ALIEN YOU ARE. YOUR SKIN SHINES SO BRIGHTLY! IT PLEASES ME.
THIS IS NOT MY TRUE FORM. IT IS A SUIT THAT MAKES IT SO I CAN BREATHE MY AIR, WHICH IS DIFFERENT THAN YOURS. WITHOUT IT, I MIGHT DIE.

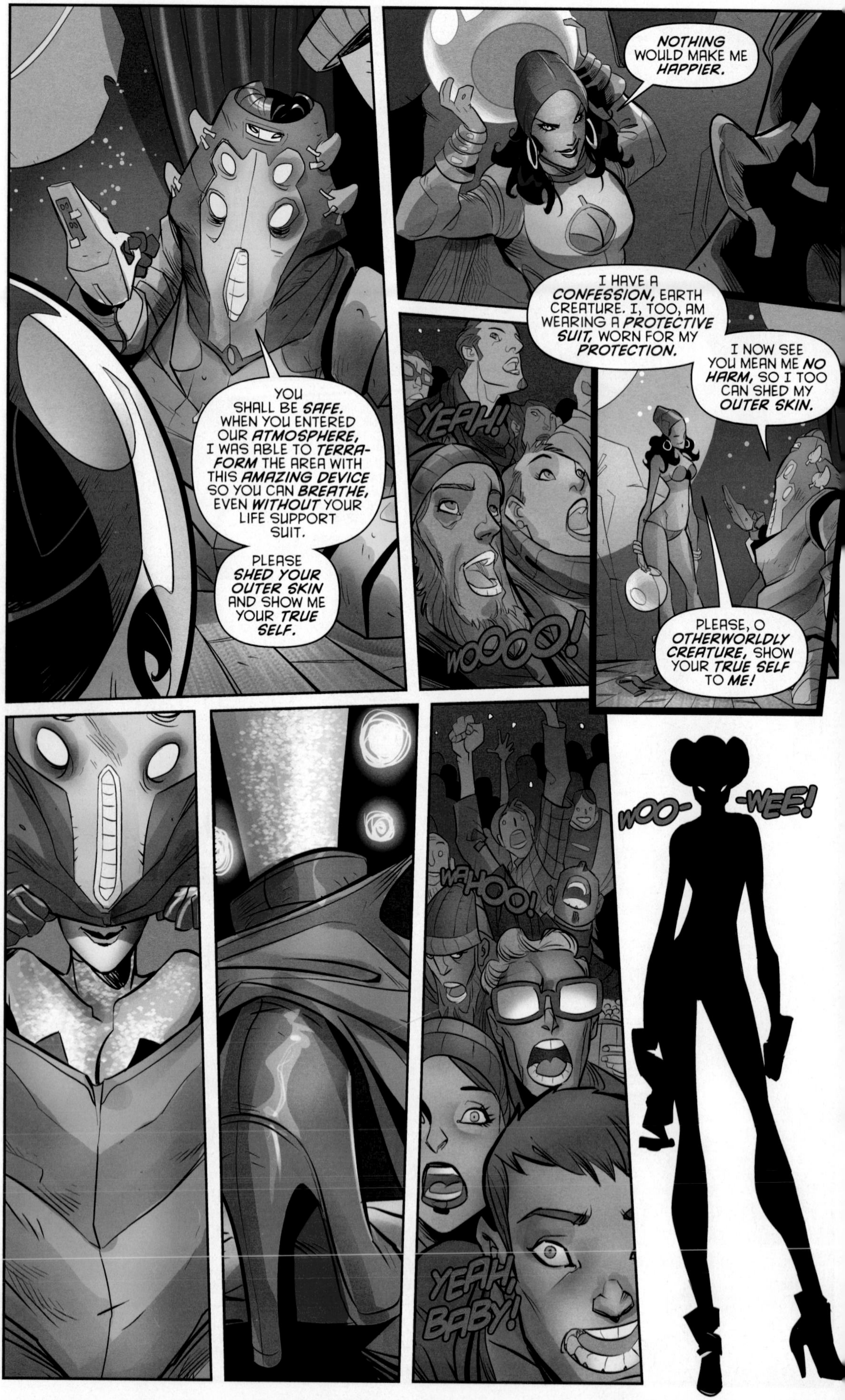
YOU SHALL BE SAFE. WHEN YOU ENTERED OUR ATMOSPHERE, I WAS ABLE TO TERRA-FORM THE AREA WITH THIS AMAZING DEVICE SO YOU CAN BREATHE, EVEN WITHOUT YOUR LIFE SUPPORT SUIT.
PLEASE SHED YOUR OUTER SKIN AND SHOW ME YOUR TRUE SELF.
NOTHING WOULD MAKE ME HAPPIER.
I HAVE A CONFESSION, EARTH CREATURE. I, TOO, AM WEARING A PROTECTIVE SUIT, WORN FOR MY PROTECTION.
YEAH!
WOOOOO!
I NOW SEE YOU MEAN ME NO HARM, SO I TOO CAN SHED MY OUTER SKIN.
PLEASE, O OTHERWORLDLY CREATURE, SHOW YOUR TRUE SELF TO ME!
WAHOO!
YEAH, BABY!
WOO-
-WEE!

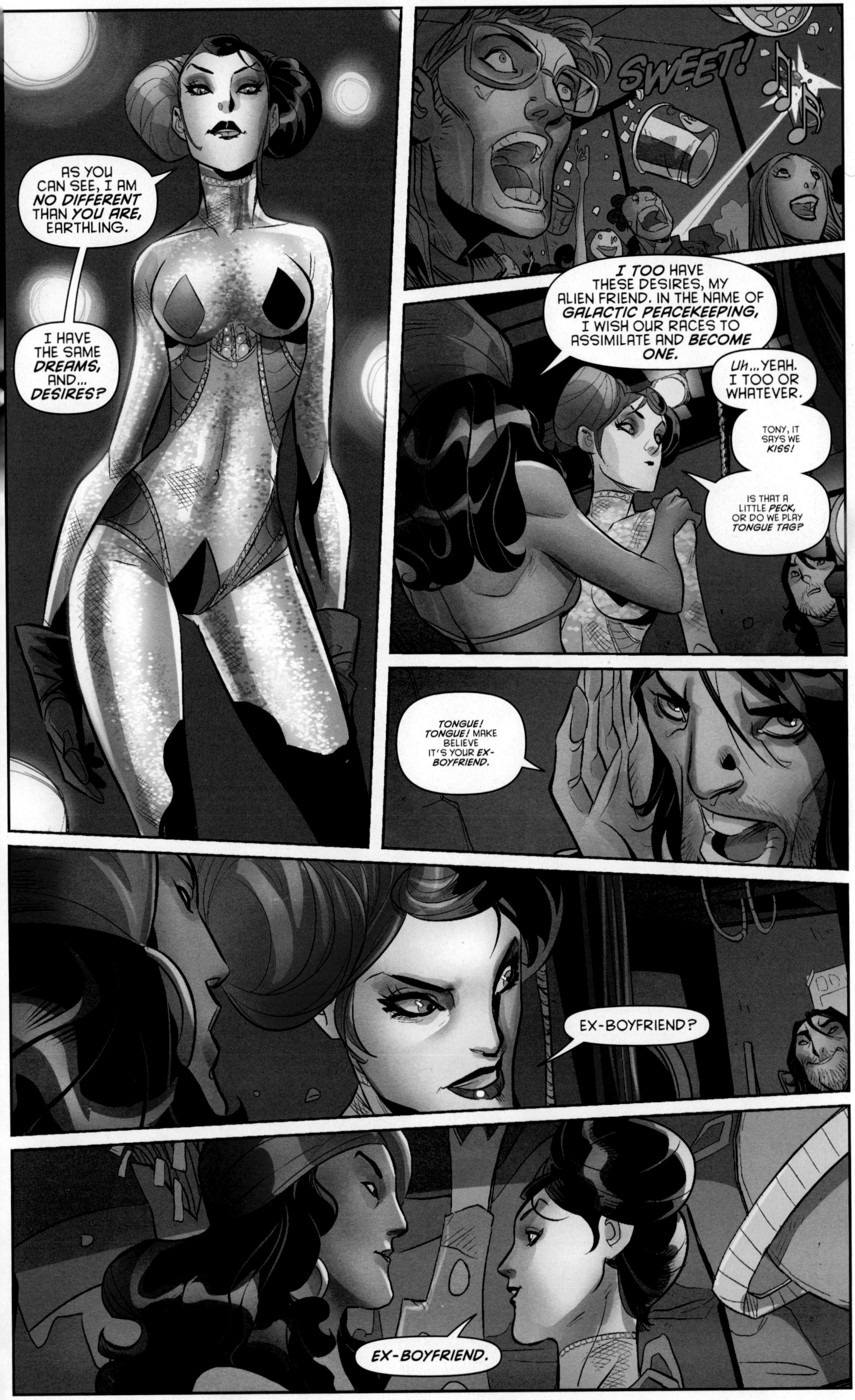
AS YOU CAN SEE, I AM NO DIFFERENT THAN YOU ARE, EARTHLING.
I HAVE THE SAME DREAMS, AND... DESIRES?
SWEET!
I TOO HAVE THESE DESIRES, MY ALIEN FRIEND. IN THE NAME OF GALACTIC PEACEKEEPING, I WISH OUR RACES TO ASSIMILATE AND BECOME ONE.
Uh...YEAH. I TOO OR WHATEVER.
TONY, IT SAYS WE KISS!
IS THAT A LITTLE PECK, OR DO WE PLAY TONGUE TAG?
TONGUE! TONGUE! MAKE BELIEVE IT'S YOUR EX-BOYFRIEND.
EX-BOYFRIEND?
EX-BOYFRIEND.

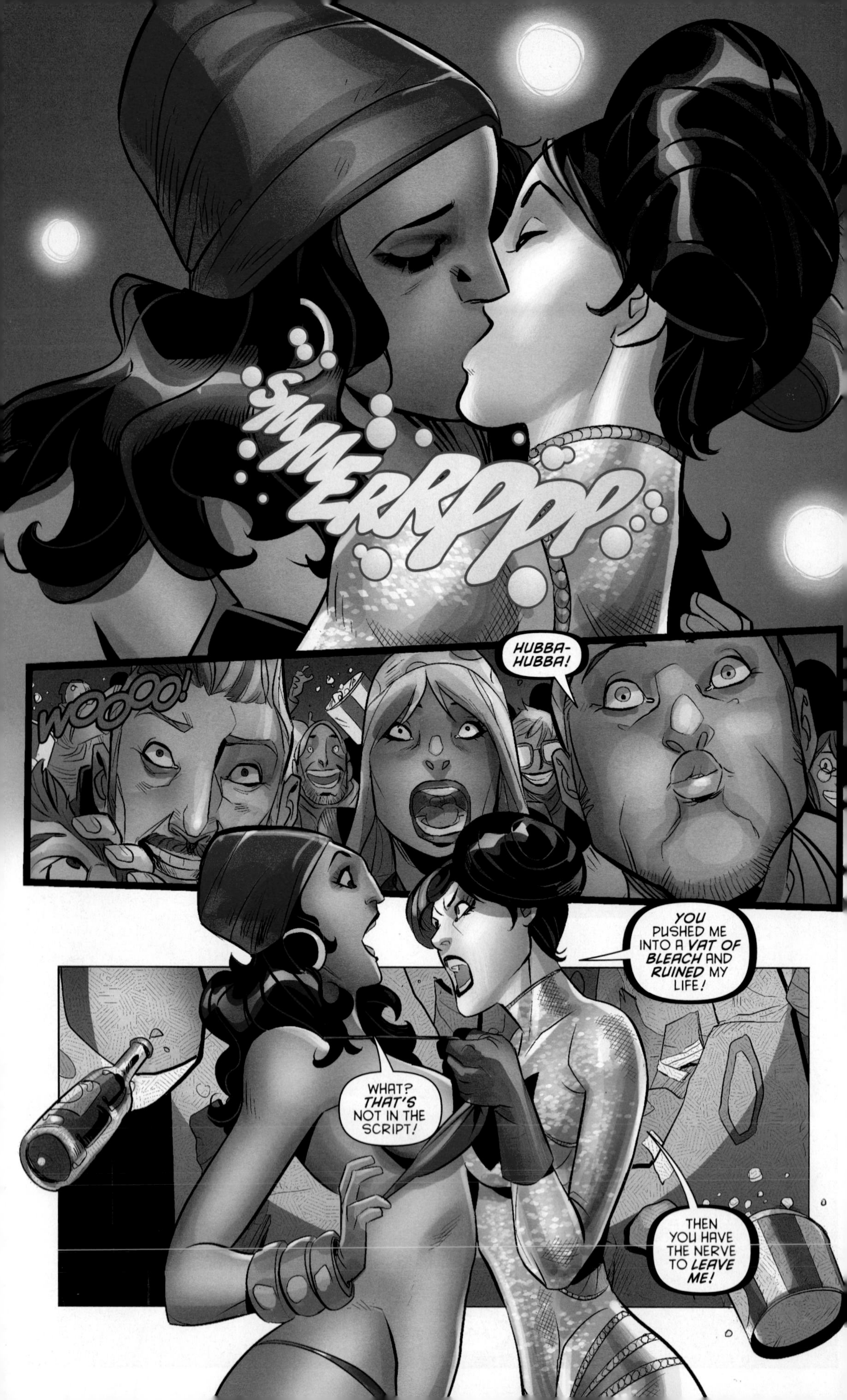
SMMERRPPP
WOOOO!
HUBBA-HUBBA!
YOU PUSHED ME INTO A VAT OF BLEACH AND RUINED MY LIFE!
WHAT? THAT'S NOT IN THE SCRIPT!
THEN YOU HAVE THE NERVE TO LEAVE ME!

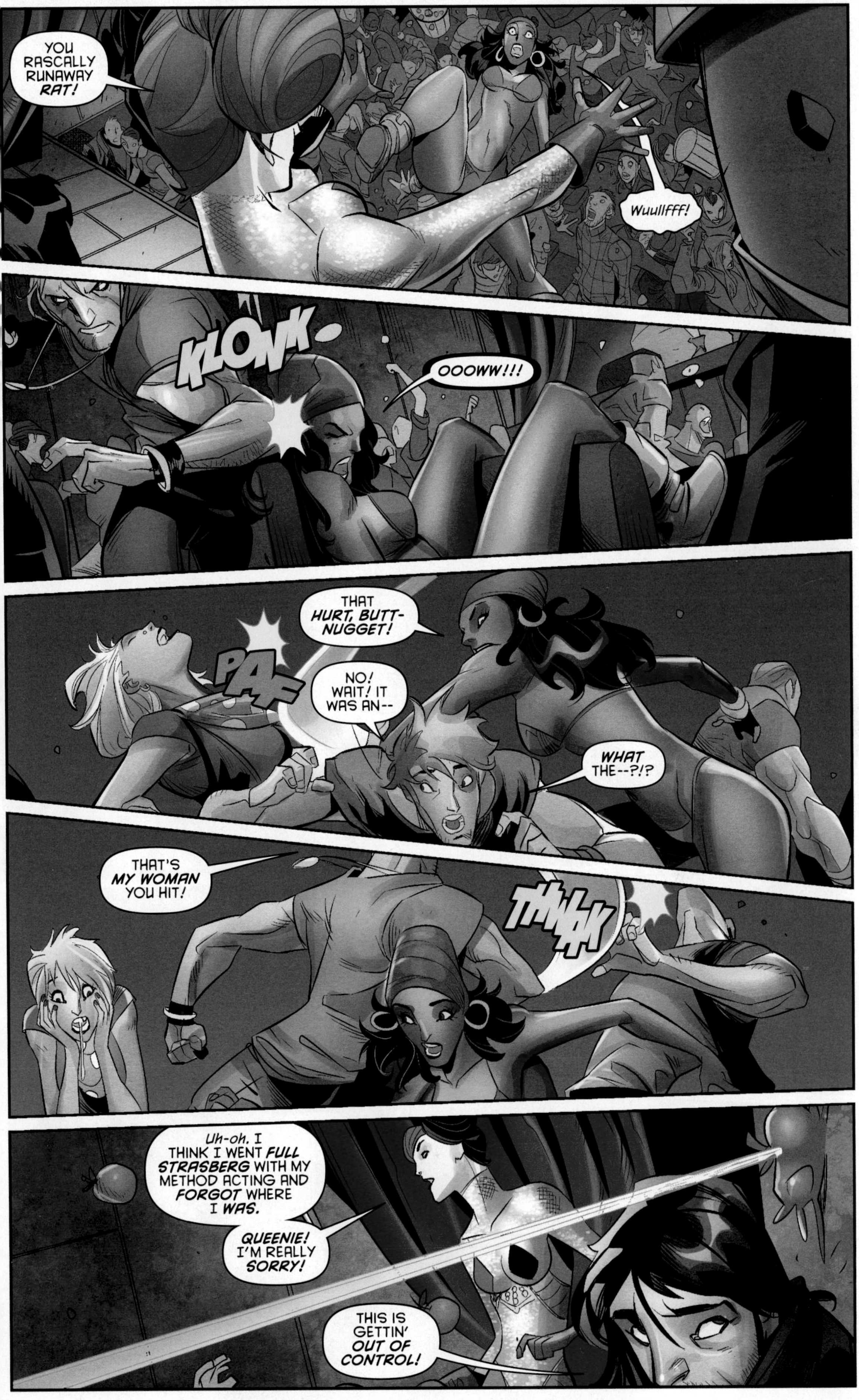
YOU RASCALLY RUNAWAY RAT!
Wuullfff!
KLONK
OOOWW!!!
THAT HURT, BUTT-NUGGET!
PAF
NO! WAIT! IT WAS AN--
WHAT THE--?!?
THAT'S MY WOMAN YOU HIT!
THWAK
Uh-oh. I THINK I WENT FULL STRASBERG WITH MY METHOD ACTING AND FORGOT WHERE I WAS.
QUEENIE! I'M REALLY SORRY!
THIS IS GETTIN' OUT OF CONTROL!

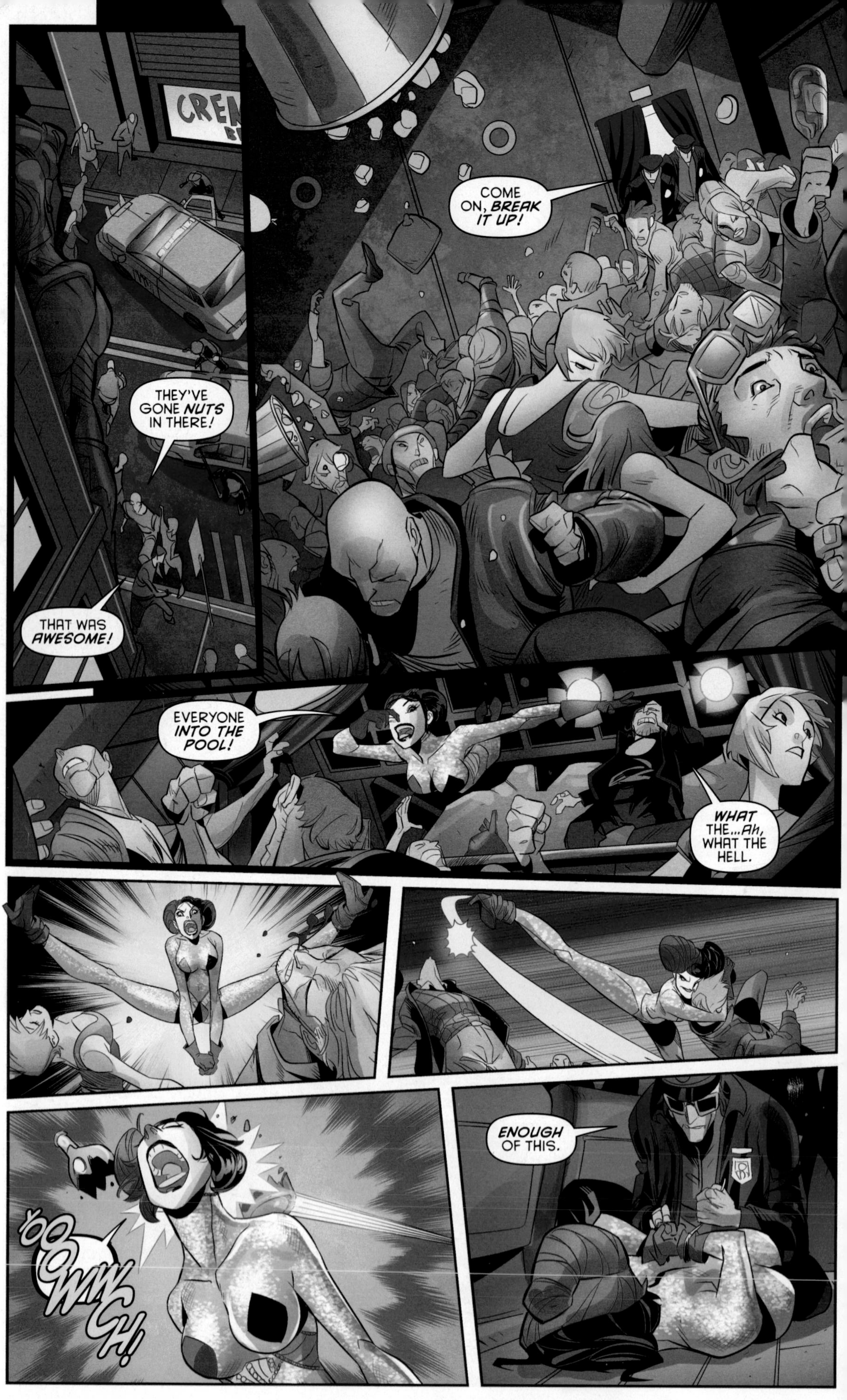

CREM
COME ON, BREAK IT UP!
THEY'VE GONE NUTS IN THERE!
THAT WAS AWESOME!
EVERYONE INTO THE POOL!
WHAT THE...Ah, WHAT THE HELL.
OOWWCH!
ENOUGH OF THIS.

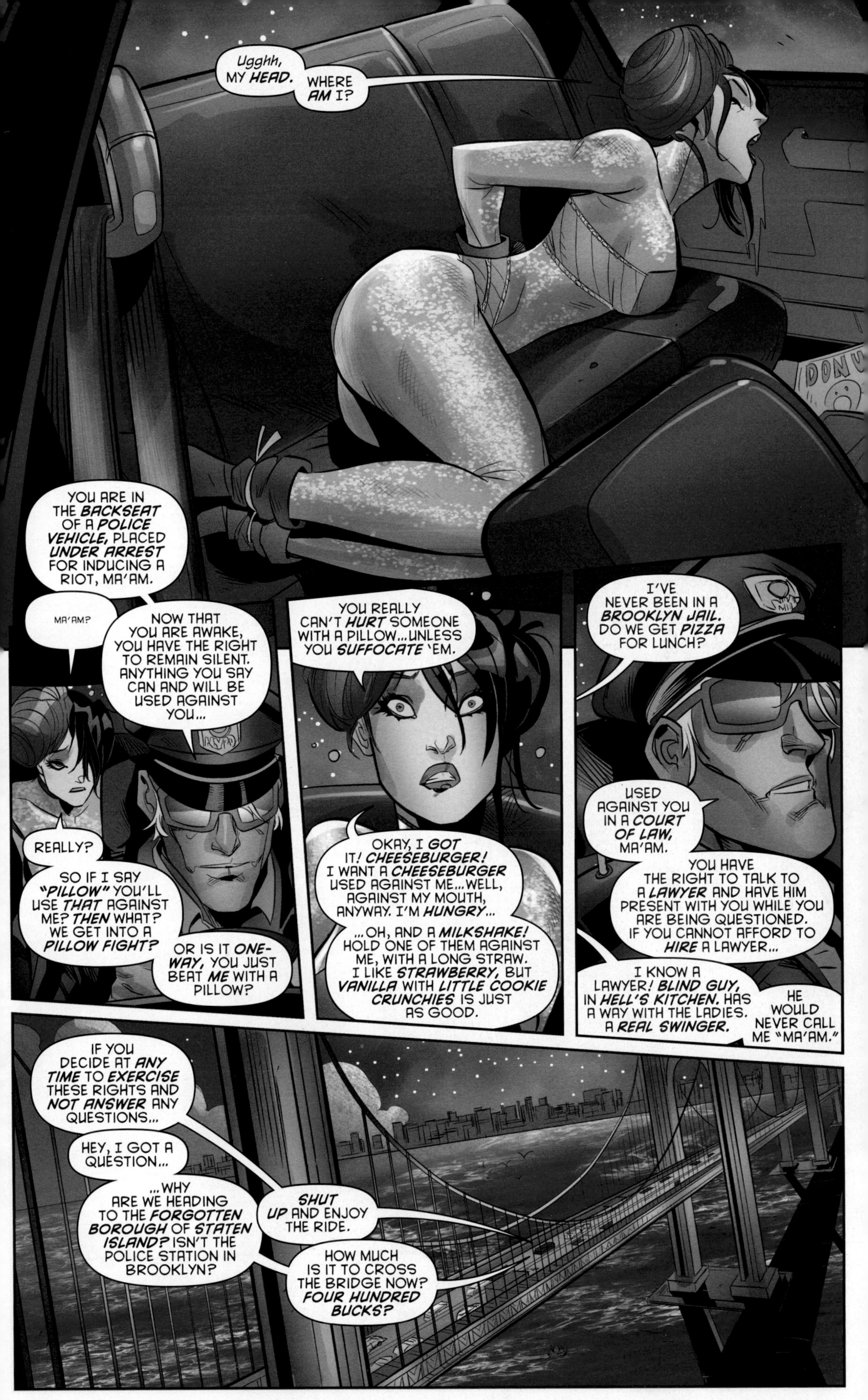

Ugghh, MY HEAD.
WHERE AM I?
YOU ARE IN THE BACKSEAT OF A POLICE VEHICLE, PLACED UNDER ARREST FOR INDUCING A RIOT, MA'AM.
MA'AM?
NOW THAT YOU ARE AWAKE, YOU HAVE THE RIGHT TO REMAIN SILENT. ANYTHING YOU SAY CAN AND WILL BE USED AGAINST YOU...
REALLY?
SO IF I SAY "PILLOW" YOU'LL USE THAT AGAINST ME? THEN WHAT? WE GET INTO A PILLOW FIGHT?
OR IS IT ONE-WAY, YOU JUST BEAT ME WITH A PILLOW?
YOU REALLY CAN'T HURT SOMEONE WITH A PILLOW...UNLESS YOU SUFFOCATE 'EM.
OKAY, I GOT IT! CHEESEBURGER! I WANT A CHEESEBURGER USED AGAINST ME...WELL, AGAINST MY MOUTH, ANYWAY. I'M HUNGRY...
...OH, AND A MILKSHAKE! HOLD ONE OF THEM AGAINST ME, WITH A LONG STRAW. I LIKE STRAWBERRY, BUT VANILLA WITH LITTLE COOKIE CRUNCHIES IS JUST AS GOOD.
I'VE NEVER BEEN IN A BROOKLYN JAIL. DO WE GET PIZZA FOR LUNCH?
USED AGAINST YOU IN A COURT OF LAW, MA'AM.
YOU HAVE THE RIGHT TO TALK TO A LAWYER AND HAVE HIM PRESENT WITH YOU WHILE YOU ARE BEING QUESTIONED. IF YOU CANNOT AFFORD TO HIRE A LAWYER...
I KNOW A LAWYER! BLIND GUY, IN HELL'S KITCHEN. HAS A WAY WITH THE LADIES. A REAL SWINGER.
HE WOULD NEVER CALL ME "MA'AM."
IF YOU DECIDE AT ANY TIME TO EXERCISE THESE RIGHTS AND NOT ANSWER ANY QUESTIONS...
HEY, I GOT A QUESTION...
...WHY ARE WE HEADING TO THE FORGOTTEN BOROUGH OF STATEN ISLAND? ISN'T THE POLICE STATION IN BROOKLYN?
SHUT UP AND ENJOY THE RIDE.
HOW MUCH IS IT TO CROSS THE BRIDGE NOW? FOUR HUNDRED BUCKS?

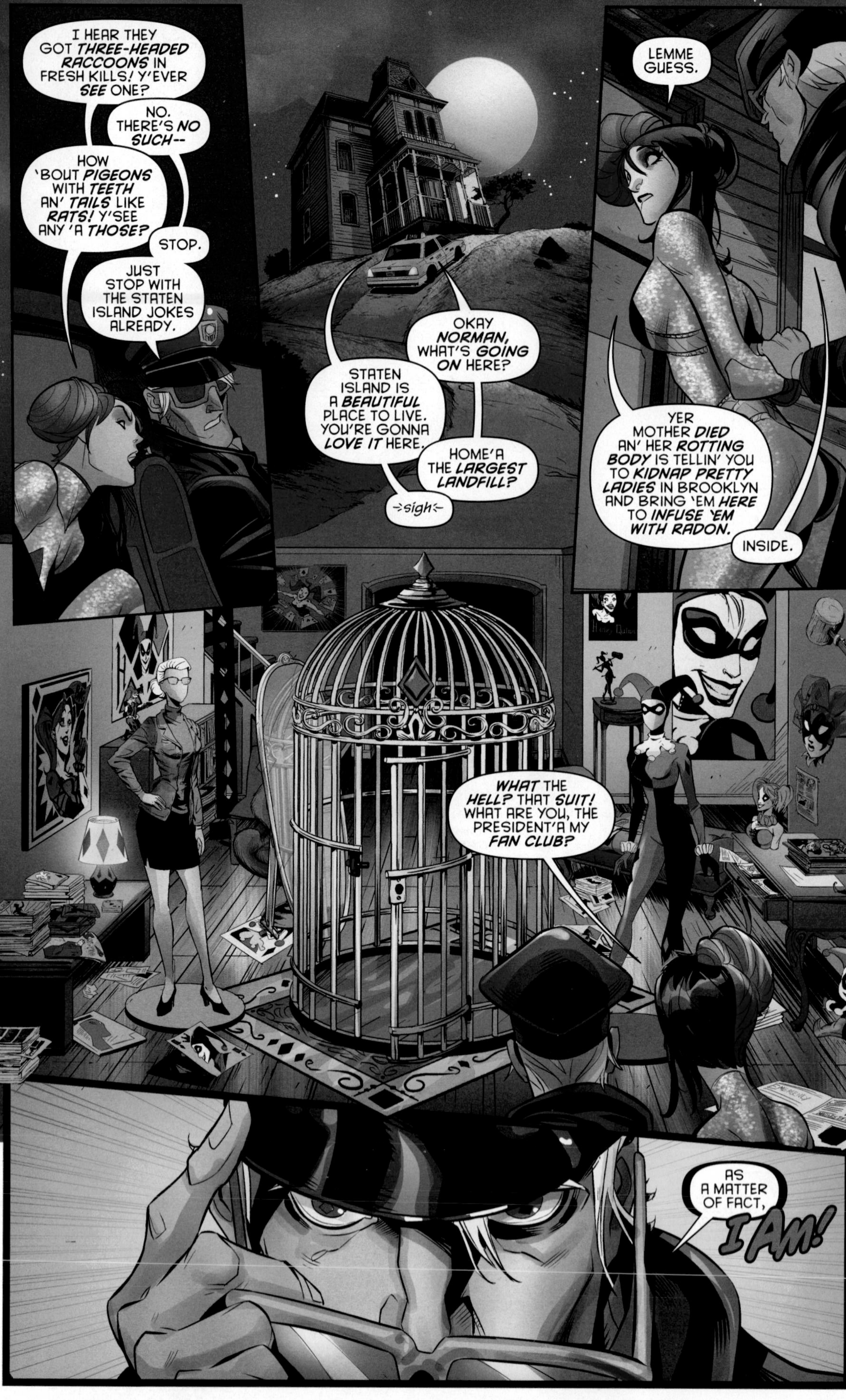
I HEAR THEY GOT THREE-HEADED RACCOONS IN FRESH KILLS! Y'EVER SEE ONE?
NO. THERE'S NO SUCH--
HOW 'BOUT PIGEONS WITH TEETH AN' TAILS LIKE RATS! Y'SEE ANY 'A THOSE?
STOP.
JUST STOP WITH THE STATEN ISLAND JOKES ALREADY.
STATEN ISLAND IS A BEAUTIFUL PLACE TO LIVE. YOU'RE GONNA LOVE IT HERE.
HOME'A THE LARGEST LANDFILL?
~sigh~
OKAY NORMAN, WHAT'S GOING ON HERE?
LEMME GUESS.
YER MOTHER DIED AN' HER ROTTING BODY IS TELLIN' YOU TO KIDNAP PRETTY LADIES IN BROOKLYN AND BRING 'EM HERE TO INFUSE 'EM WITH RADON.
INSIDE.
WHAT THE HELL? THAT SUIT! WHAT ARE YOU, THE PRESIDENT'A MY FAN CLUB?
AS A MATTER OF FACT,
I AM!

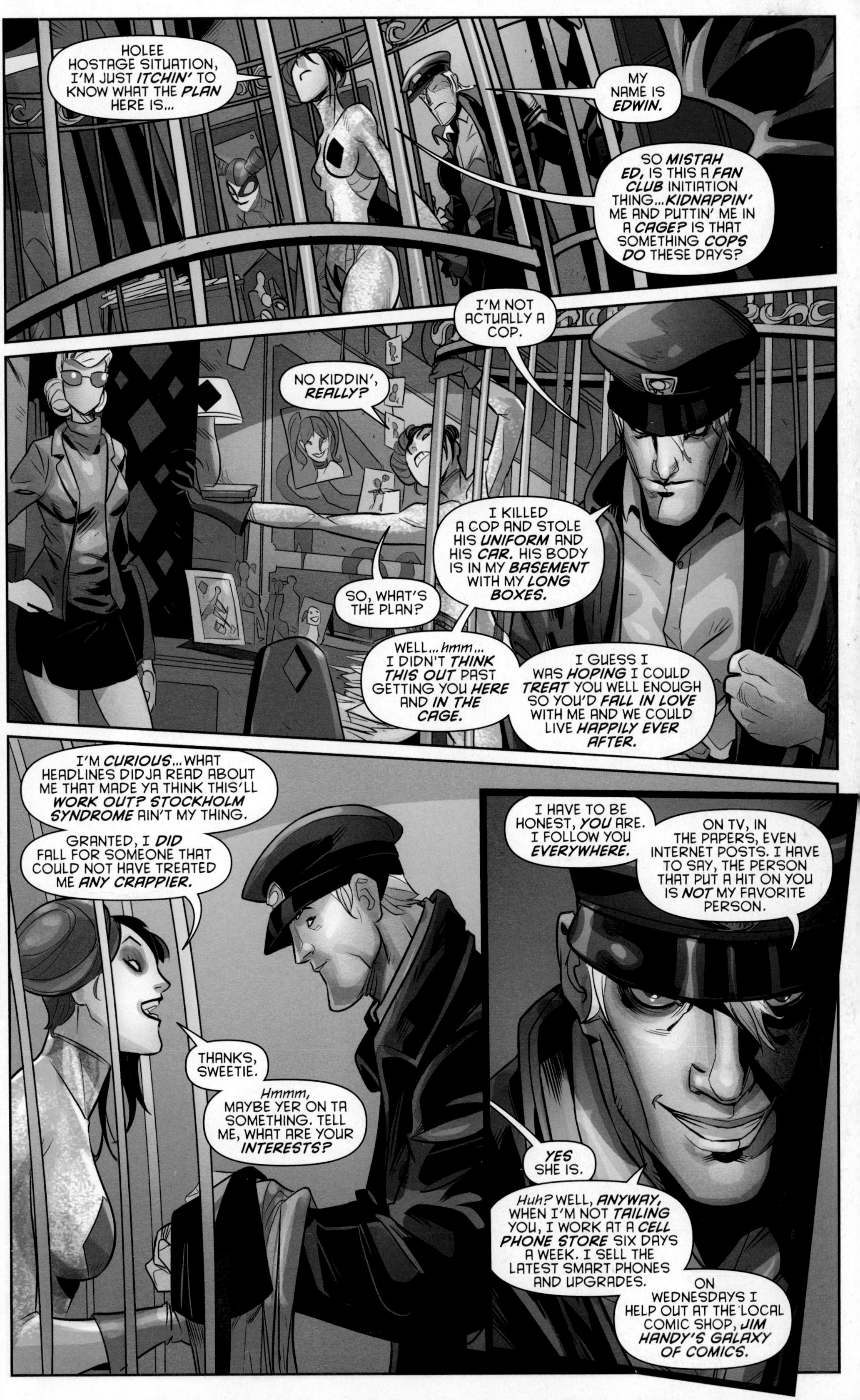
HOLEE HOSTAGE SITUATION, I'M JUST *ITCHIN'* TO KNOW WHAT THE *PLAN* HERE IS...
MY NAME IS *EDWIN.*
SO *MISTAH ED,* IS THIS A *FAN CLUB* INITIATION THING... *KIDNAPPIN'* ME AND PUTTIN' ME IN A *CAGE?* IS THAT SOMETHING *COPS DO* THESE DAYS?
I'M NOT ACTUALLY A COP.
NO KIDDIN', *REALLY?*
I KILLED A COP AND STOLE HIS *UNIFORM* AND HIS *CAR.* HIS BODY IS IN MY *BASEMENT* WITH MY *LONG BOXES.*
SO, WHAT'S THE PLAN?
WELL... *hmm...* I DIDN'T *THINK THIS OUT* PAST GETTING YOU *HERE* AND *IN THE CAGE.*
I GUESS I WAS *HOPING* I COULD *TREAT* YOU WELL ENOUGH SO YOU'D *FALL IN LOVE* WITH ME AND WE COULD LIVE *HAPPILY EVER AFTER.*
I'M *CURIOUS*... WHAT HEADLINES DIDJA READ ABOUT ME THAT MADE YA THINK THIS'LL *WORK OUT? STOCKHOLM SYNDROME* AIN'T MY THING.
GRANTED, I *DID* FALL FOR SOMEONE THAT COULD NOT HAVE TREATED ME *ANY CRAPPIER.*
THANKS, SWEETIE.
Hmmm, MAYBE YER ON TA SOMETHING. TELL ME, WHAT ARE YOUR *INTERESTS?*
I HAVE TO BE HONEST, *YOU* ARE. I FOLLOW YOU *EVERYWHERE.*
ON TV, IN THE PAPERS, EVEN INTERNET POSTS. I HAVE TO SAY, THE PERSON THAT PUT A HIT ON YOU IS *NOT* MY FAVORITE PERSON.
YES SHE IS.
Huh? WELL, *ANYWAY,* WHEN I'M NOT *TAILING* YOU, I WORK AT A *CELL PHONE STORE* SIX DAYS A WEEK. I SELL THE LATEST SMART PHONES AND UPGRADES.
ON WEDNESDAYS I HELP OUT AT THE LOCAL COMIC SHOP, *JIM HANDY'S GALAXY OF COMICS.*

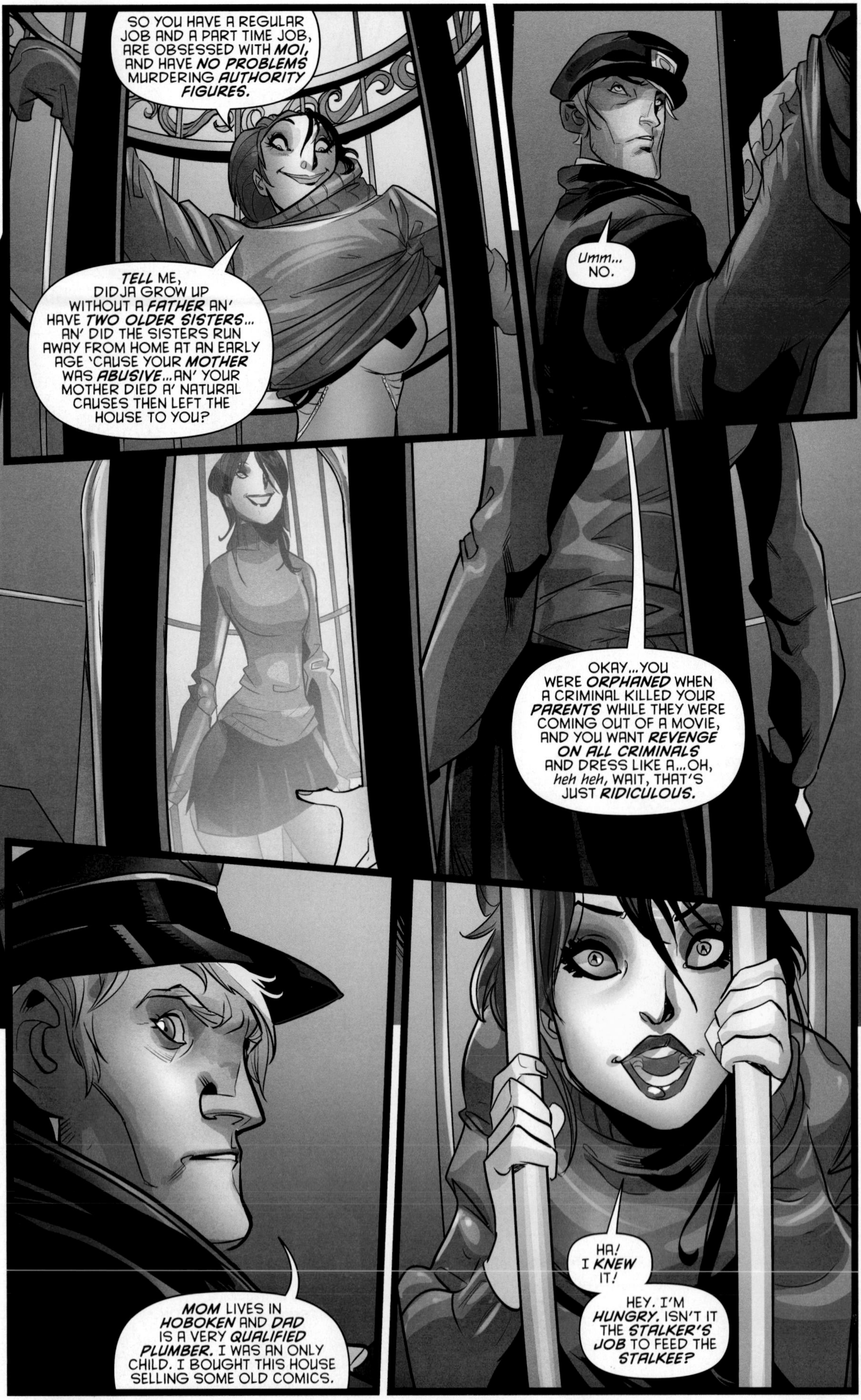
SO YOU HAVE A REGULAR JOB AND A PART TIME JOB, ARE OBSESSED WITH MOI, AND HAVE NO PROBLEMS MURDERING AUTHORITY FIGURES.
TELL ME, DIDJA GROW UP WITHOUT A FATHER AN' HAVE TWO OLDER SISTERS... AN' DID THE SISTERS RUN AWAY FROM HOME AT AN EARLY AGE 'CAUSE YOUR MOTHER WAS ABUSIVE...AN' YOUR MOTHER DIED A' NATURAL CAUSES THEN LEFT THE HOUSE TO YOU?
Umm... NO.
OKAY...YOU WERE ORPHANED WHEN A CRIMINAL KILLED YOUR PARENTS WHILE THEY WERE COMING OUT OF A MOVIE, AND YOU WANT REVENGE ON ALL CRIMINALS AND DRESS LIKE A...OH, heh heh, WAIT, THAT'S JUST RIDICULOUS.
MOM LIVES IN HOBOKEN AND DAD IS A VERY QUALIFIED PLUMBER. I WAS AN ONLY CHILD. I BOUGHT THIS HOUSE SELLING SOME OLD COMICS.
HA! I KNEW IT!
HEY. I'M HUNGRY. ISN'T IT THE STALKER'S JOB TO FEED THE STALKEE?

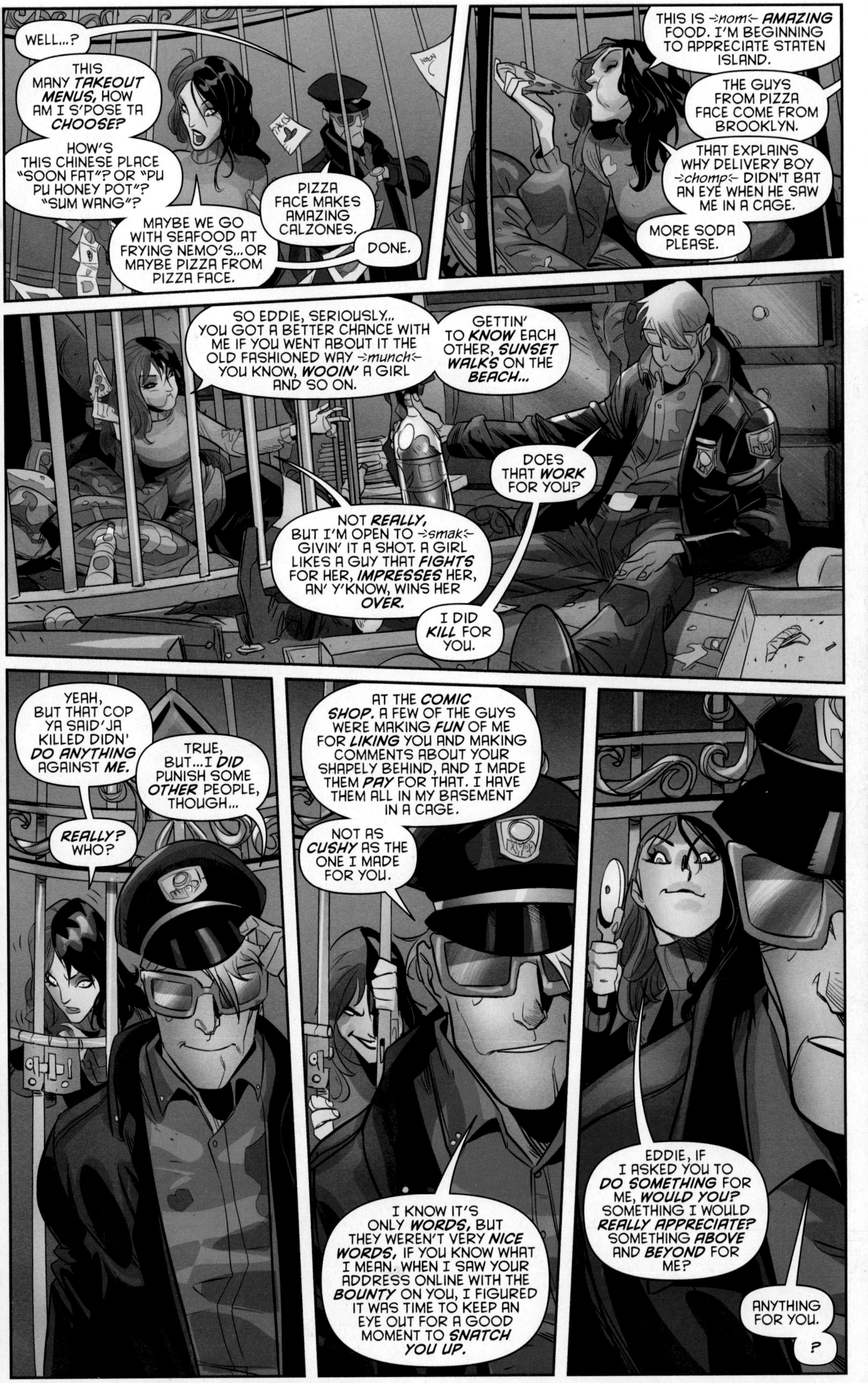
WELL...?
THIS MANY TAKEOUT MENUS, HOW AM I S'POSE TA CHOOSE?
HOW'S THIS CHINESE PLACE "SOON FAT"? OR "PU PU HONEY POT"? "SUM WANG"?
MAYBE WE GO WITH SEAFOOD AT FRYING NEMO'S...OR MAYBE PIZZA FROM PIZZA FACE.
PIZZA FACE MAKES AMAZING CALZONES.
DONE.
THIS IS →nom← AMAZING FOOD. I'M BEGINNING TO APPRECIATE STATEN ISLAND.
THE GUYS FROM PIZZA FACE COME FROM BROOKLYN.
THAT EXPLAINS WHY DELIVERY BOY →chomp← DIDN'T BAT AN EYE WHEN HE SAW ME IN A CAGE.
MORE SODA PLEASE.
SO EDDIE, SERIOUSLY... YOU GOT A BETTER CHANCE WITH ME IF YOU WENT ABOUT IT THE OLD FASHIONED WAY →munch← YOU KNOW, WOOIN' A GIRL AND SO ON.
GETTIN' TO KNOW EACH OTHER, SUNSET WALKS ON THE BEACH...
DOES THAT WORK FOR YOU?
NOT REALLY, BUT I'M OPEN TO →smak← GIVIN' IT A SHOT. A GIRL LIKES A GUY THAT FIGHTS FOR HER, IMPRESSES HER, AN' Y'KNOW, WINS HER OVER.
I DID KILL FOR YOU.
YEAH, BUT THAT COP YA SAID'JA KILLED DIDN' DO ANYTHING AGAINST ME.
TRUE, BUT...I DID PUNISH SOME OTHER PEOPLE, THOUGH...
REALLY? WHO?
AT THE COMIC SHOP. A FEW OF THE GUYS WERE MAKING FUN OF ME FOR LIKING YOU AND MAKING COMMENTS ABOUT YOUR SHAPELY BEHIND, AND I MADE THEM PAY FOR THAT. I HAVE THEM ALL IN MY BASEMENT IN A CAGE.
NOT AS CUSHY AS THE ONE I MADE FOR YOU.
I KNOW IT'S ONLY WORDS, BUT THEY WEREN'T VERY NICE WORDS, IF YOU KNOW WHAT I MEAN. WHEN I SAW YOUR ADDRESS ONLINE WITH THE BOUNTY ON YOU, I FIGURED IT WAS TIME TO KEEP AN EYE OUT FOR A GOOD MOMENT TO SNATCH YOU UP.
EDDIE, IF I ASKED YOU TO DO SOMETHING FOR ME, WOULD YOU? SOMETHING I WOULD REALLY APPRECIATE? SOMETHING ABOVE AND BEYOND FOR ME?
ANYTHING FOR YOU.
?

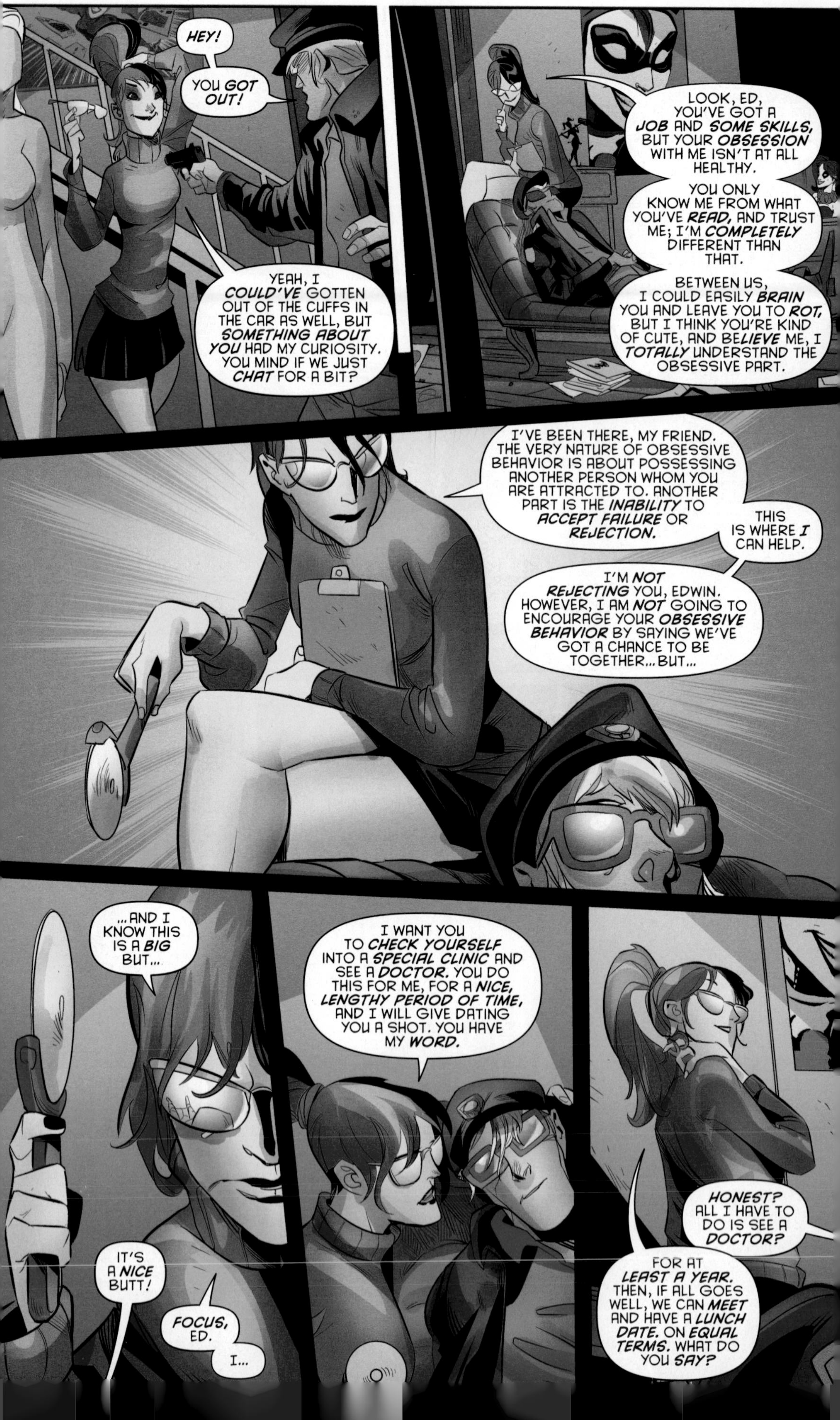
HEY!
YOU GOT OUT!
YEAH, I COULD'VE GOTTEN OUT OF THE CUFFS IN THE CAR AS WELL, BUT SOMETHING ABOUT YOU HAD MY CURIOSITY. YOU MIND IF WE JUST CHAT FOR A BIT?
LOOK, ED, YOU'VE GOT A JOB AND SOME SKILLS, BUT YOUR OBSESSION WITH ME ISN'T AT ALL HEALTHY.
YOU ONLY KNOW ME FROM WHAT YOU'VE READ, AND TRUST ME; I'M COMPLETELY DIFFERENT THAN THAT.
BETWEEN US, I COULD EASILY BRAIN YOU AND LEAVE YOU TO ROT, BUT I THINK YOU'RE KIND OF CUTE, AND BELIEVE ME, I TOTALLY UNDERSTAND THE OBSESSIVE PART.
I'VE BEEN THERE, MY FRIEND. THE VERY NATURE OF OBSESSIVE BEHAVIOR IS ABOUT POSSESSING ANOTHER PERSON WHOM YOU ARE ATTRACTED TO. ANOTHER PART IS THE INABILITY TO ACCEPT FAILURE OR REJECTION.
THIS IS WHERE I CAN HELP.
I'M NOT REJECTING YOU, EDWIN. HOWEVER, I AM NOT GOING TO ENCOURAGE YOUR OBSESSIVE BEHAVIOR BY SAYING WE'VE GOT A CHANCE TO BE TOGETHER... BUT...
...AND I KNOW THIS IS A BIG BUT...
IT'S A NICE BUTT!
FOCUS, ED.
I...
I WANT YOU TO CHECK YOURSELF INTO A SPECIAL CLINIC AND SEE A DOCTOR. YOU DO THIS FOR ME, FOR A NICE, LENGTHY PERIOD OF TIME, AND I WILL GIVE DATING YOU A SHOT. YOU HAVE MY WORD.
HONEST? ALL I HAVE TO DO IS SEE A DOCTOR?
FOR AT LEAST A YEAR. THEN, IF ALL GOES WELL, WE CAN MEET AND HAVE A LUNCH DATE. ON EQUAL TERMS. WHAT DO YOU SAY?

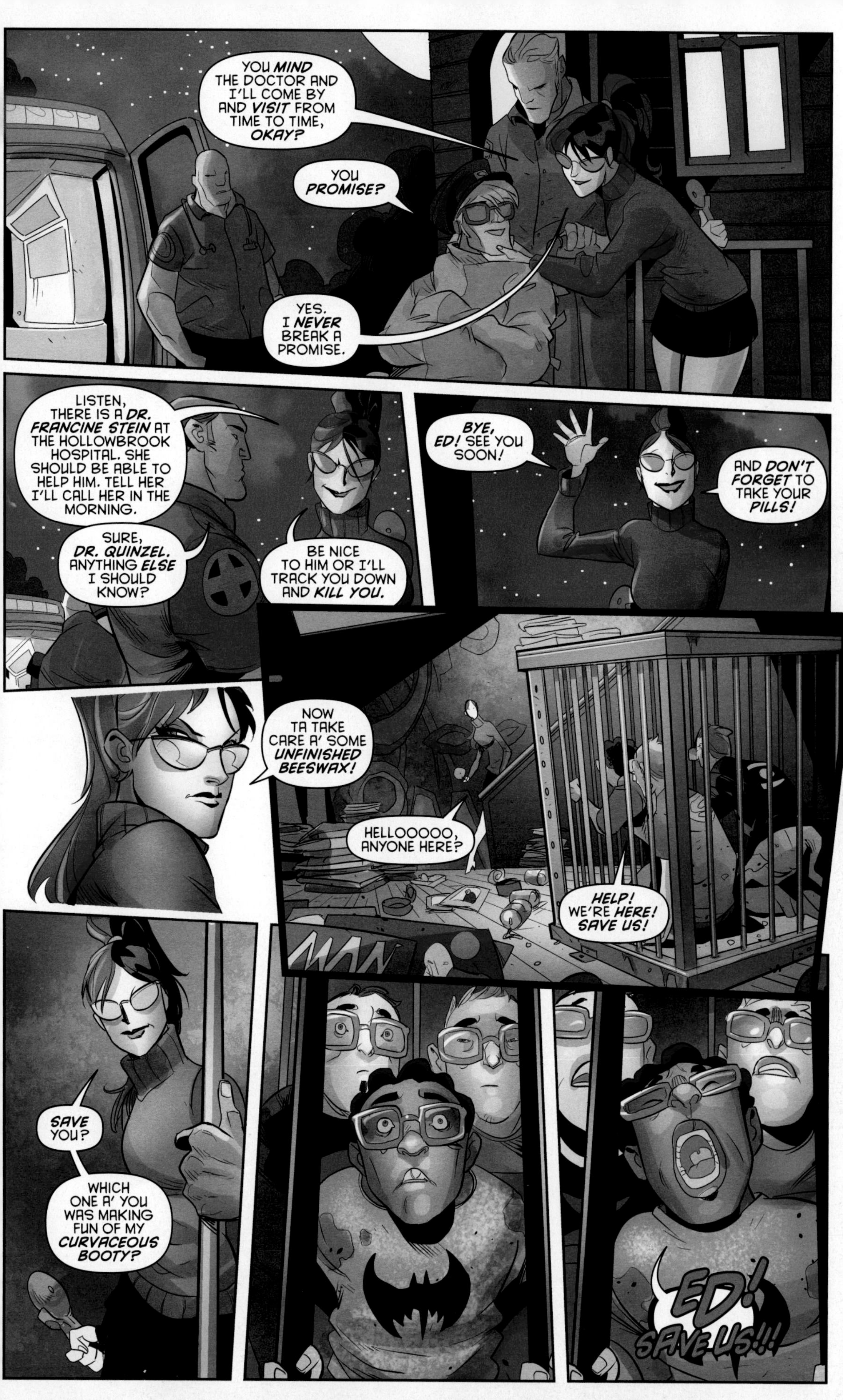
YOU MIND THE DOCTOR AND I'LL COME BY AND VISIT FROM TIME TO TIME, OKAY?
YOU PROMISE?
YES. I NEVER BREAK A PROMISE.
LISTEN, THERE IS A DR. FRANCINE STEIN AT THE HOLLOWBROOK HOSPITAL. SHE SHOULD BE ABLE TO HELP HIM. TELL HER I'LL CALL HER IN THE MORNING.
SURE, DR. QUINZEL. ANYTHING ELSE I SHOULD KNOW?
BE NICE TO HIM OR I'LL TRACK YOU DOWN AND KILL YOU.
BYE, ED! SEE YOU SOON!
AND DON'T FORGET TO TAKE YOUR PILLS!
NOW TA TAKE CARE A' SOME UNFINISHED BEESWAX!
HELLOOOOO, ANYONE HERE?
HELP! WE'RE HERE! SAVE US!
MAN
SAVE YOU?
WHICH ONE A' YOU WAS MAKING FUN OF MY CURVACEOUS BOOTY?
ED! SAVE US!!!

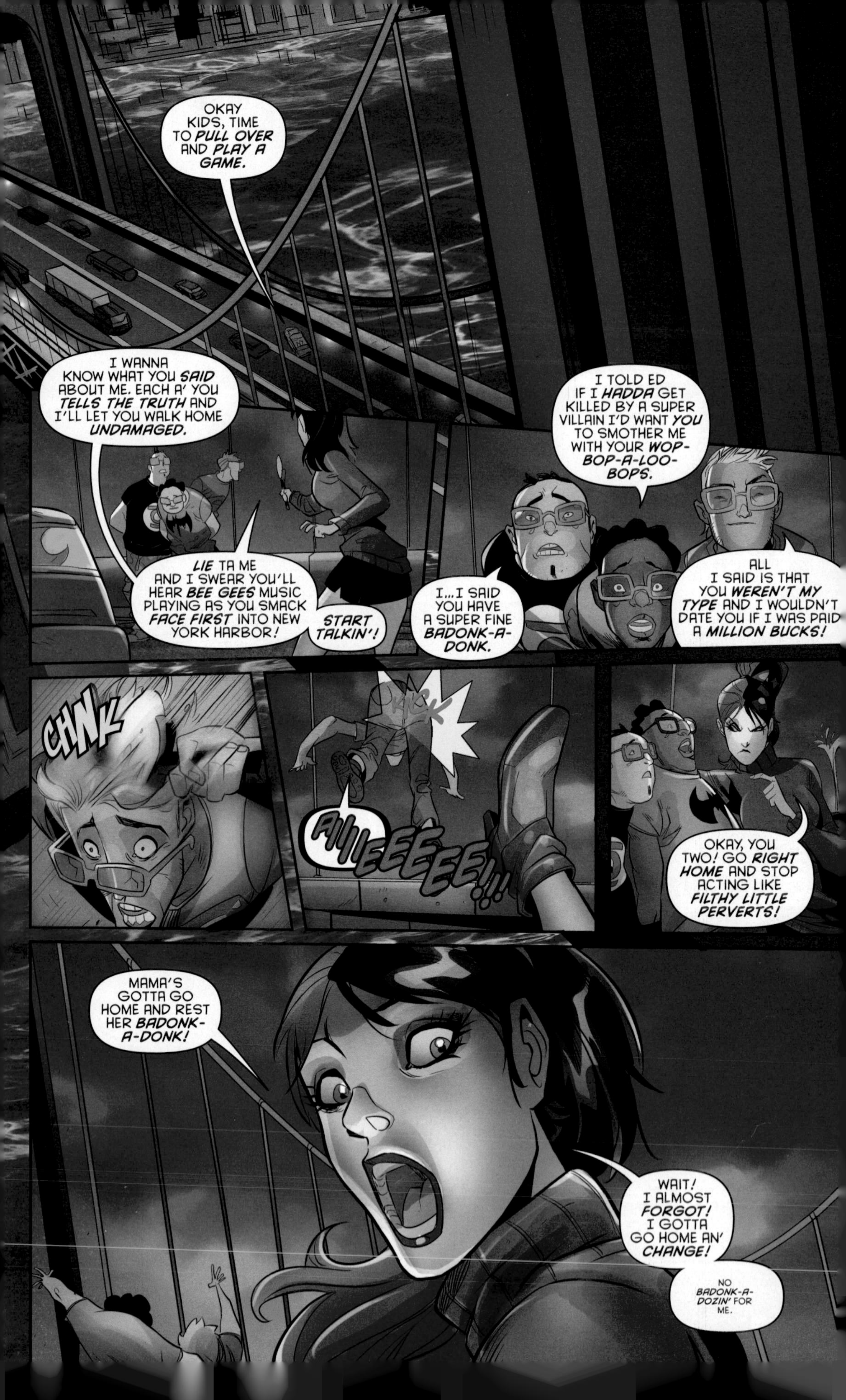
OKAY KIDS, TIME TO PULL OVER AND PLAY A GAME.
I WANNA KNOW WHAT YOU SAID ABOUT ME. EACH A' YOU TELLS THE TRUTH AND I'LL LET YOU WALK HOME UNDAMAGED.
LIE TA ME AND I SWEAR YOU'LL HEAR BEE GEES MUSIC PLAYING AS YOU SMACK FACE FIRST INTO NEW YORK HARBOR!
START TALKIN'!
I TOLD ED IF I HADDA GET KILLED BY A SUPER VILLAIN I'D WANT YOU TO SMOTHER ME WITH YOUR WOP-BOP-A-LOO-BOPS.
I...I SAID YOU HAVE A SUPER FINE BADONK-A-DONK.
ALL I SAID IS THAT YOU WEREN'T MY TYPE AND I WOULDN'T DATE YOU IF I WAS PAID A MILLION BUCKS!
CHNK
KICK
AIIIEEEEEE!!!
OKAY, YOU TWO! GO RIGHT HOME AND STOP ACTING LIKE FILTHY LITTLE PERVERTS!
MAMA'S GOTTA GO HOME AND REST HER BADONK-A-DONK!
WAIT! I ALMOST FORGOT! I GOTTA GO HOME AN' CHANGE!
NO BADONK-A-DOZIN' FOR ME.

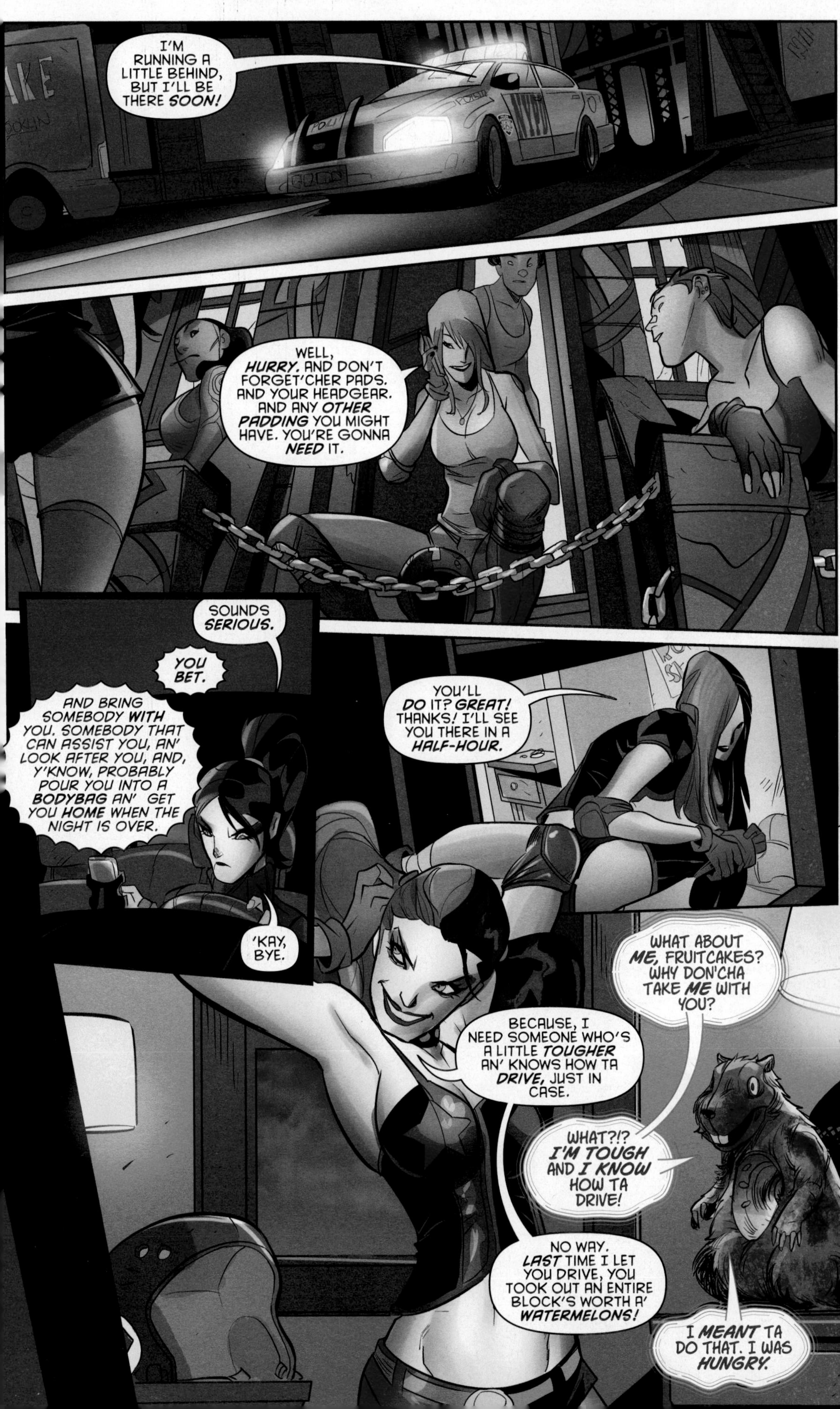
I'M RUNNING A LITTLE BEHIND, BUT I'LL BE THERE SOON!
WELL, HURRY. AND DON'T FORGET'CHER PADS. AND YOUR HEADGEAR. AND ANY OTHER PADDING YOU MIGHT HAVE. YOU'RE GONNA NEED IT.
SOUNDS SERIOUS.
YOU BET.
AND BRING SOMEBODY WITH YOU. SOMEBODY THAT CAN ASSIST YOU, AN' LOOK AFTER YOU, AND, Y'KNOW, PROBABLY POUR YOU INTO A BODYBAG AN' GET YOU HOME WHEN THE NIGHT IS OVER.
YOU'LL DO IT? GREAT! THANKS! I'LL SEE YOU THERE IN A HALF-HOUR.
'KAY, BYE.
WHAT ABOUT ME, FRUITCAKES? WHY DON'CHA TAKE ME WITH YOU?
BECAUSE, I NEED SOMEONE WHO'S A LITTLE TOUGHER AN' KNOWS HOW TA DRIVE, JUST IN CASE.
WHAT?!? I'M TOUGH AND I KNOW HOW TA DRIVE!
NO WAY. LAST TIME I LET YOU DRIVE, YOU TOOK OUT AN ENTIRE BLOCK'S WORTH A' WATERMELONS!
I MEANT TA DO THAT. I WAS HUNGRY.

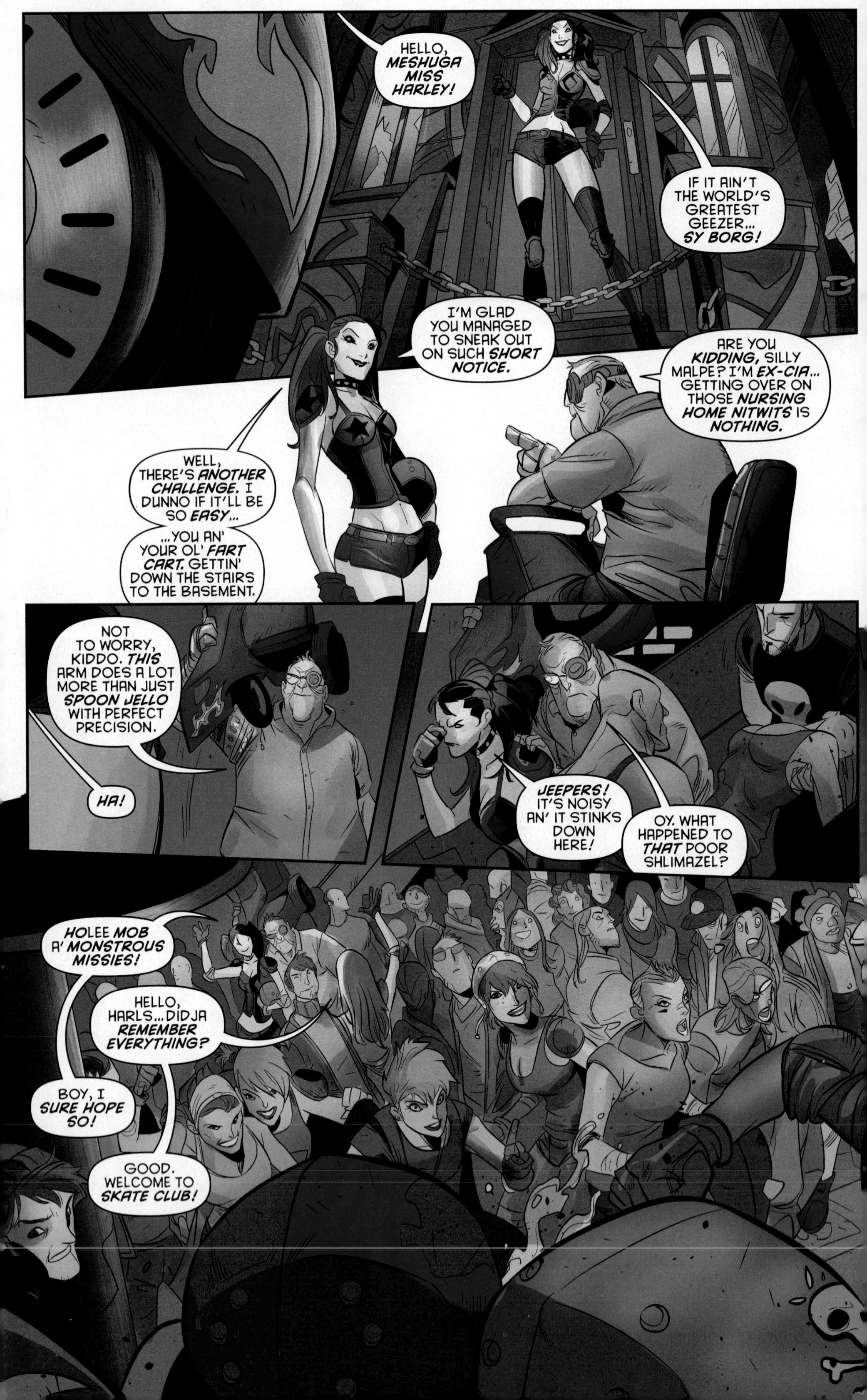
HELLO, MESHUGA MISS HARLEY!
IF IT AIN'T THE WORLD'S GREATEST GEEZER... SY BORG!
I'M GLAD YOU MANAGED TO SNEAK OUT ON SUCH SHORT NOTICE.
ARE YOU KIDDING, SILLY MALPE? I'M EX-CIA... GETTING OVER ON THOSE NURSING HOME NITWITS IS NOTHING.
WELL, THERE'S ANOTHER CHALLENGE. I DUNNO IF IT'LL BE SO EASY...
...YOU AN' YOUR OL' FART CART, GETTIN' DOWN THE STAIRS TO THE BASEMENT.
NOT TO WORRY, KIDDO. THIS ARM DOES A LOT MORE THAN JUST SPOON JELLO WITH PERFECT PRECISION.
HA!
JEEPERS! IT'S NOISY AN' IT STINKS DOWN HERE!
OY. WHAT HAPPENED TO THAT POOR SHLIMAZEL?
HOLEE MOB A' MONSTROUS MISSIES!
HELLO, HARLS...DIDJA REMEMBER EVERYTHING?
BOY, I SURE HOPE SO!
GOOD. WELCOME TO SKATE CLUB!

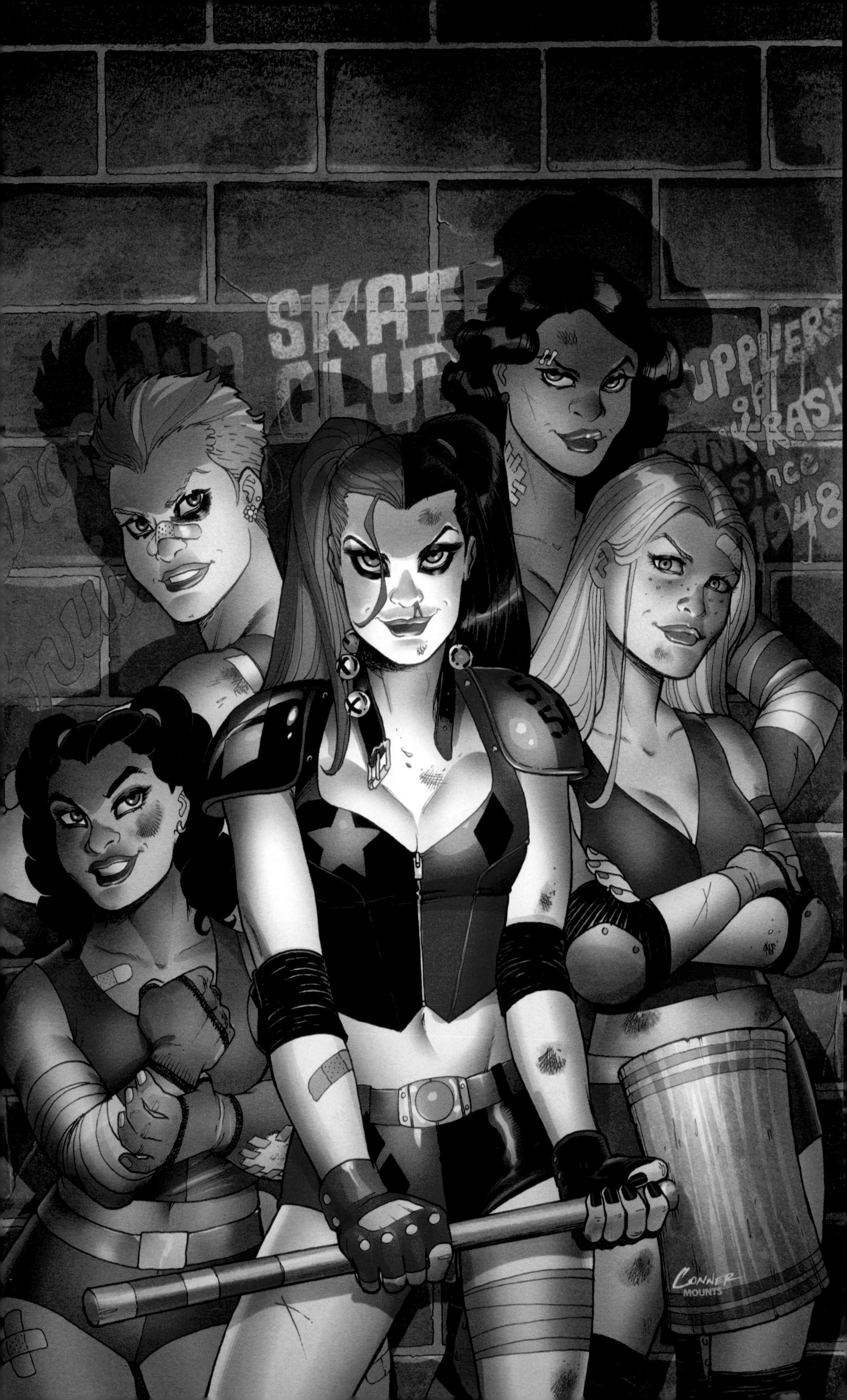
SKATE
since
1948
CONNER
MOUNTS

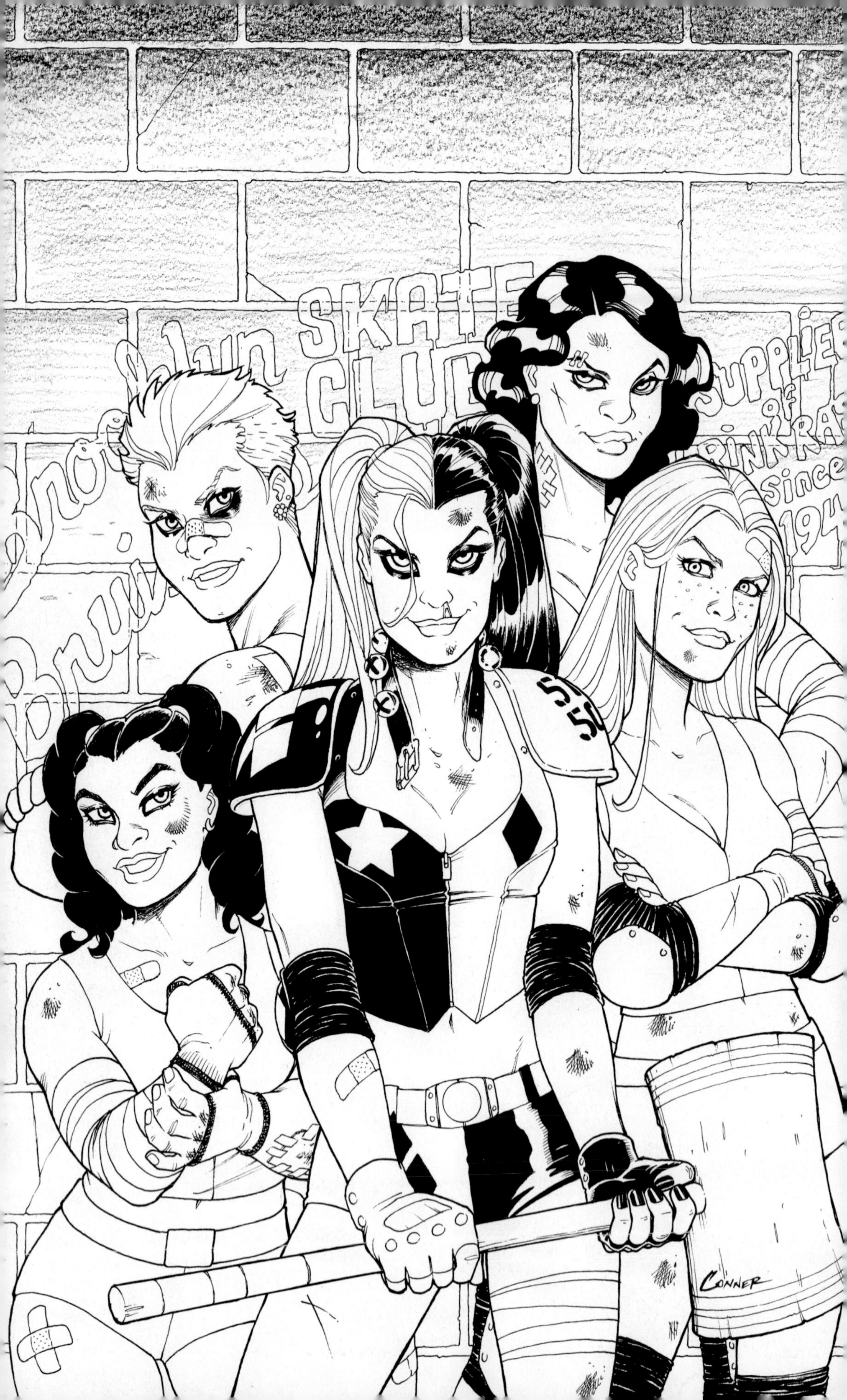

SKATE
of
since
CONNER

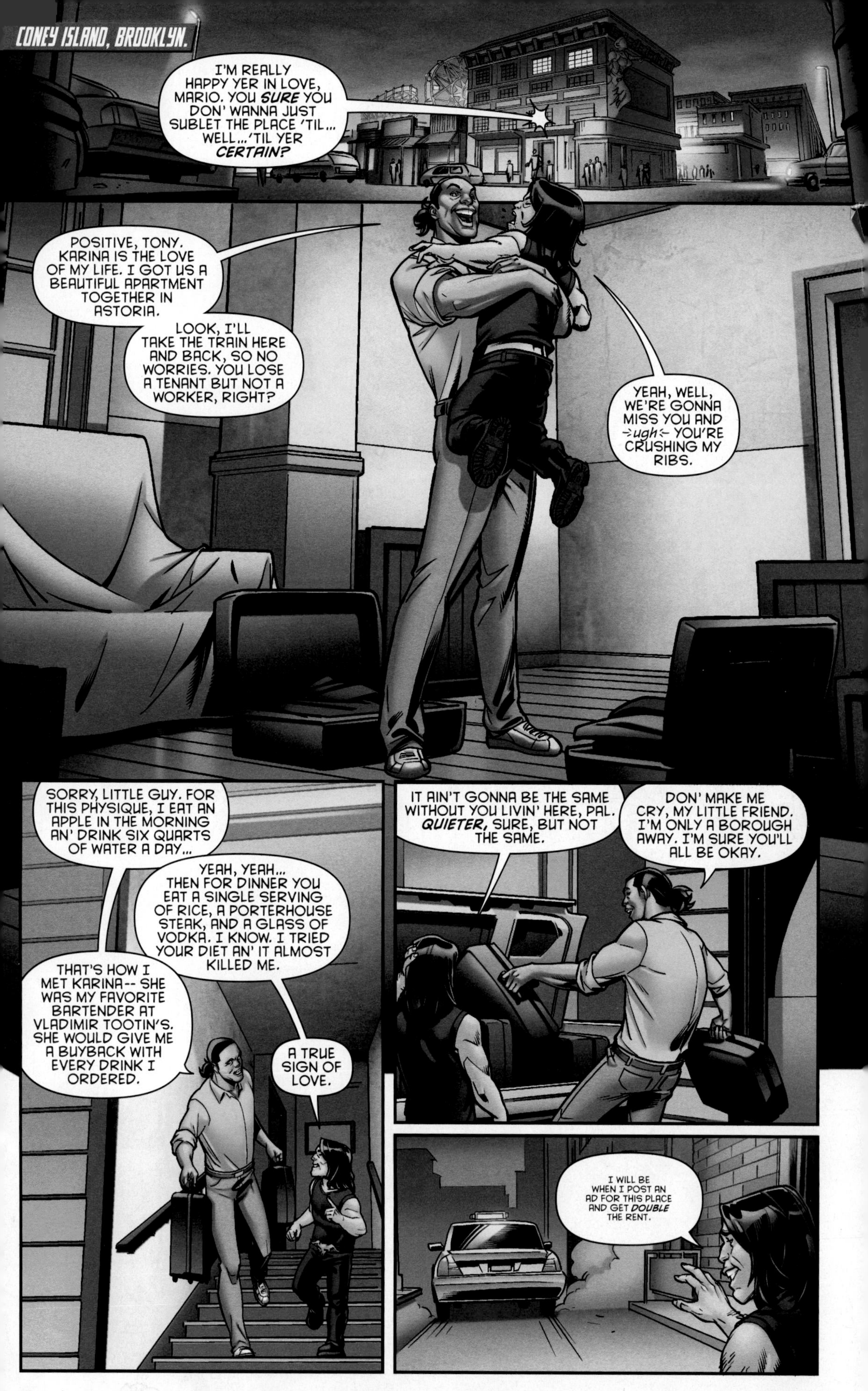
CONEY ISLAND, BROOKLYN.
I'M REALLY HAPPY YER IN LOVE, MARIO. YOU *SURE* YOU DON' WANNA JUST SUBLET THE PLACE 'TIL... WELL...'TIL YER *CERTAIN?*
POSITIVE, TONY. KARINA IS THE LOVE OF MY LIFE. I GOT US A BEAUTIFUL APARTMENT TOGETHER IN ASTORIA.
LOOK, I'LL TAKE THE TRAIN HERE AND BACK, SO NO WORRIES. YOU LOSE A TENANT BUT NOT A WORKER, RIGHT?
YEAH, WELL, WE'RE GONNA MISS YOU AND *ugh* YOU'RE CRUSHING MY RIBS.
SORRY, LITTLE GUY. FOR THIS PHYSIQUE, I EAT AN APPLE IN THE MORNING AN' DRINK SIX QUARTS OF WATER A DAY...
YEAH, YEAH... THEN FOR DINNER YOU EAT A SINGLE SERVING OF RICE, A PORTERHOUSE STEAK, AND A GLASS OF VODKA. I KNOW. I TRIED YOUR DIET AN' IT ALMOST KILLED ME.
THAT'S HOW I MET KARINA-- SHE WAS MY FAVORITE BARTENDER AT VLADIMIR TOOTIN'S. SHE WOULD GIVE ME A BUYBACK WITH EVERY DRINK I ORDERED.
A TRUE SIGN OF LOVE.
IT AIN'T GONNA BE THE SAME WITHOUT YOU LIVIN' HERE, PAL. *QUIETER,* SURE, BUT NOT THE SAME.
DON' MAKE ME CRY, MY LITTLE FRIEND. I'M ONLY A BOROUGH AWAY. I'M SURE YOU'LL ALL BE OKAY.
I WILL BE WHEN I POST AN AD FOR THIS PLACE AND GET *DOUBLE* THE RENT.

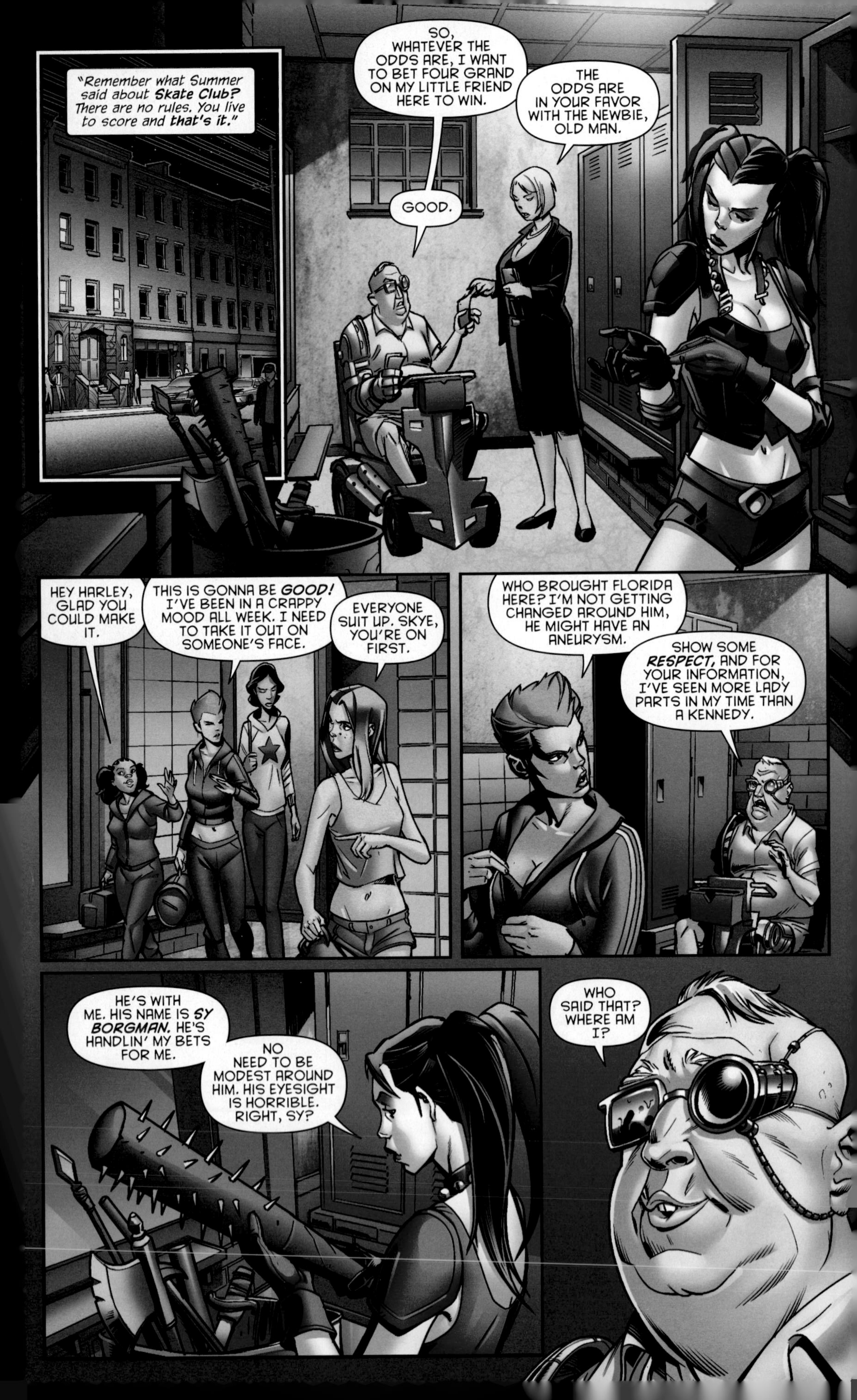
"Remember what Summer said about Skate Club? There are no rules. You live to score and that's it."
SO, WHATEVER THE ODDS ARE, I WANT TO BET FOUR GRAND ON MY LITTLE FRIEND HERE TO WIN.
THE ODDS ARE IN YOUR FAVOR WITH THE NEWBIE, OLD MAN.
GOOD.
HEY HARLEY, GLAD YOU COULD MAKE IT.
THIS IS GONNA BE GOOD! I'VE BEEN IN A CRAPPY MOOD ALL WEEK. I NEED TO TAKE IT OUT ON SOMEONE'S FACE.
EVERYONE SUIT UP. SKYE, YOU'RE ON FIRST.
WHO BROUGHT FLORIDA HERE? I'M NOT GETTING CHANGED AROUND HIM, HE MIGHT HAVE AN ANEURYSM.
SHOW SOME RESPECT, AND FOR YOUR INFORMATION, I'VE SEEN MORE LADY PARTS IN MY TIME THAN A KENNEDY.
HE'S WITH ME. HIS NAME IS SY BORGMAN. HE'S HANDLIN' MY BETS FOR ME.
NO NEED TO BE MODEST AROUND HIM. HIS EYESIGHT IS HORRIBLE. RIGHT, SY?
WHO SAID THAT? WHERE AM I?

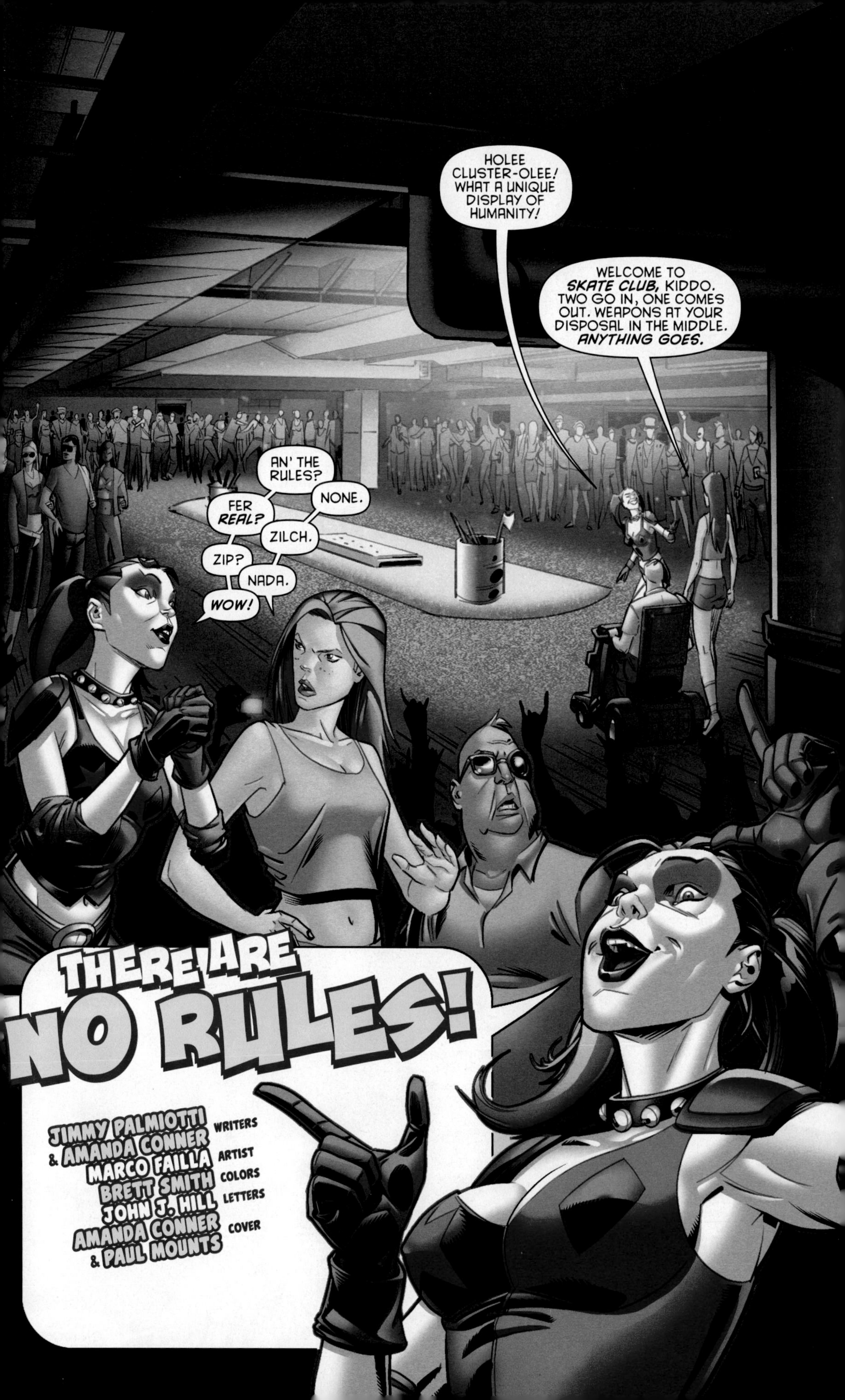

HOLEE CLUSTER-OLEE! WHAT A UNIQUE DISPLAY OF HUMANITY!
WELCOME TO SKATE CLUB, KIDDO. TWO GO IN, ONE COMES OUT. WEAPONS AT YOUR DISPOSAL IN THE MIDDLE. ANYTHING GOES.
AN' THE RULES?
NONE.
FER REAL?
ZILCH.
ZIP?
NADA.
WOW!
THERE ARE NO RULES!
JIMMY PALMIOTTI & AMANDA CONNER WRITERS
MARCO FAILLA ARTIST
BRETT SMITH COLORS
JOHN J. HILL LETTERS
AMANDA CONNER & PAUL MOUNTS COVER

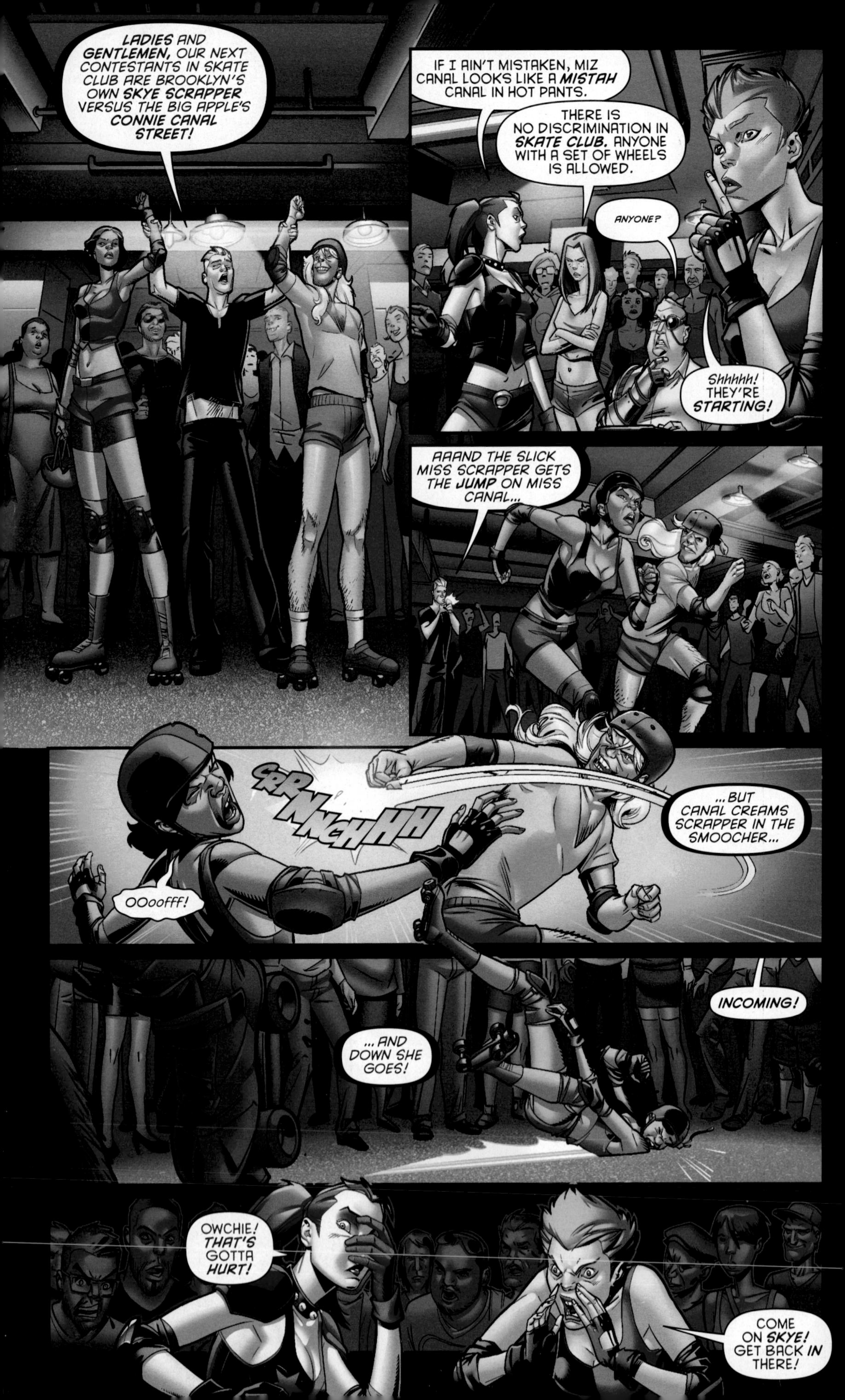

LADIES AND GENTLEMEN, OUR NEXT CONTESTANTS IN SKATE CLUB ARE BROOKLYN'S OWN SKYE SCRAPPER VERSUS THE BIG APPLE'S CONNIE CANAL STREET!
IF I AIN'T MISTAKEN, MIZ CANAL LOOKS LIKE A MISTAH CANAL IN HOT PANTS.
THERE IS NO DISCRIMINATION IN SKATE CLUB. ANYONE WITH A SET OF WHEELS IS ALLOWED.
ANYONE?
Shhhhh! THEY'RE STARTING!
AAAND THE SLICK MISS SCRAPPER GETS THE JUMP ON MISS CANAL...
CRRNNCHHHH
...BUT CANAL CREAMS SCRAPPER IN THE SMOOCHER...
OOoofff!
INCOMING!
...AND DOWN SHE GOES!
OWCHIE! THAT'S GOTTA HURT!
COME ON SKYE! GET BACK IN THERE!

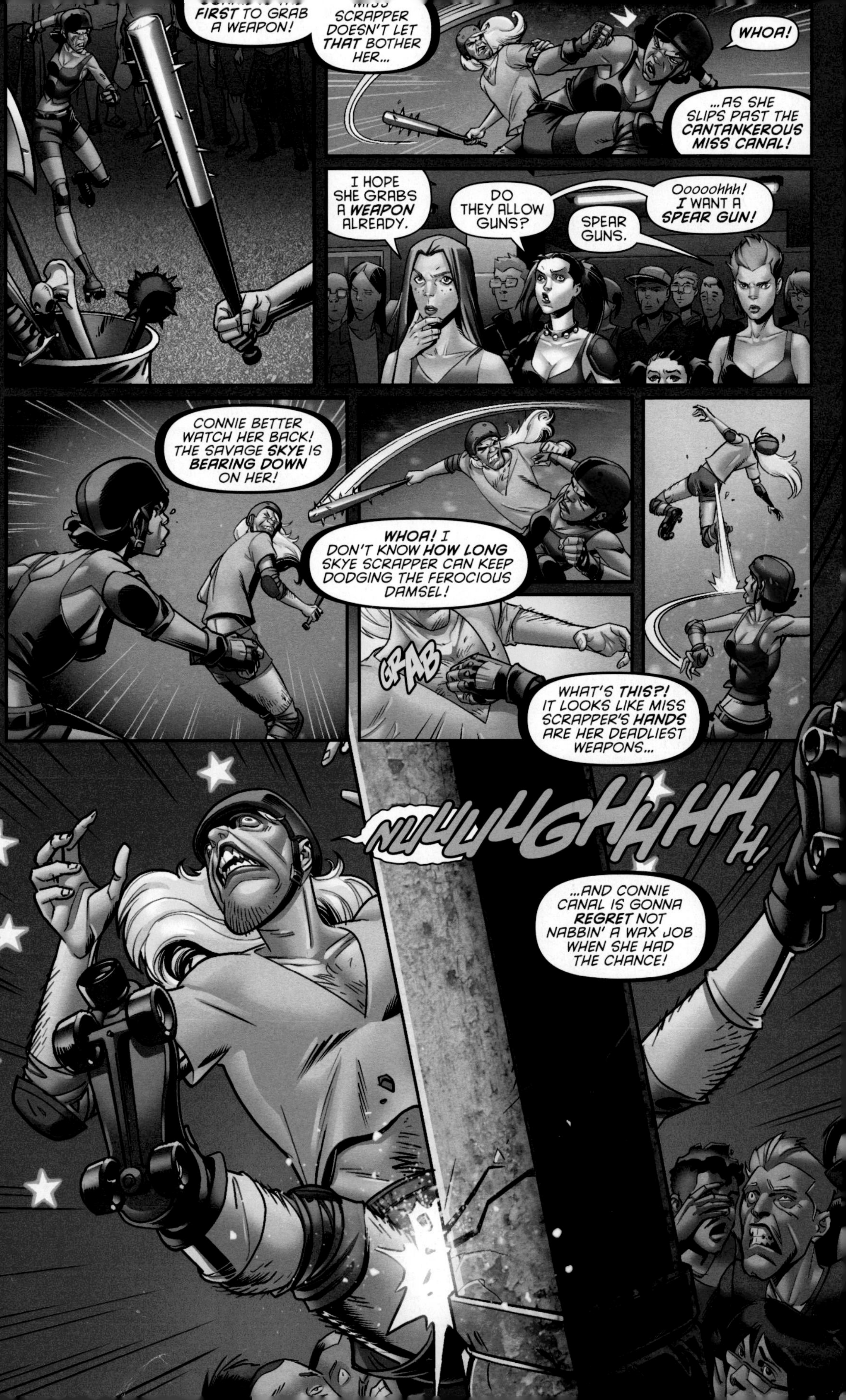

FIRST TO GRAB A WEAPON!
SCRAPPER DOESN'T LET THAT BOTHER HER...
WHOA!
...AS SHE SLIPS PAST THE CANTANKEROUS MISS CANAL!
I HOPE SHE GRABS A WEAPON ALREADY.
DO THEY ALLOW GUNS?
SPEAR GUNS.
Ooooohhh! I WANT A SPEAR GUN!
CONNIE BETTER WATCH HER BACK! THE SAVAGE SKYE IS BEARING DOWN ON HER!
WHOA! I DON'T KNOW HOW LONG SKYE SCRAPPER CAN KEEP DODGING THE FEROCIOUS DAMSEL!
GRAB
WHAT'S THIS?! IT LOOKS LIKE MISS SCRAPPER'S HANDS ARE HER DEADLIEST WEAPONS...
NUUUUGHHHHH!
...AND CONNIE CANAL IS GONNA REGRET NOT NABBIN' A WAX JOB WHEN SHE HAD THE CHANCE!

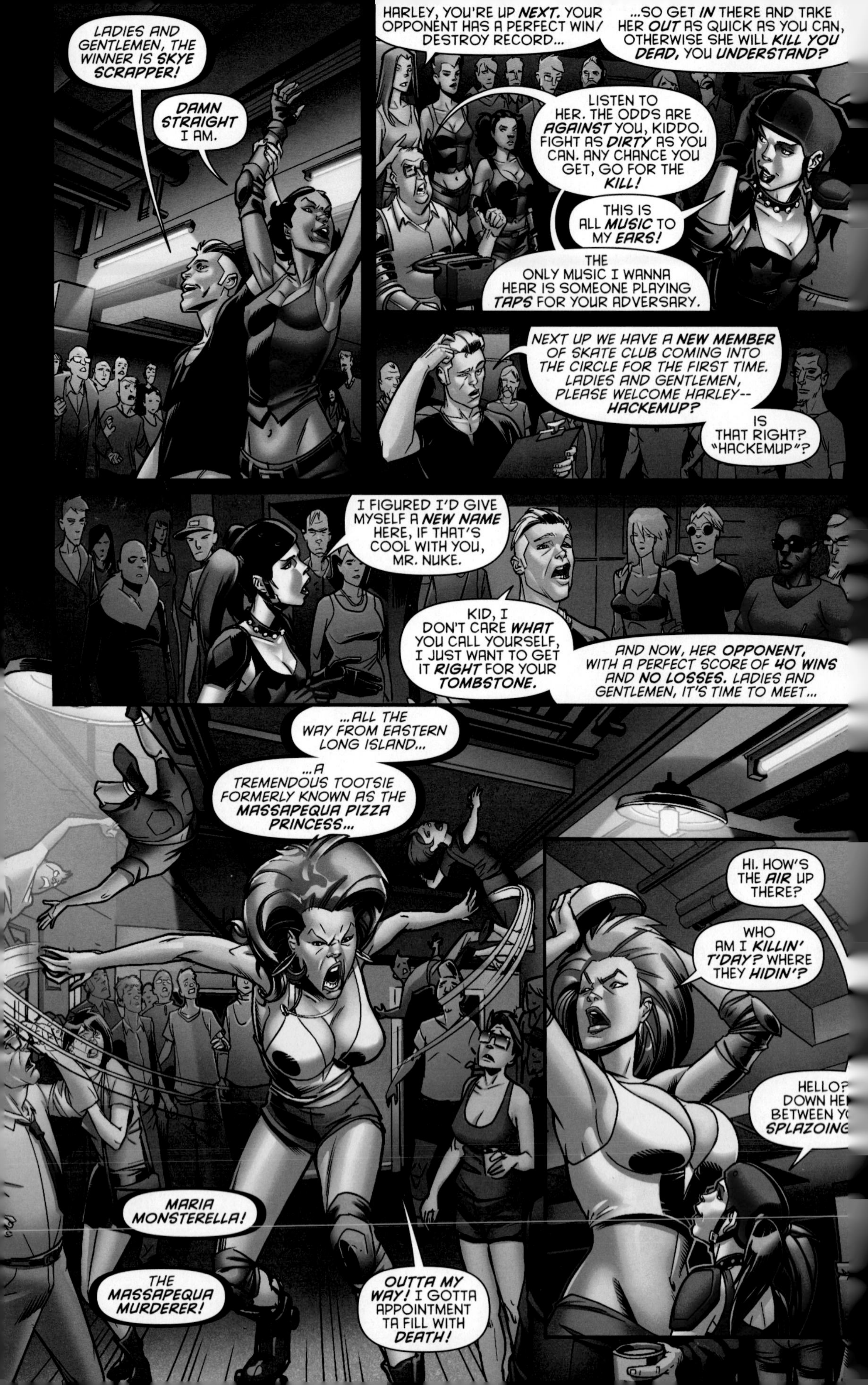
LADIES AND GENTLEMEN, THE WINNER IS SKYE SCRAPPER!
DAMN STRAIGHT I AM.
HARLEY, YOU'RE UP NEXT. YOUR OPPONENT HAS A PERFECT WIN/ DESTROY RECORD...
...SO GET IN THERE AND TAKE HER OUT AS QUICK AS YOU CAN, OTHERWISE SHE WILL KILL YOU DEAD, YOU UNDERSTAND?
LISTEN TO HER. THE ODDS ARE AGAINST YOU, KIDDO. FIGHT AS DIRTY AS YOU CAN. ANY CHANCE YOU GET, GO FOR THE KILL!
THIS IS ALL MUSIC TO MY EARS!
THE ONLY MUSIC I WANNA HEAR IS SOMEONE PLAYING TAPS FOR YOUR ADVERSARY.
NEXT UP WE HAVE A NEW MEMBER OF SKATE CLUB COMING INTO THE CIRCLE FOR THE FIRST TIME. LADIES AND GENTLEMEN, PLEASE WELCOME HARLEY-- HACKEMUP?
IS THAT RIGHT? "HACKEMUP"?
I FIGURED I'D GIVE MYSELF A NEW NAME HERE, IF THAT'S COOL WITH YOU, MR. NUKE.
KID, I DON'T CARE WHAT YOU CALL YOURSELF, I JUST WANT TO GET IT RIGHT FOR YOUR TOMBSTONE.
AND NOW, HER OPPONENT, WITH A PERFECT SCORE OF 40 WINS AND NO LOSSES. LADIES AND GENTLEMEN, IT'S TIME TO MEET...
...ALL THE WAY FROM EASTERN LONG ISLAND...
...A TREMENDOUS TOOTSIE FORMERLY KNOWN AS THE MASSAPEQUA PIZZA PRINCESS...
MARIA MONSTERELLA!
THE MASSAPEQUA MURDERER!
OUTTA MY WAY! I GOTTA APPOINTMENT TA FILL WITH DEATH!
HI. HOW'S THE AIR UP THERE?
WHO AM I KILLIN' T'DAY? WHERE THEY HIDIN'?

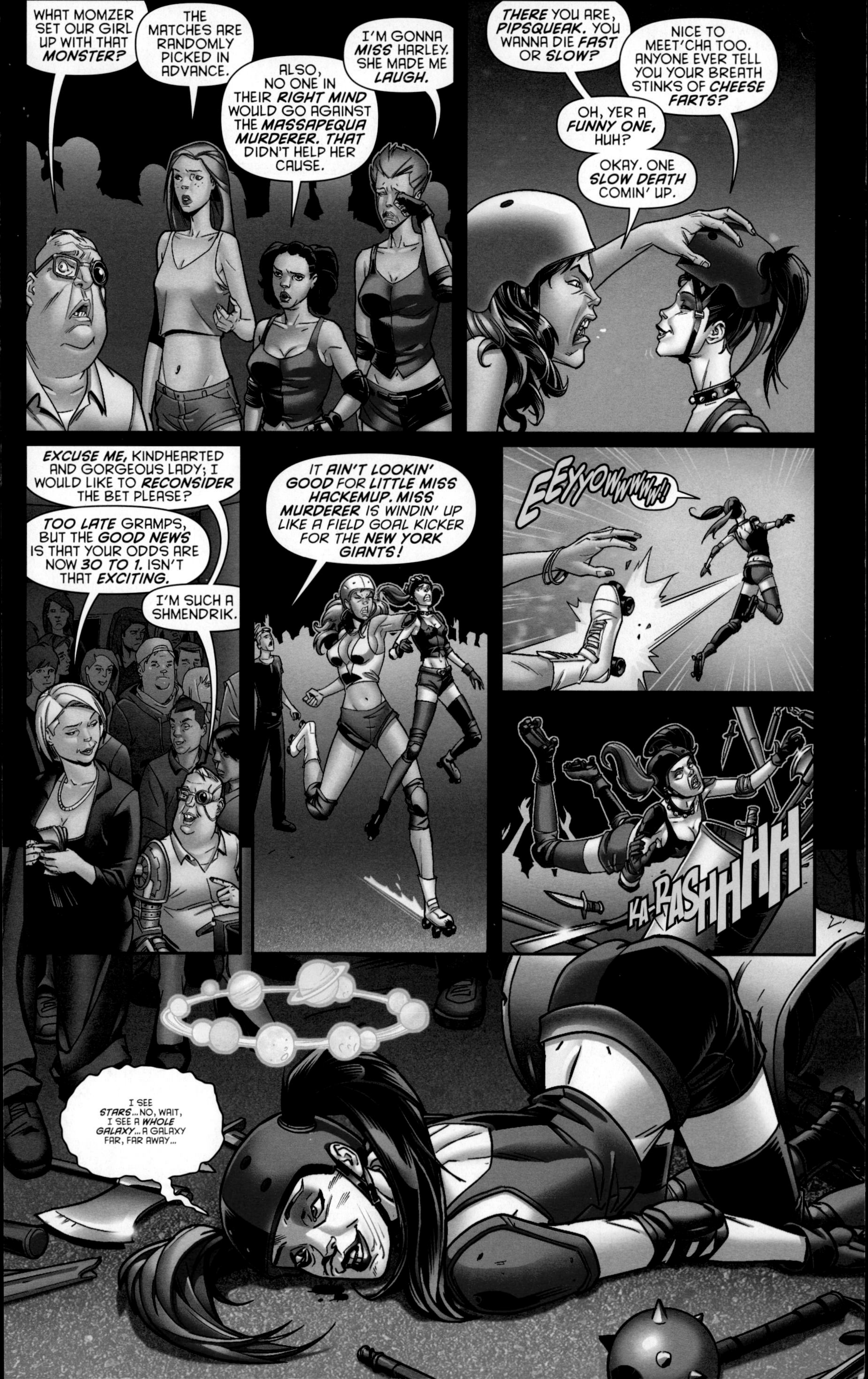
WHAT MOMZER SET OUR GIRL UP WITH THAT MONSTER?
THE MATCHES ARE RANDOMLY PICKED IN ADVANCE.
ALSO, NO ONE IN THEIR RIGHT MIND WOULD GO AGAINST THE MASSAPEQUA MURDERER. THAT DIDN'T HELP HER CAUSE.
I'M GONNA MISS HARLEY. SHE MADE ME LAUGH.
THERE YOU ARE, PIPSQUEAK. YOU WANNA DIE FAST OR SLOW?
NICE TO MEET'CHA TOO. ANYONE EVER TELL YOU YOUR BREATH STINKS OF CHEESE FARTS?
OH, YER A FUNNY ONE, HUH?
OKAY. ONE SLOW DEATH COMIN' UP.
EXCUSE ME, KINDHEARTED AND GORGEOUS LADY; I WOULD LIKE TO RECONSIDER THE BET PLEASE?
TOO LATE GRAMPS, BUT THE GOOD NEWS IS THAT YOUR ODDS ARE NOW 30 TO 1. ISN'T THAT EXCITING.
I'M SUCH A SHMENDRIK.
IT AIN'T LOOKIN' GOOD FOR LITTLE MISS HACKEMUP. MISS MURDERER IS WINDIN' UP LIKE A FIELD GOAL KICKER FOR THE NEW YORK GIANTS!
EEYYOWWWWW!
KA-RASHHHH
I SEE STARS...NO, WAIT, I SEE A WHOLE GALAXY...A GALAXY FAR, FAR AWAY...

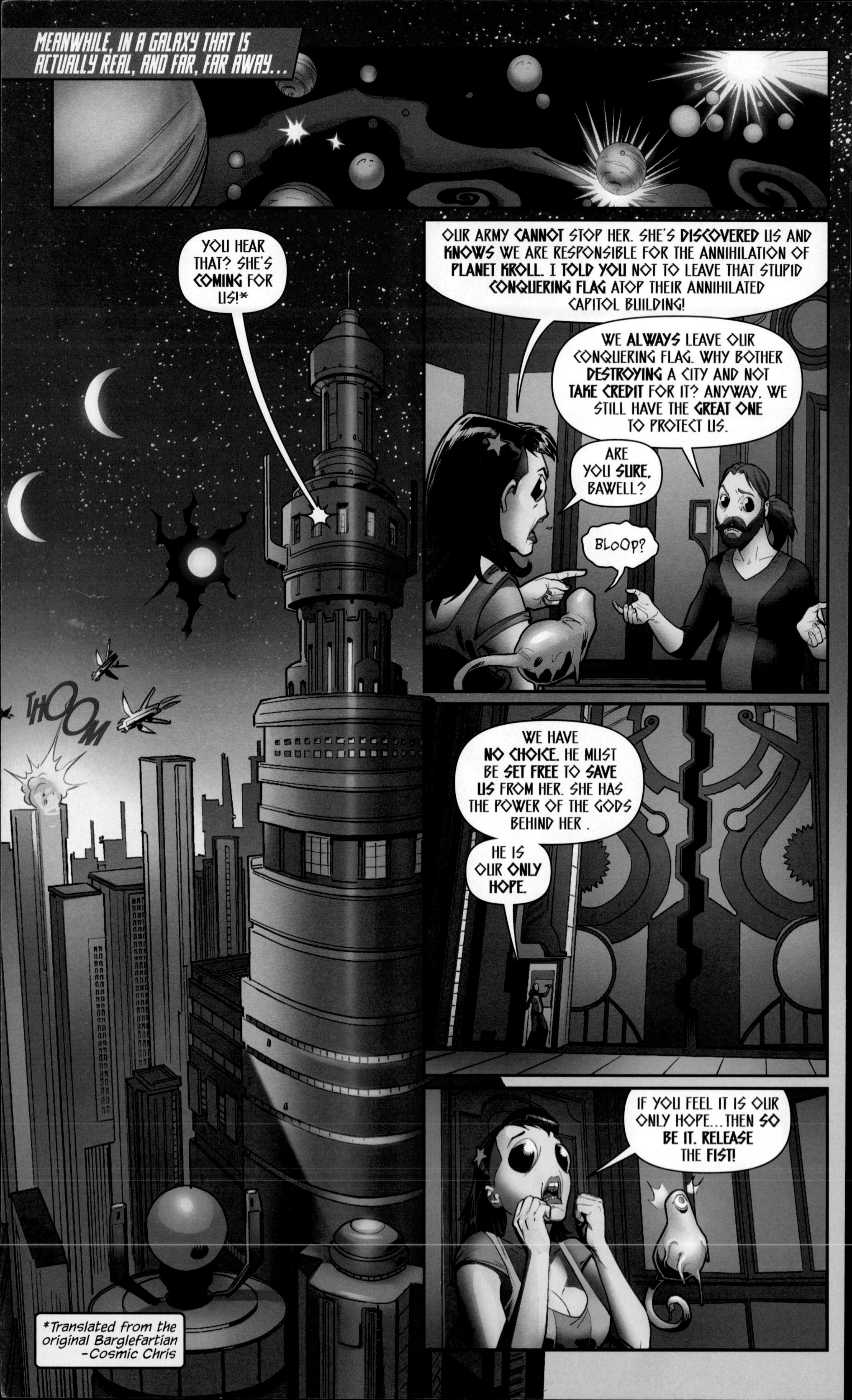
MEANWHILE, IN A GALAXY THAT IS ACTUALLY REAL, AND FAR, FAR AWAY...
YOU HEAR THAT? SHE'S COMING FOR US!*
THOOOM
OUR ARMY CANNOT STOP HER. SHE'S DISCOVERED US AND KNOWS WE ARE RESPONSIBLE FOR THE ANNIHILATION OF PLANET KROLL. I TOLD YOU NOT TO LEAVE THAT STUPID CONQUERING FLAG ATOP THEIR ANNIHILATED CAPITOL BUILDING!
WE ALWAYS LEAVE OUR CONQUERING FLAG. WHY BOTHER DESTROYING A CITY AND NOT TAKE CREDIT FOR IT? ANYWAY, WE STILL HAVE THE GREAT ONE TO PROTECT US.
ARE YOU SURE, BAWELL?
BLOOP?
WE HAVE NO CHOICE. HE MUST BE SET FREE TO SAVE US FROM HER. SHE HAS THE POWER OF THE GODS BEHIND HER .
HE IS OUR ONLY HOPE.
IF YOU FEEL IT IS OUR ONLY HOPE...THEN SO BE IT. RELEASE THE FIST!
*Translated from the original Barglefartian -Cosmic Chris

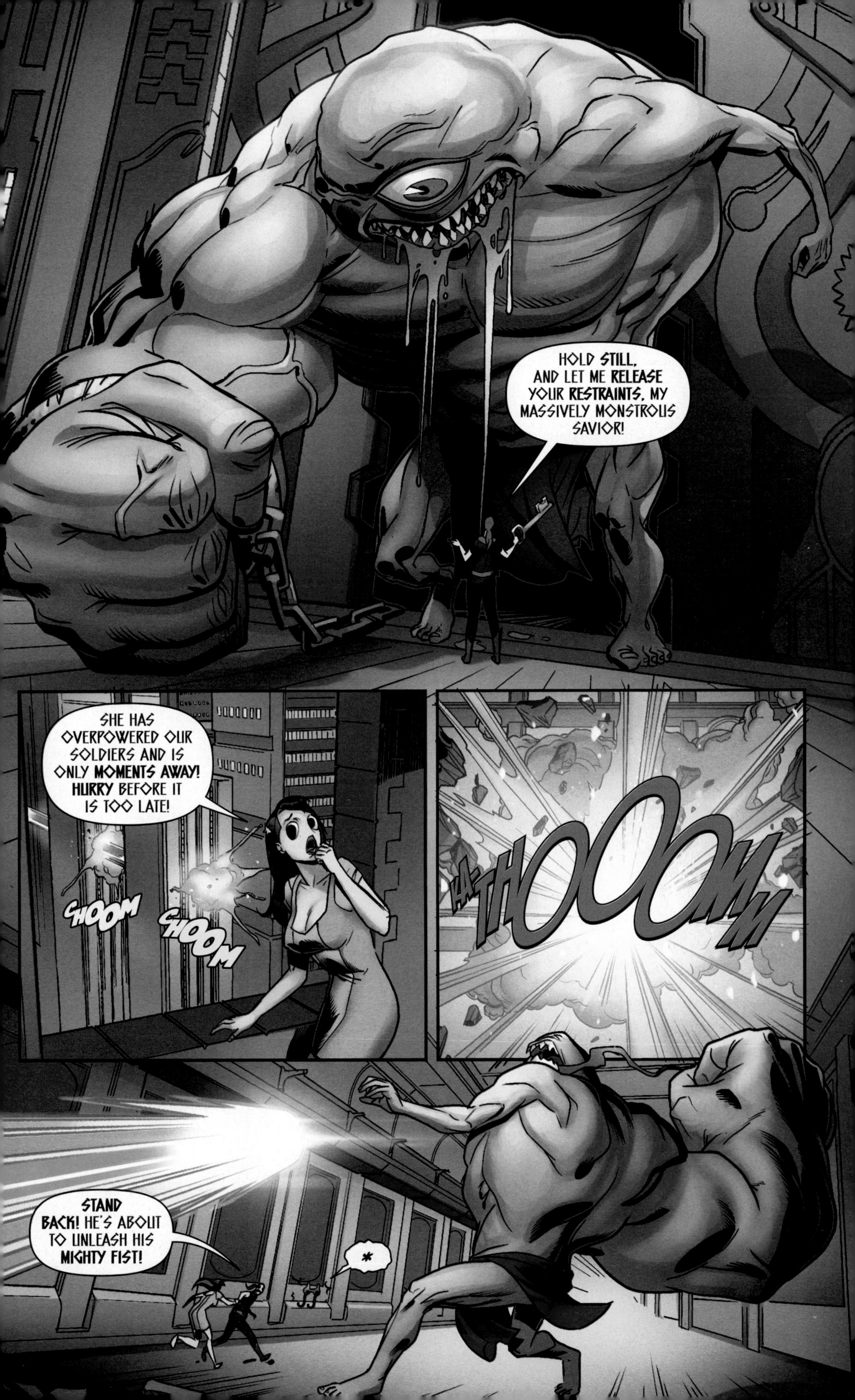
HOLD STILL, AND LET ME RELEASE YOUR RESTRAINTS, MY MASSIVELY MONSTROUS SAVIOR!
SHE HAS OVERPOWERED OUR SOLDIERS AND IS ONLY MOMENTS AWAY! HURRY BEFORE IT IS TOO LATE!
CHOOM
CHOOM
KATHOOOMM
STAND BACK! HE'S ABOUT TO UNLEASH HIS MIGHTY FIST!
*

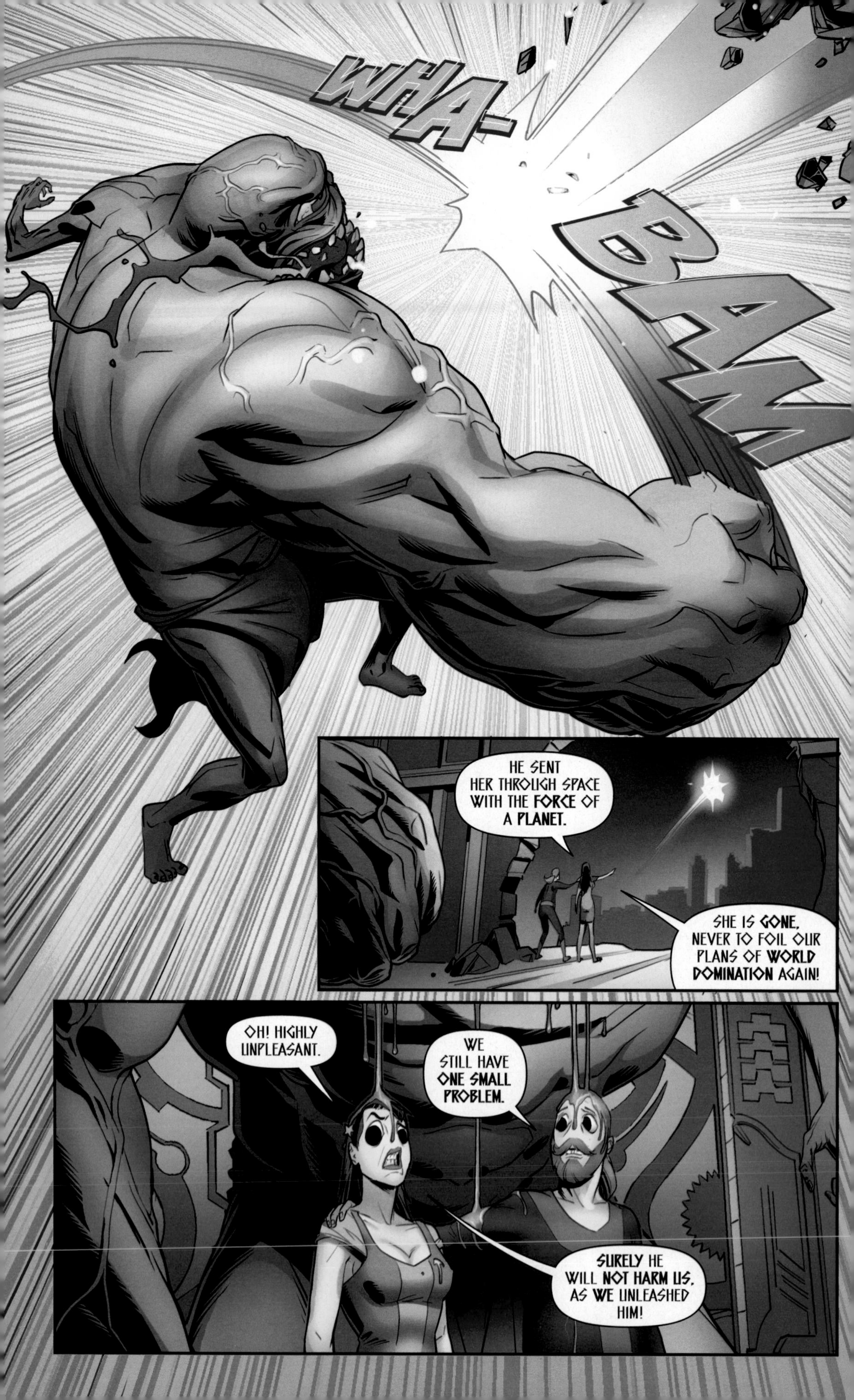
WHA-
BAM
HE SENT HER THROUGH SPACE WITH THE FORCE OF A PLANET.
SHE IS GONE, NEVER TO FOIL OUR PLANS OF WORLD DOMINATION AGAIN!
OH! HIGHLY UNPLEASANT.
WE STILL HAVE ONE SMALL PROBLEM.
SURELY HE WILL NOT HARM US, AS WE UNLEASHED HIM!

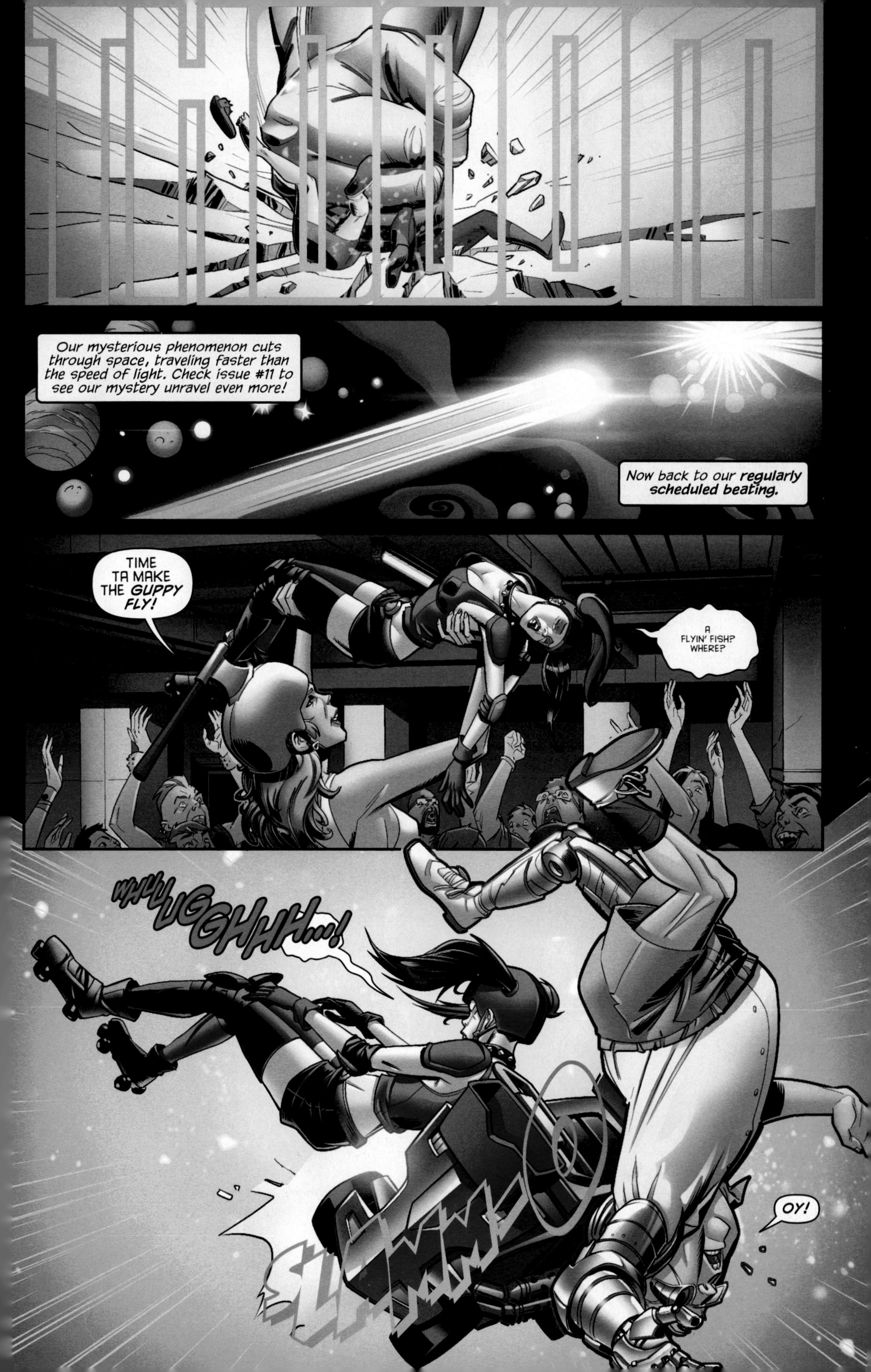
THOOOOM
Our mysterious phenomenon cuts through space, traveling faster than the speed of light. Check issue #11 to see our mystery unravel even more!
Now back to our regularly scheduled beating.
TIME TA MAKE THE GUPPY FLY!
A FLYIN' FISH? WHERE?
WHUUGGHHH...!
OY!

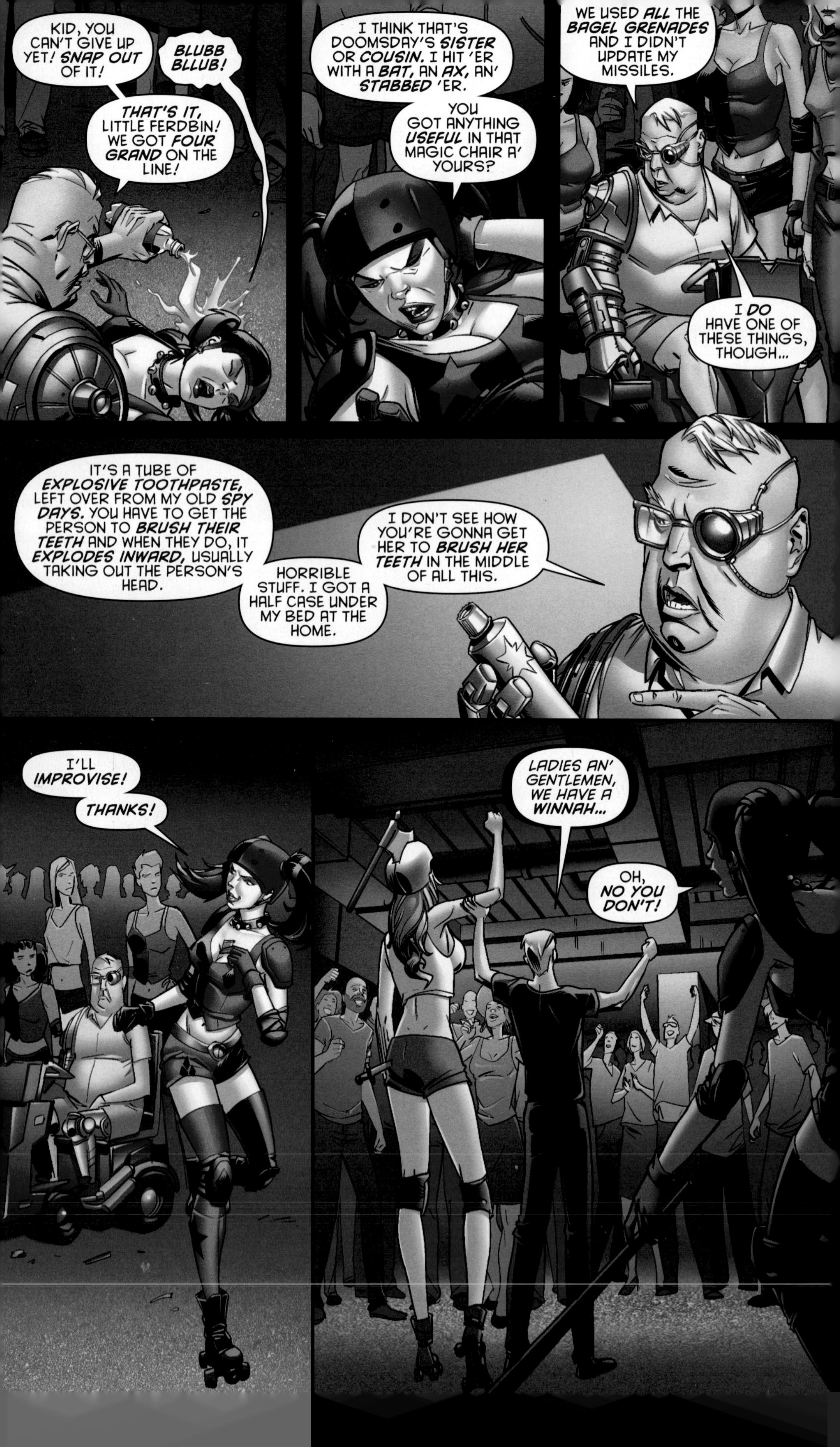

KID, YOU CAN'T GIVE UP YET! SNAP OUT OF IT!
BLUBB BLLUB!
THAT'S IT, LITTLE FERDBIN! WE GOT FOUR GRAND ON THE LINE!
I THINK THAT'S DOOMSDAY'S SISTER OR COUSIN. I HIT 'ER WITH A BAT, AN AX, AN' STABBED 'ER.
YOU GOT ANYTHING USEFUL IN THAT MAGIC CHAIR A' YOURS?
WE USED ALL THE BAGEL GRENADES AND I DIDN'T UPDATE MY MISSILES.
I DO HAVE ONE OF THESE THINGS, THOUGH...
IT'S A TUBE OF EXPLOSIVE TOOTHPASTE, LEFT OVER FROM MY OLD SPY DAYS. YOU HAVE TO GET THE PERSON TO BRUSH THEIR TEETH AND WHEN THEY DO, IT EXPLODES INWARD, USUALLY TAKING OUT THE PERSON'S HEAD.
HORRIBLE STUFF. I GOT A HALF CASE UNDER MY BED AT THE HOME.
I DON'T SEE HOW YOU'RE GONNA GET HER TO BRUSH HER TEETH IN THE MIDDLE OF ALL THIS.
I'LL IMPROVISE!
THANKS!
LADIES AN' GENTLEMEN, WE HAVE A WINNAH...
OH, NO YOU DON'T!

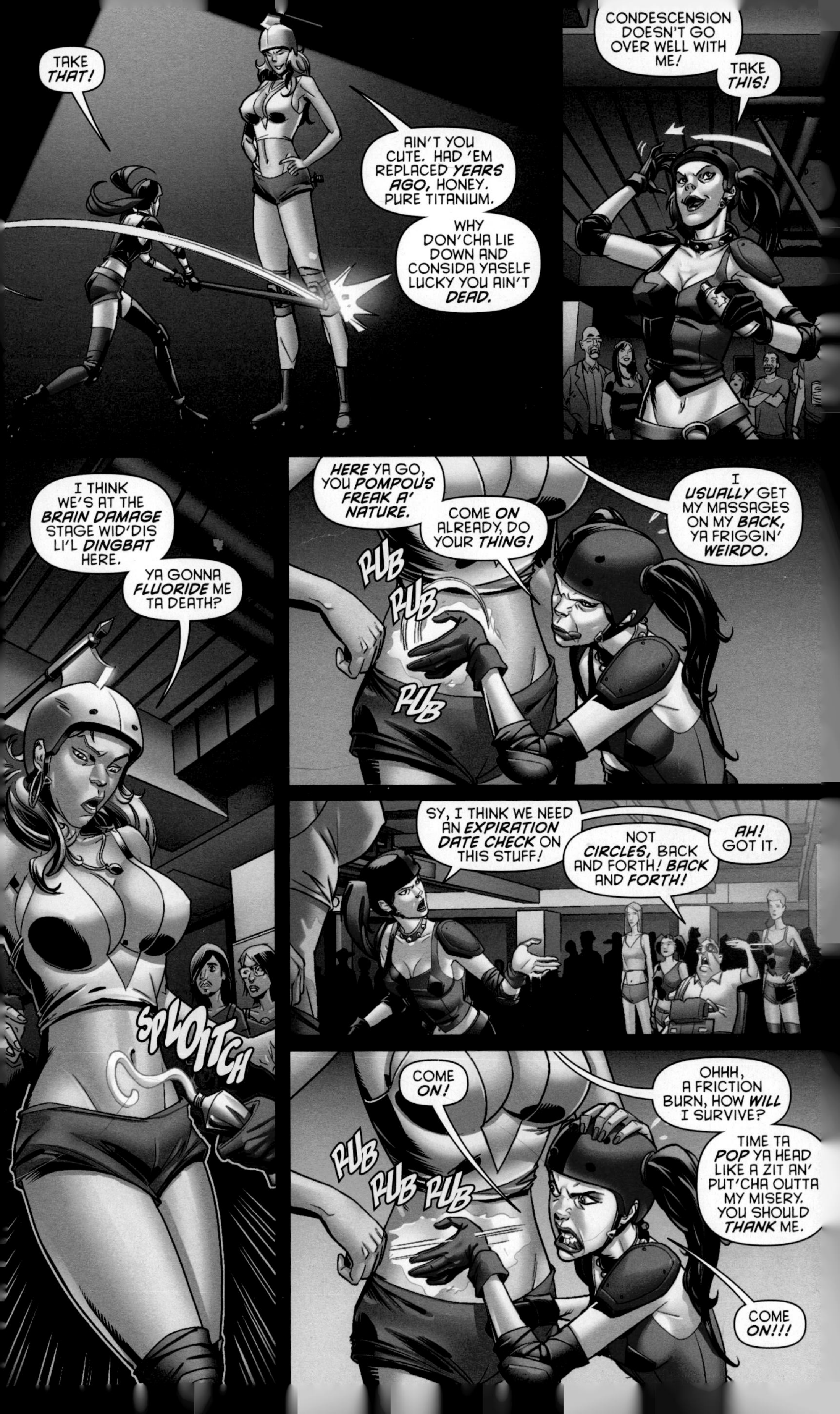

TAKE THAT!
AIN'T YOU CUTE. HAD 'EM REPLACED YEARS AGO, HONEY. PURE TITANIUM.
WHY DON'CHA LIE DOWN AND CONSIDA YASELF LUCKY YOU AIN'T DEAD.
CONDESCENSION DOESN'T GO OVER WELL WITH ME!
TAKE THIS!
I THINK WE'S AT THE BRAIN DAMAGE STAGE WID'DIS LI'L DINGBAT HERE.
YA GONNA FLUORIDE ME TA DEATH?
SPLOITCH
HERE YA GO, YOU POMPOUS FREAK A' NATURE.
COME ON ALREADY, DO YOUR THING!
I USUALLY GET MY MASSAGES ON MY BACK, YA FRIGGIN' WEIRDO.
RUB RUB RUB
SY, I THINK WE NEED AN EXPIRATION DATE CHECK ON THIS STUFF!
NOT CIRCLES, BACK AND FORTH! BACK AND FORTH!
AH! GOT IT.
COME ON!
OHHH, A FRICTION BURN, HOW WILL I SURVIVE?
TIME TA POP YA HEAD LIKE A ZIT AN' PUT'CHA OUTTA MY MISERY. YOU SHOULD THANK ME.
RUB RUB RUB
COME ON!!!

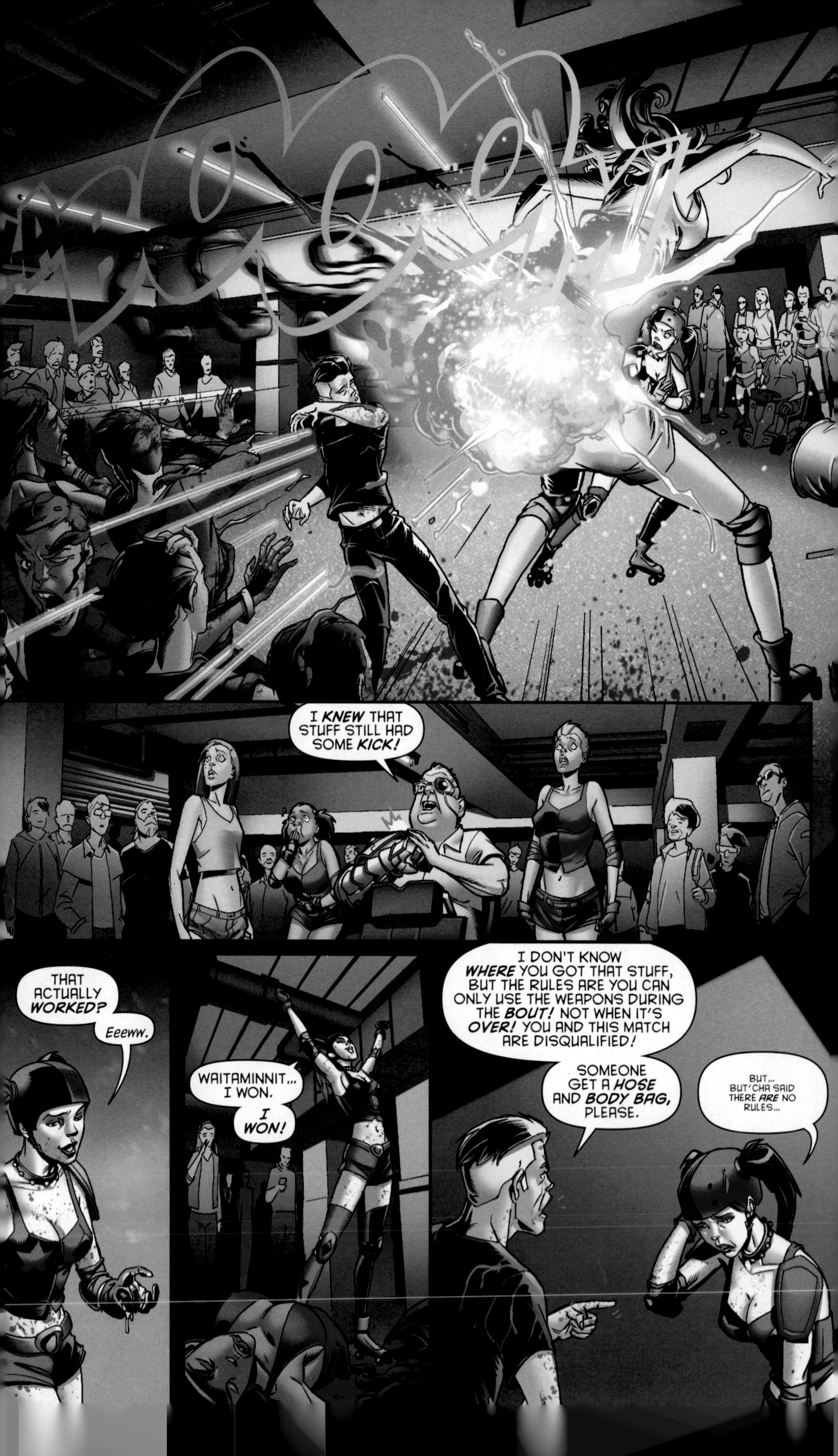
I KNEW THAT STUFF STILL HAD SOME KICK!
THAT ACTUALLY WORKED?
Eeeww.
WAITAMINNIT... I WON.
I WON!
I DON'T KNOW WHERE YOU GOT THAT STUFF, BUT THE RULES ARE YOU CAN ONLY USE THE WEAPONS DURING THE BOUT! NOT WHEN IT'S OVER! YOU AND THIS MATCH ARE DISQUALIFIED!
SOMEONE GET A HOSE AND BODY BAG, PLEASE.
BUT... BUT'CHA SAID THERE ARE NO RULES...

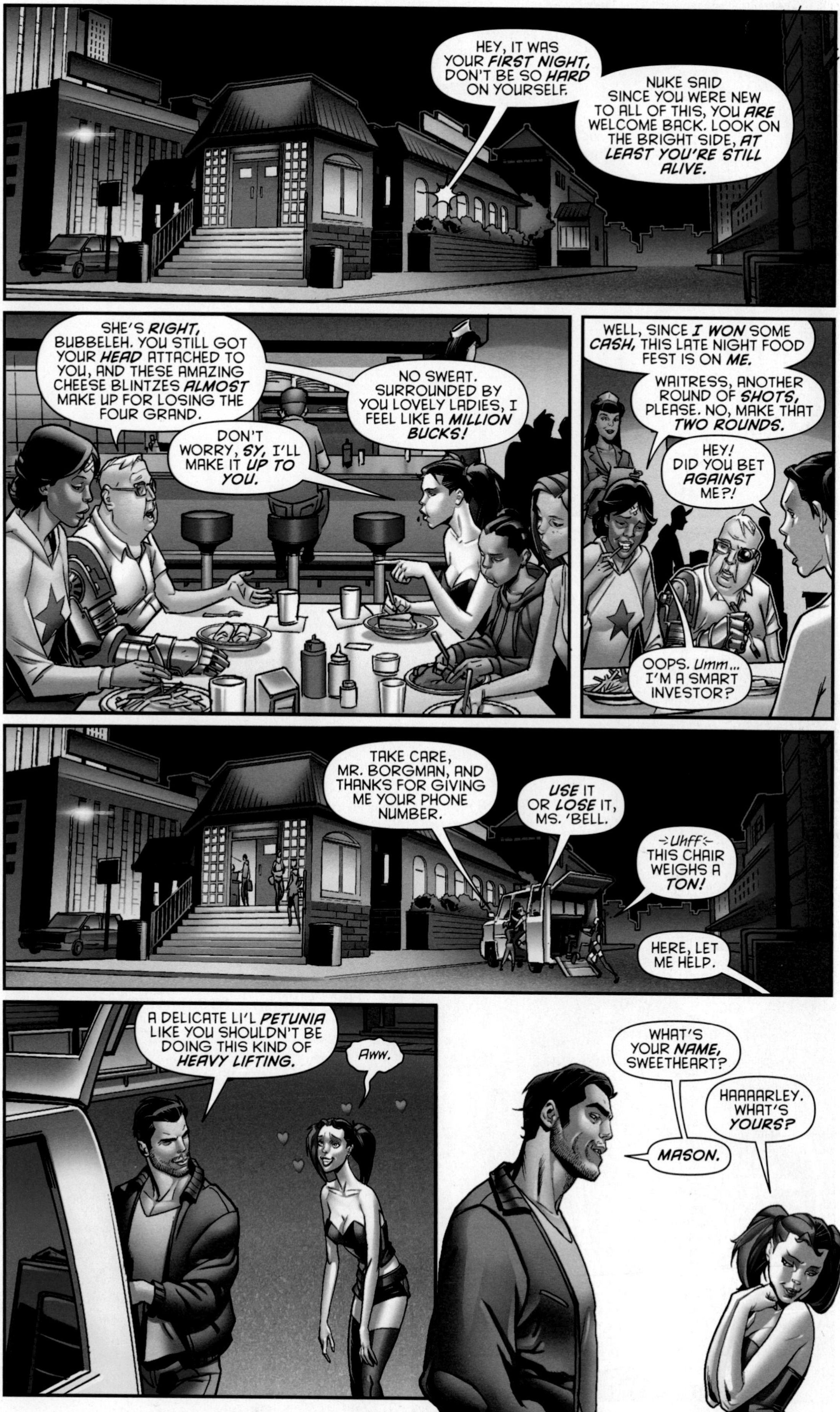
HEY, IT WAS YOUR FIRST NIGHT, DON'T BE SO HARD ON YOURSELF.
NUKE SAID SINCE YOU WERE NEW TO ALL OF THIS, YOU ARE WELCOME BACK. LOOK ON THE BRIGHT SIDE, AT LEAST YOU'RE STILL ALIVE.
SHE'S RIGHT, BUBBELEH. YOU STILL GOT YOUR HEAD ATTACHED TO YOU, AND THESE AMAZING CHEESE BLINTZES ALMOST MAKE UP FOR LOSING THE FOUR GRAND.
DON'T WORRY, SY, I'LL MAKE IT UP TO YOU.
NO SWEAT. SURROUNDED BY YOU LOVELY LADIES, I FEEL LIKE A MILLION BUCKS!
WELL, SINCE I WON SOME CASH, THIS LATE NIGHT FOOD FEST IS ON ME.
WAITRESS, ANOTHER ROUND OF SHOTS, PLEASE. NO, MAKE THAT TWO ROUNDS.
HEY! DID YOU BET AGAINST ME?!
OOPS. Umm... I'M A SMART INVESTOR?
TAKE CARE, MR. BORGMAN, AND THANKS FOR GIVING ME YOUR PHONE NUMBER.
USE IT OR LOSE IT, MS. 'BELL.
Uhff THIS CHAIR WEIGHS A TON!
HERE, LET ME HELP.
A DELICATE LI'L PETUNIA LIKE YOU SHOULDN'T BE DOING THIS KIND OF HEAVY LIFTING.
Aww.
WHAT'S YOUR NAME, SWEETHEART?
HAAAARLEY. WHAT'S YOURS?
MASON.

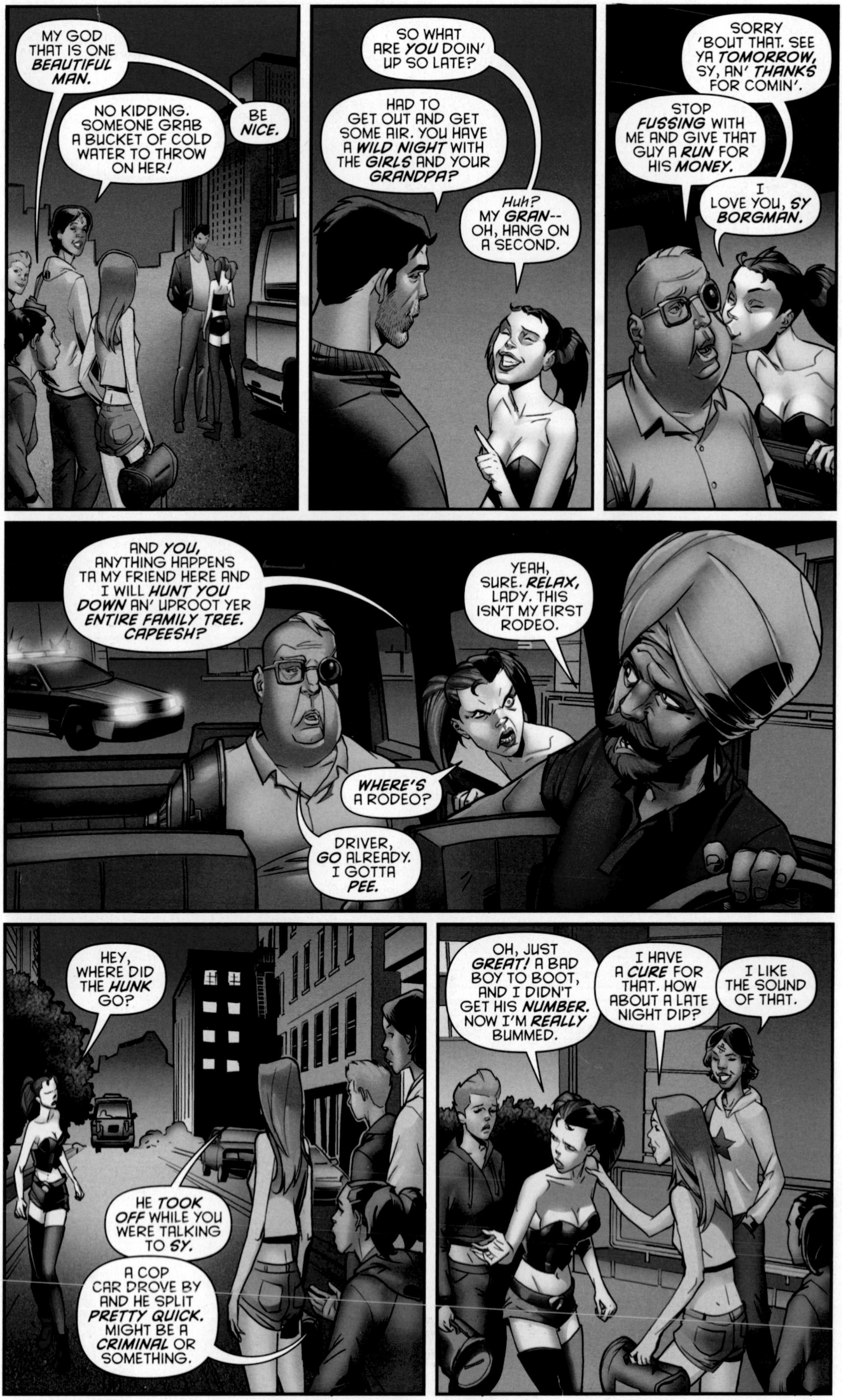
MY GOD THAT IS ONE BEAUTIFUL MAN.
BE NICE.
NO KIDDING. SOMEONE GRAB A BUCKET OF COLD WATER TO THROW ON HER!
SO WHAT ARE YOU DOIN' UP SO LATE?
HAD TO GET OUT AND GET SOME AIR. YOU HAVE A WILD NIGHT WITH THE GIRLS AND YOUR GRANDPA?
Huh? MY GRAN-- OH, HANG ON A SECOND.
SORRY 'BOUT THAT. SEE YA TOMORROW, SY, AN' THANKS FOR COMIN'.
STOP FUSSING WITH ME AND GIVE THAT GUY A RUN FOR HIS MONEY.
I LOVE YOU, SY BORGMAN.
AND YOU, ANYTHING HAPPENS TA MY FRIEND HERE AND I WILL HUNT YOU DOWN AN' UPROOT YER ENTIRE FAMILY TREE. CAPEESH?
YEAH, SURE. RELAX, LADY. THIS ISN'T MY FIRST RODEO.
WHERE'S A RODEO?
DRIVER, GO ALREADY. I GOTTA PEE.
HEY, WHERE DID THE HUNK GO?
HE TOOK OFF WHILE YOU WERE TALKING TO SY.
A COP CAR DROVE BY AND HE SPLIT PRETTY QUICK. MIGHT BE A CRIMINAL OR SOMETHING.
OH, JUST GREAT! A BAD BOY TO BOOT, AND I DIDN'T GET HIS NUMBER. NOW I'M REALLY BUMMED.
I HAVE A CURE FOR THAT. HOW ABOUT A LATE NIGHT DIP?
I LIKE THE SOUND OF THAT.

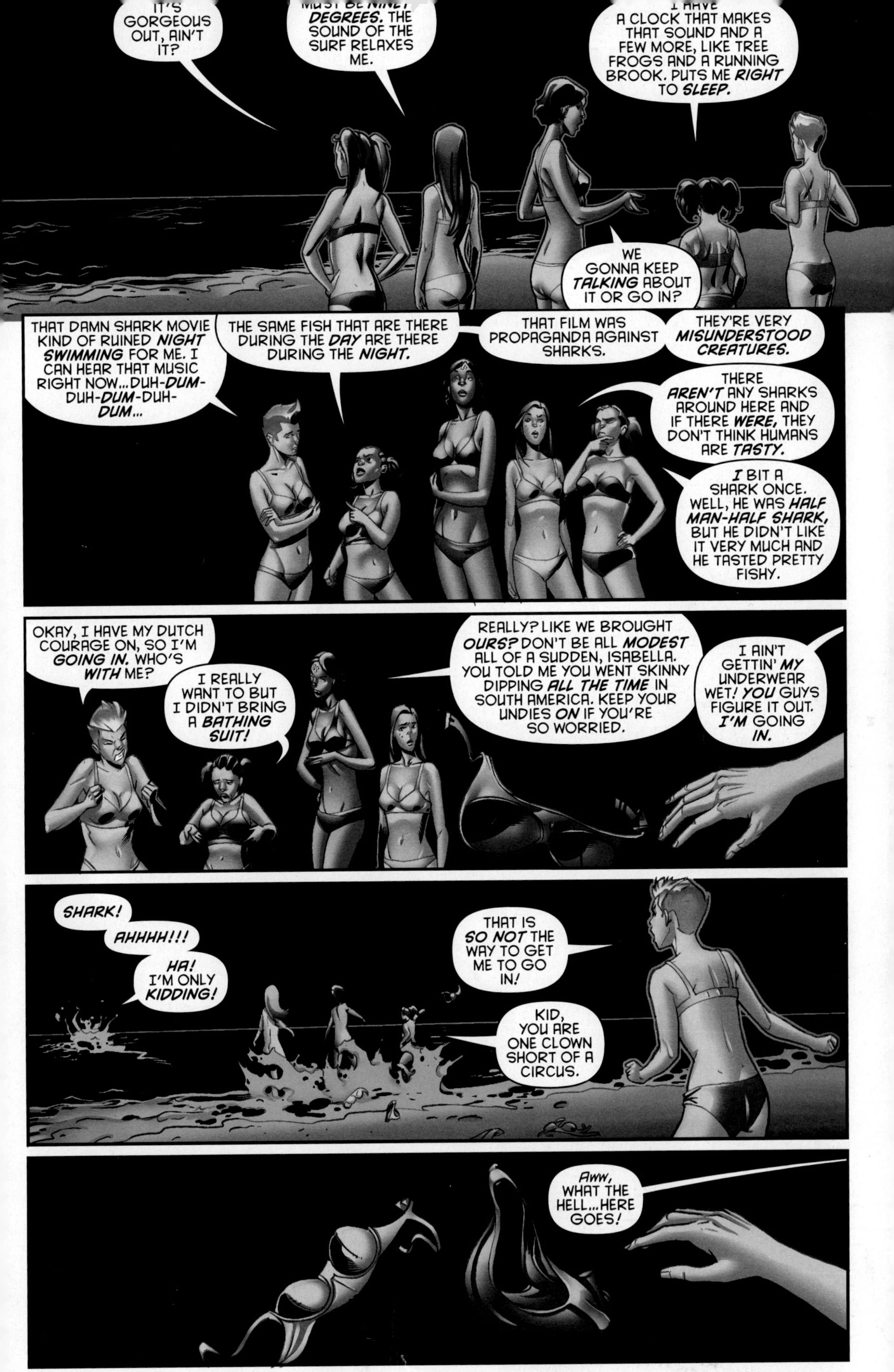

IT'S GORGEOUS OUT, AIN'T IT?
DEGREES. THE SOUND OF THE SURF RELAXES ME.
A CLOCK THAT MAKES THAT SOUND AND A FEW MORE, LIKE TREE FROGS AND A RUNNING BROOK. PUTS ME RIGHT TO SLEEP.
WE GONNA KEEP TALKING ABOUT IT OR GO IN?
THAT DAMN SHARK MOVIE KIND OF RUINED NIGHT SWIMMING FOR ME. I CAN HEAR THAT MUSIC RIGHT NOW...DUH-DUM-DUH-DUM-DUH-DUM...
THE SAME FISH THAT ARE THERE DURING THE DAY ARE THERE DURING THE NIGHT.
THAT FILM WAS PROPAGANDA AGAINST SHARKS.
THEY'RE VERY MISUNDERSTOOD CREATURES.
THERE AREN'T ANY SHARKS AROUND HERE AND IF THERE WERE, THEY DON'T THINK HUMANS ARE TASTY.
I BIT A SHARK ONCE. WELL, HE WAS HALF MAN-HALF SHARK, BUT HE DIDN'T LIKE IT VERY MUCH AND HE TASTED PRETTY FISHY.
OKAY, I HAVE MY DUTCH COURAGE ON, SO I'M GOING IN. WHO'S WITH ME?
I REALLY WANT TO BUT I DIDN'T BRING A BATHING SUIT!
REALLY? LIKE WE BROUGHT OURS? DON'T BE ALL MODEST ALL OF A SUDDEN, ISABELLA. YOU TOLD ME YOU WENT SKINNY DIPPING ALL THE TIME IN SOUTH AMERICA. KEEP YOUR UNDIES ON IF YOU'RE SO WORRIED.
I AIN'T GETTIN' MY UNDERWEAR WET! YOU GUYS FIGURE IT OUT. I'M GOING IN.
SHARK!
AHHHH!!!
HA! I'M ONLY KIDDING!
THAT IS SO NOT THE WAY TO GET ME TO GO IN!
KID, YOU ARE ONE CLOWN SHORT OF A CIRCUS.
AWW, WHAT THE HELL...HERE GOES!

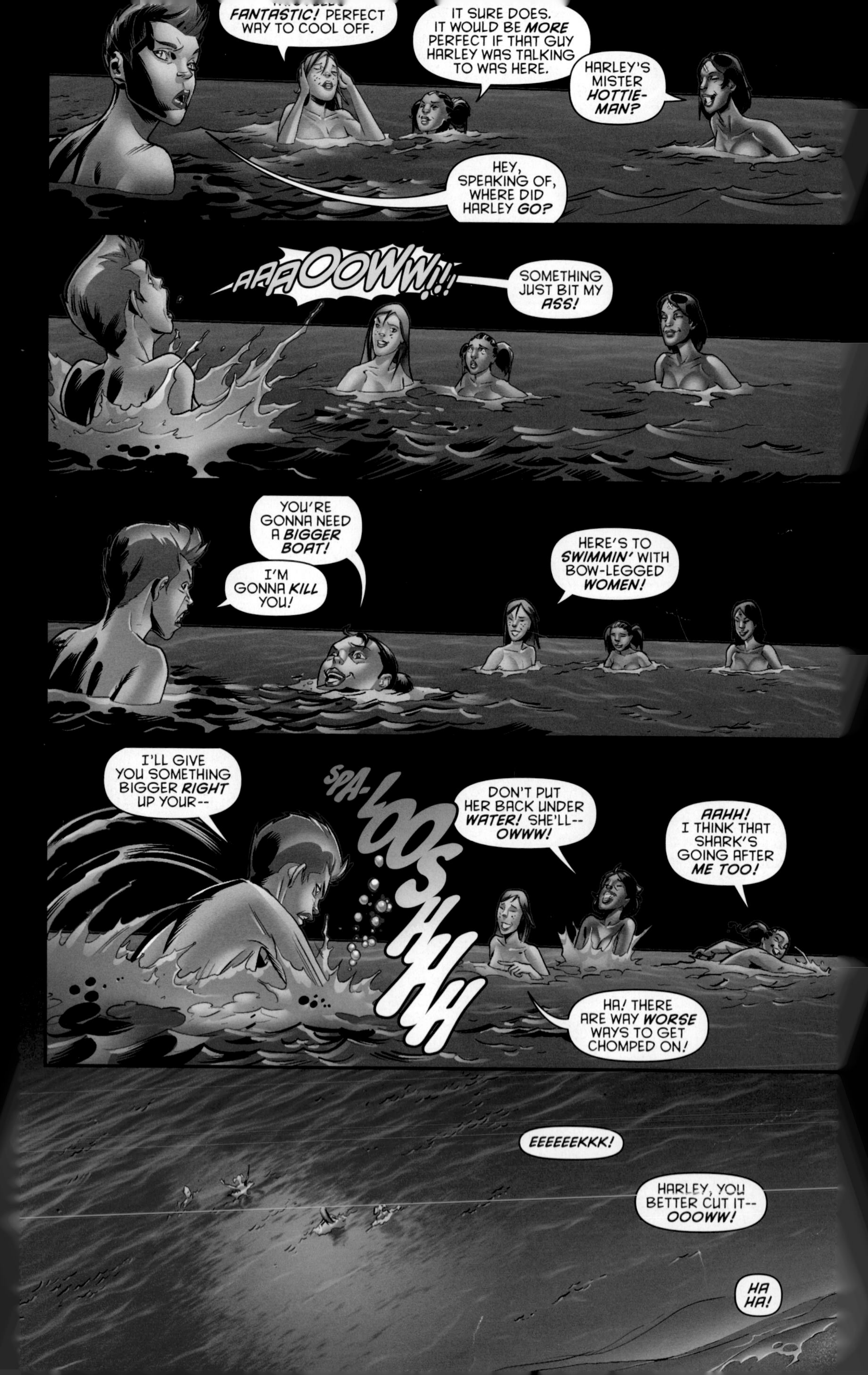
FANTASTIC! PERFECT WAY TO COOL OFF.
IT SURE DOES. IT WOULD BE MORE PERFECT IF THAT GUY HARLEY WAS TALKING TO WAS HERE.
HARLEY'S MISTER HOTTIE-MAN?
HEY, SPEAKING OF, WHERE DID HARLEY GO?
AAAOOOWW!!!
SOMETHING JUST BIT MY ASS!
YOU'RE GONNA NEED A BIGGER BOAT!
I'M GONNA KILL YOU!
HERE'S TO SWIMMIN' WITH BOW-LEGGED WOMEN!
I'LL GIVE YOU SOMETHING BIGGER RIGHT UP YOUR--
SPA-LOOSHHH
DON'T PUT HER BACK UNDER WATER! SHE'LL-- OWWW!
AAHH! I THINK THAT SHARK'S GOING AFTER ME TOO!
HA! THERE ARE WAY WORSE WAYS TO GET CHOMPED ON!
EEEEEEKKK!
HARLEY, YOU BETTER CUT IT-- OOOWW!
HA HA!

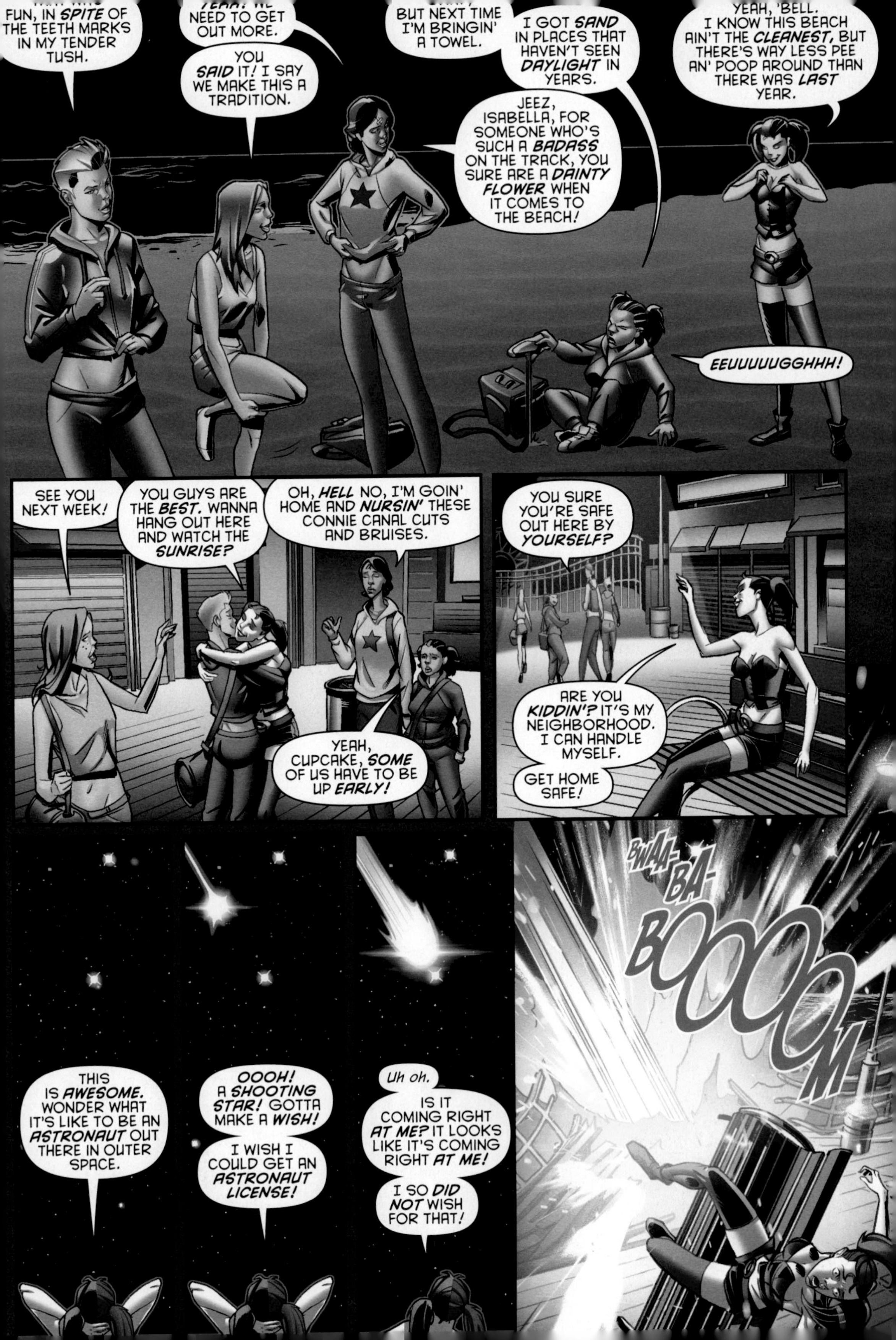
FUN, IN SPITE OF THE TEETH MARKS IN MY TENDER TUSH.
NEED TO GET OUT MORE.
YOU SAID IT! I SAY WE MAKE THIS A TRADITION.
BUT NEXT TIME I'M BRINGIN' A TOWEL.
I GOT SAND IN PLACES THAT HAVEN'T SEEN DAYLIGHT IN YEARS.
JEEZ, ISABELLA, FOR SOMEONE WHO'S SUCH A BADASS ON THE TRACK, YOU SURE ARE A DAINTY FLOWER WHEN IT COMES TO THE BEACH!
YEAH, 'BELL. I KNOW THIS BEACH AIN'T THE CLEANEST, BUT THERE'S WAY LESS PEE AN' POOP AROUND THAN THERE WAS LAST YEAR.
EEUUUUUGGHHH!
SEE YOU NEXT WEEK!
YOU GUYS ARE THE BEST. WANNA HANG OUT HERE AND WATCH THE SUNRISE?
OH, HELL NO, I'M GOIN' HOME AND NURSIN' THESE CONNIE CANAL CUTS AND BRUISES.
YEAH, CUPCAKE, SOME OF US HAVE TO BE UP EARLY!
YOU SURE YOU'RE SAFE OUT HERE BY YOURSELF?
ARE YOU KIDDIN'? IT'S MY NEIGHBORHOOD. I CAN HANDLE MYSELF.
GET HOME SAFE!
THIS IS AWESOME. WONDER WHAT IT'S LIKE TO BE AN ASTRONAUT OUT THERE IN OUTER SPACE.
OOOH! A SHOOTING STAR! GOTTA MAKE A WISH!
I WISH I COULD GET AN ASTRONAUT LICENSE!
Uh oh.
IS IT COMING RIGHT AT ME? IT LOOKS LIKE IT'S COMING RIGHT AT ME!
I SO DID NOT WISH FOR THAT!
BWAA-BA-BOOOOM

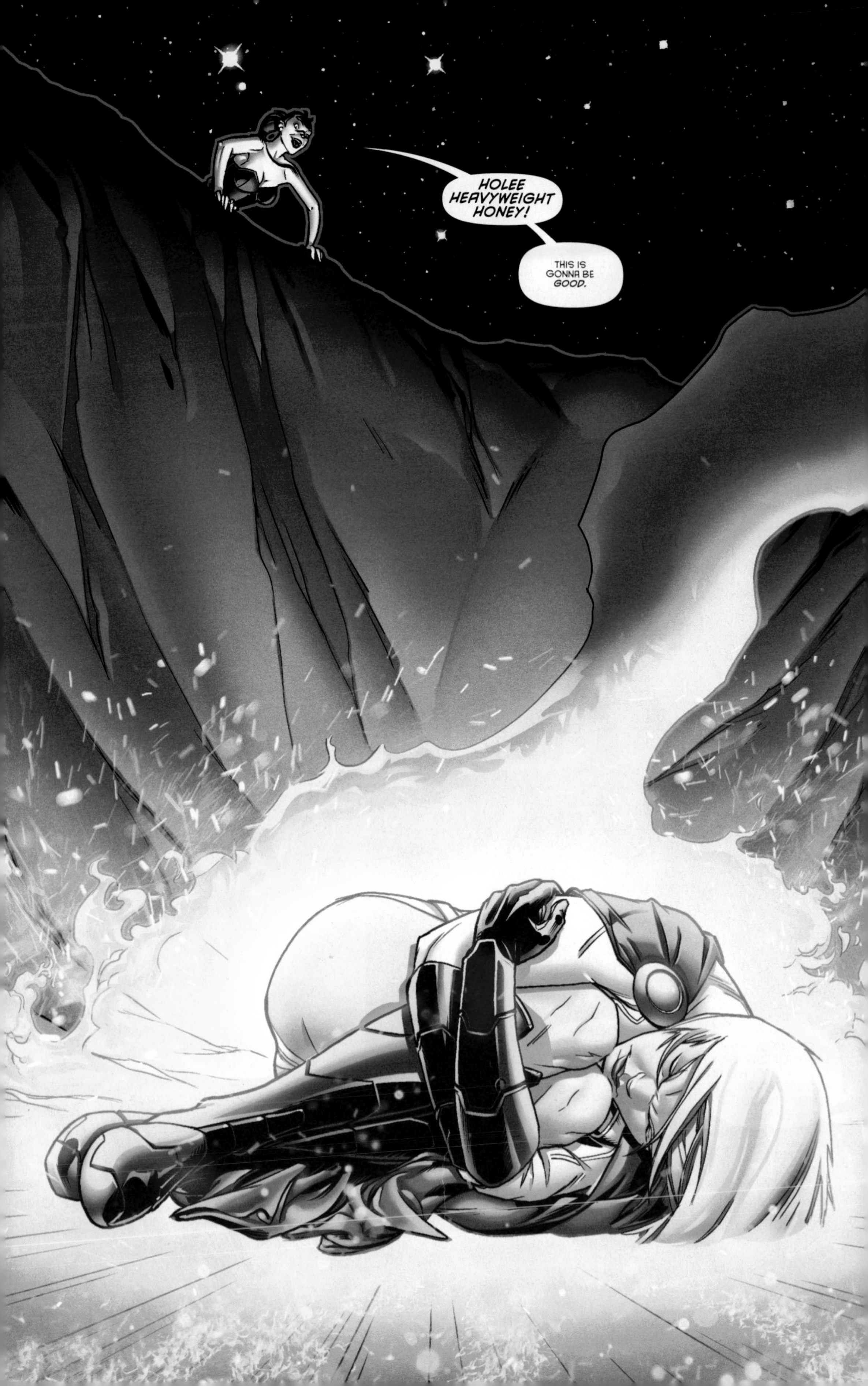
HOLEE HEAVYWEIGHT HONEY!
THIS IS GONNA BE GOOD.

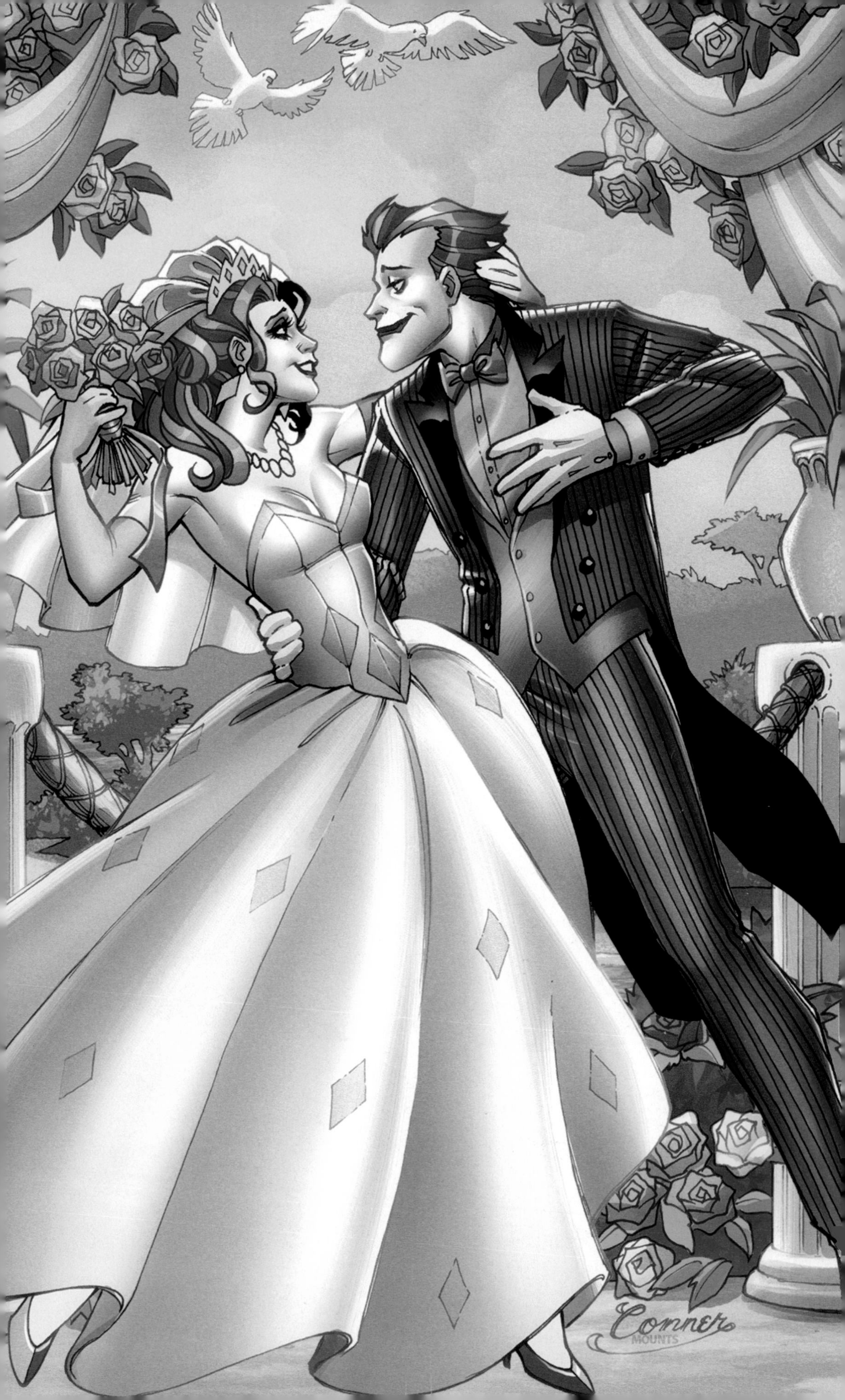
Conner
MOUNTS

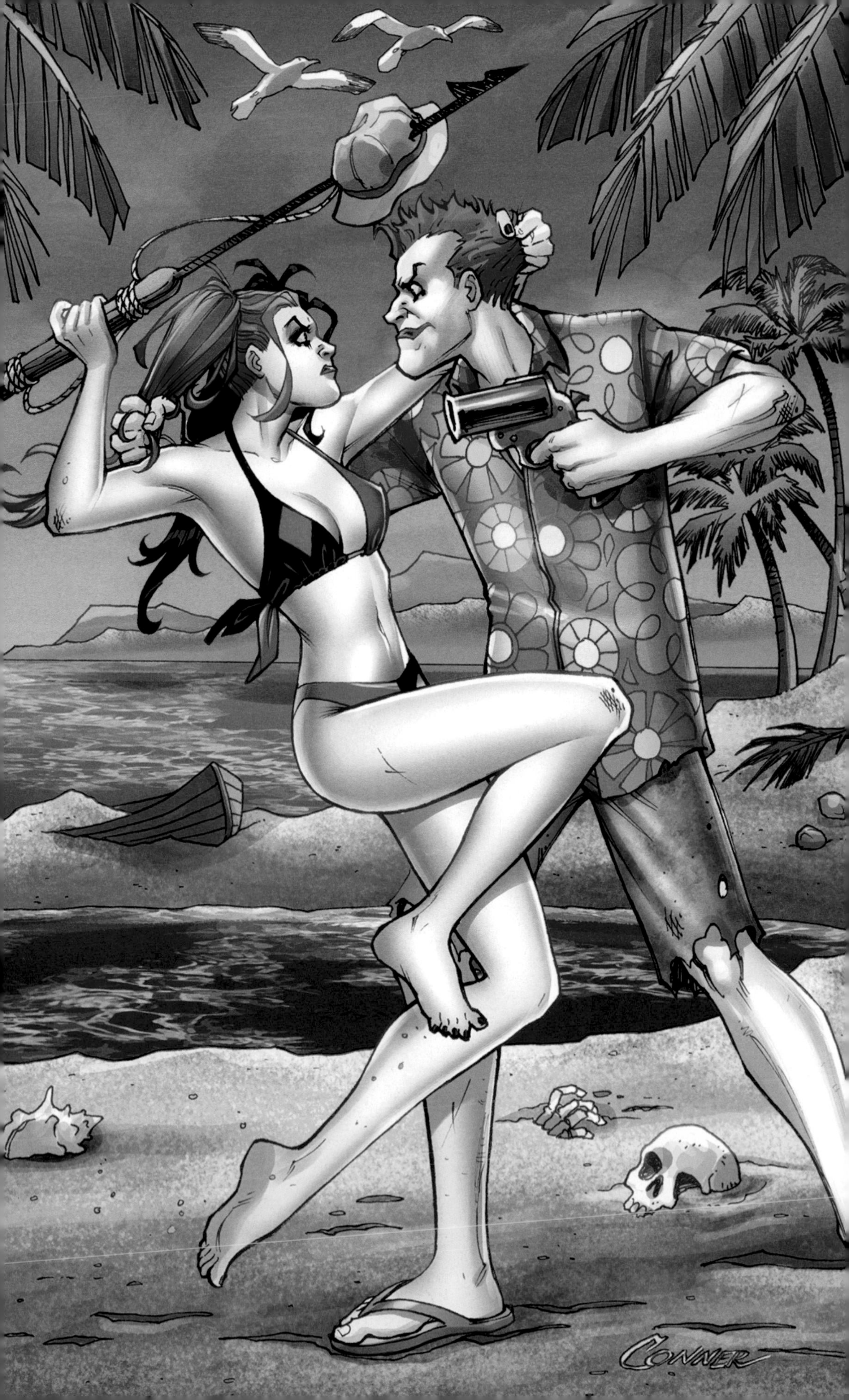
CONNER

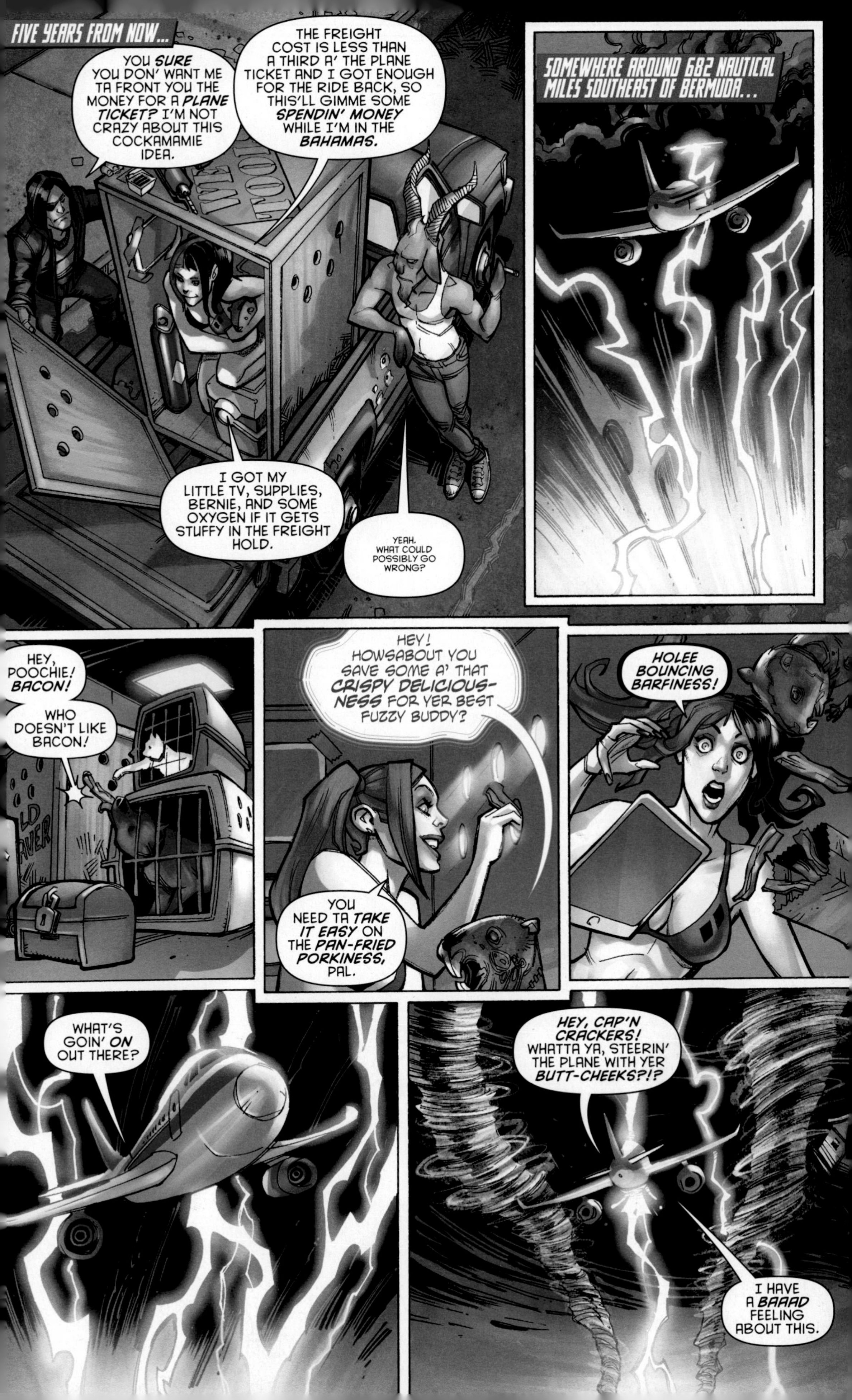
FIVE YEARS FROM NOW...
YOU SURE YOU DON' WANT ME TA FRONT YOU THE MONEY FOR A PLANE TICKET? I'M NOT CRAZY ABOUT THIS COCKAMAMIE IDEA.
THE FREIGHT COST IS LESS THAN A THIRD A' THE PLANE TICKET AND I GOT ENOUGH FOR THE RIDE BACK, SO THIS'LL GIMME SOME SPENDIN' MONEY WHILE I'M IN THE BAHAMAS.
I GOT MY LITTLE TV, SUPPLIES, BERNIE, AND SOME OXYGEN IF IT GETS STUFFY IN THE FREIGHT HOLD.
YEAH. WHAT COULD POSSIBLY GO WRONG?
SOMEWHERE AROUND 682 NAUTICAL MILES SOUTHEAST OF BERMUDA...
HEY, POOCHIE! BACON!
WHO DOESN'T LIKE BACON!
HEY! HOWSABOUT YOU SAVE SOME A' THAT CRISPY DELICIOUS-NESS FOR YER BEST FUZZY BUDDY?
YOU NEED TA TAKE IT EASY ON THE PAN-FRIED PORKINESS, PAL.
HOLEE BOUNCING BARFINESS!
WHAT'S GOIN' ON OUT THERE?
HEY, CAP'N CRACKERS! WHATTA YA, STEERIN' THE PLANE WITH YER BUTT-CHEEKS?!?
I HAVE A BAAAD FEELING ABOUT THIS.

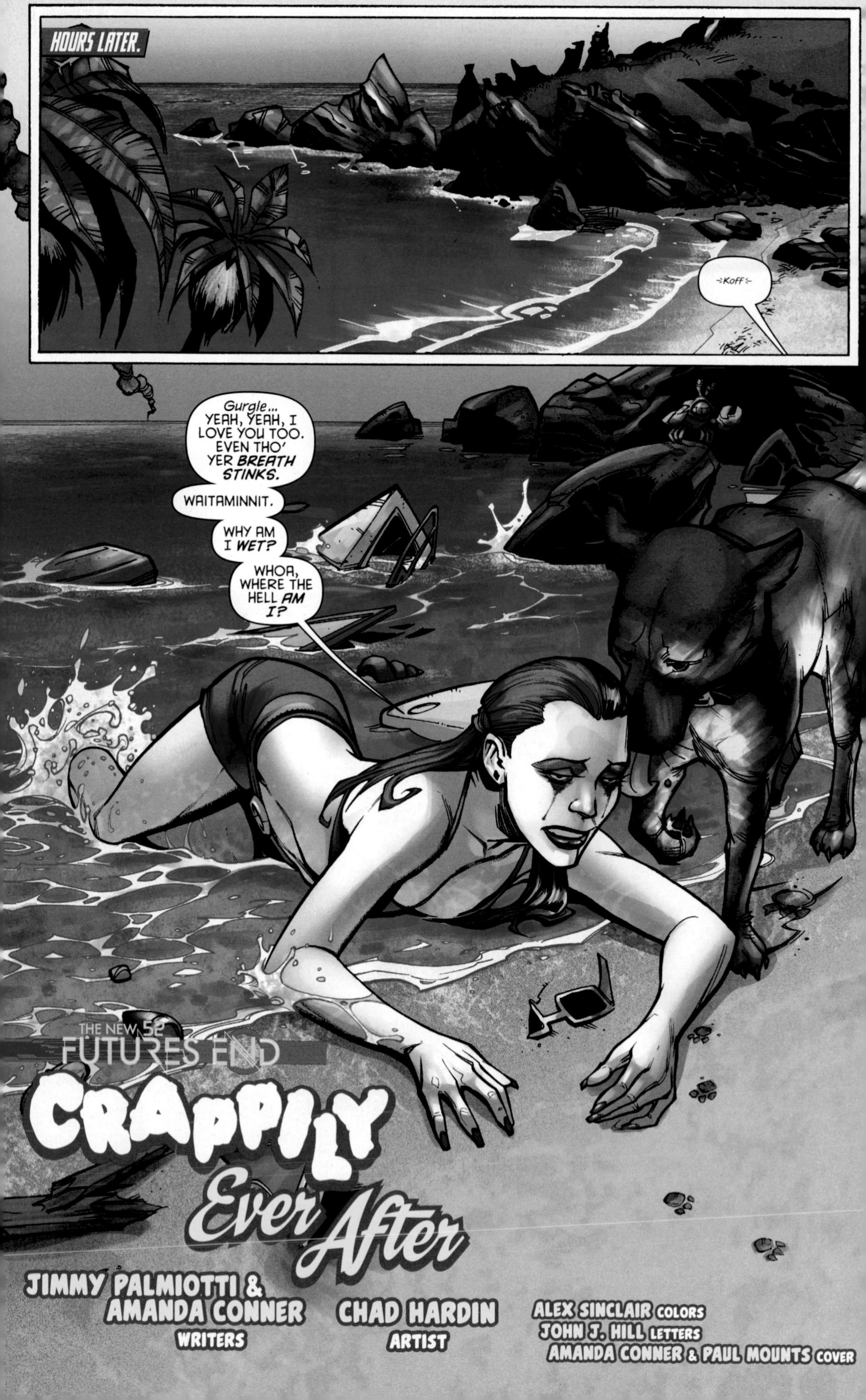
HOURS LATER.
KOFF
Gurgle... YEAH, YEAH, I LOVE YOU TOO. EVEN THO' YER BREATH STINKS.
WAITAMINNIT.
WHY AM I WET?
WHOA, WHERE THE HELL AM I?
THE NEW 52 FUTURES END
CRAPPILY Ever After
JIMMY PALMIOTTI & AMANDA CONNER WRITERS
CHAD HARDIN ARTIST
ALEX SINCLAIR COLORS
JOHN J. HILL LETTERS
AMANDA CONNER & PAUL MOUNTS COVER

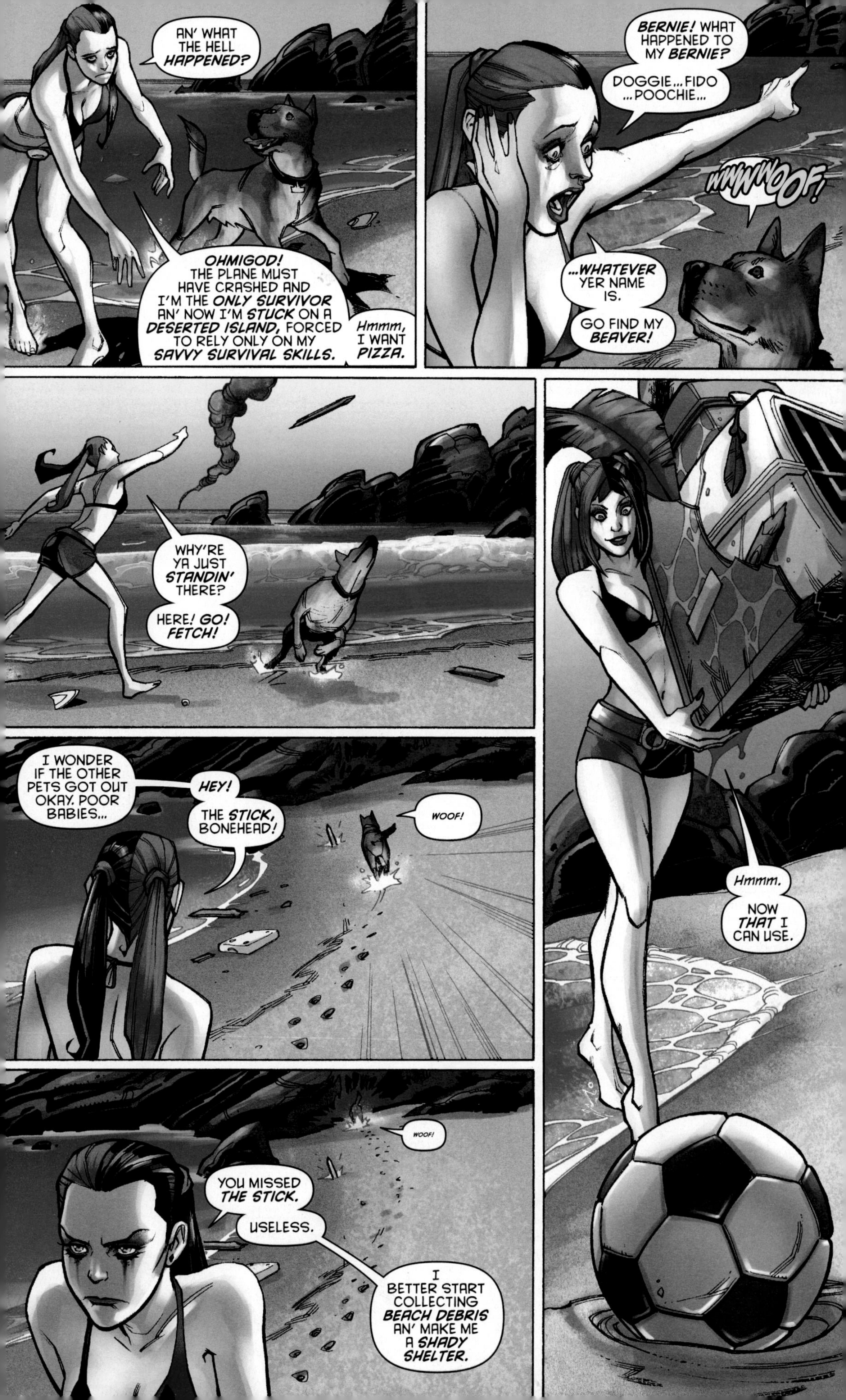
AN' WHAT THE HELL HAPPENED?
OHMIGOD! THE PLANE MUST HAVE CRASHED AND I'M THE ONLY SURVIVOR AN' NOW I'M STUCK ON A DESERTED ISLAND, FORCED TO RELY ONLY ON MY SAVVY SURVIVAL SKILLS.
Hmmm, I WANT PIZZA.
BERNIE! WHAT HAPPENED TO MY BERNIE?
DOGGIE... FIDO ...POOCHIE...
WWWWOOF!
...WHATEVER YER NAME IS.
GO FIND MY BEAVER!
WHY'RE YA JUST STANDIN' THERE?
HERE! GO! FETCH!
I WONDER IF THE OTHER PETS GOT OUT OKAY. POOR BABIES...
HEY!
THE STICK, BONEHEAD!
WOOF!
WOOF!
YOU MISSED THE STICK.
USELESS.
I BETTER START COLLECTING BEACH DEBRIS AN' MAKE ME A SHADY SHELTER.
Hmmm.
NOW THAT I CAN USE.

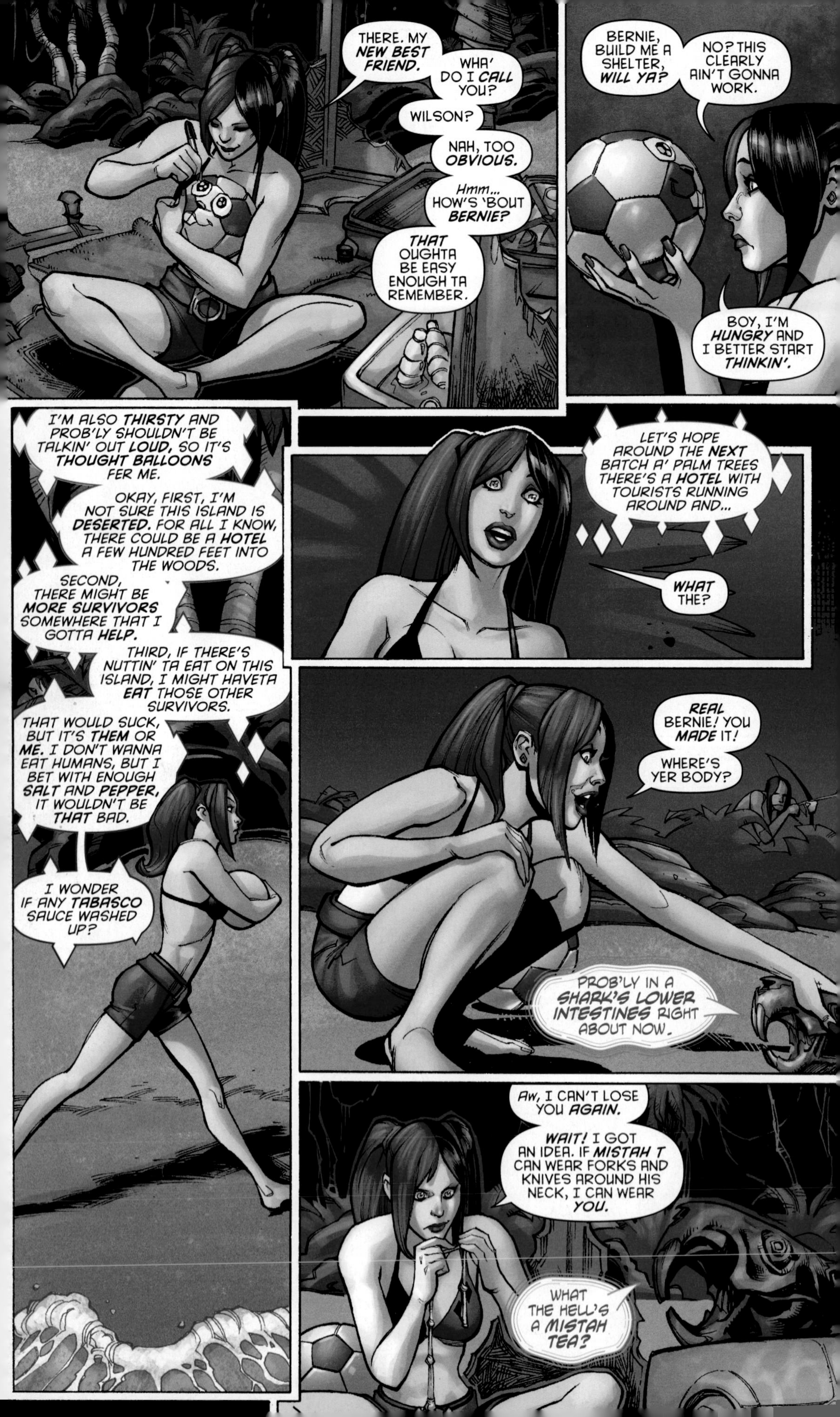
THERE. MY NEW BEST FRIEND.
WHA' DO I CALL YOU?
WILSON?
NAH, TOO OBVIOUS.
Hmm... HOW'S 'BOUT BERNIE?
THAT OUGHTA BE EASY ENOUGH TA REMEMBER.
BERNIE, BUILD ME A SHELTER, WILL YA?
NO? THIS CLEARLY AIN'T GONNA WORK.
BOY, I'M HUNGRY AND I BETTER START THINKIN'.
I'M ALSO THIRSTY AND PROB'LY SHOULDN'T BE TALKIN' OUT LOUD, SO IT'S THOUGHT BALLOONS FER ME.
OKAY, FIRST, I'M NOT SURE THIS ISLAND IS DESERTED. FOR ALL I KNOW, THERE COULD BE A HOTEL A FEW HUNDRED FEET INTO THE WOODS.
SECOND, THERE MIGHT BE MORE SURVIVORS SOMEWHERE THAT I GOTTA HELP.
THIRD, IF THERE'S NUTTIN' TA EAT ON THIS ISLAND, I MIGHT HAVETA EAT THOSE OTHER SURVIVORS.
THAT WOULD SUCK, BUT IT'S THEM OR ME. I DON'T WANNA EAT HUMANS, BUT I BET WITH ENOUGH SALT AND PEPPER, IT WOULDN'T BE THAT BAD.
I WONDER IF ANY TABASCO SAUCE WASHED UP?
LET'S HOPE AROUND THE NEXT BATCH A' PALM TREES THERE'S A HOTEL WITH TOURISTS RUNNING AROUND AND...
WHAT THE?
REAL BERNIE! YOU MADE IT!
WHERE'S YER BODY?
PROB'LY IN A SHARK'S LOWER INTESTINES RIGHT ABOUT NOW.
Aw, I CAN'T LOSE YOU AGAIN.
WAIT! I GOT AN IDEA. IF MISTAH T CAN WEAR FORKS AND KNIVES AROUND HIS NECK, I CAN WEAR YOU.
WHAT THE HELL'S A MISTAH TEA?

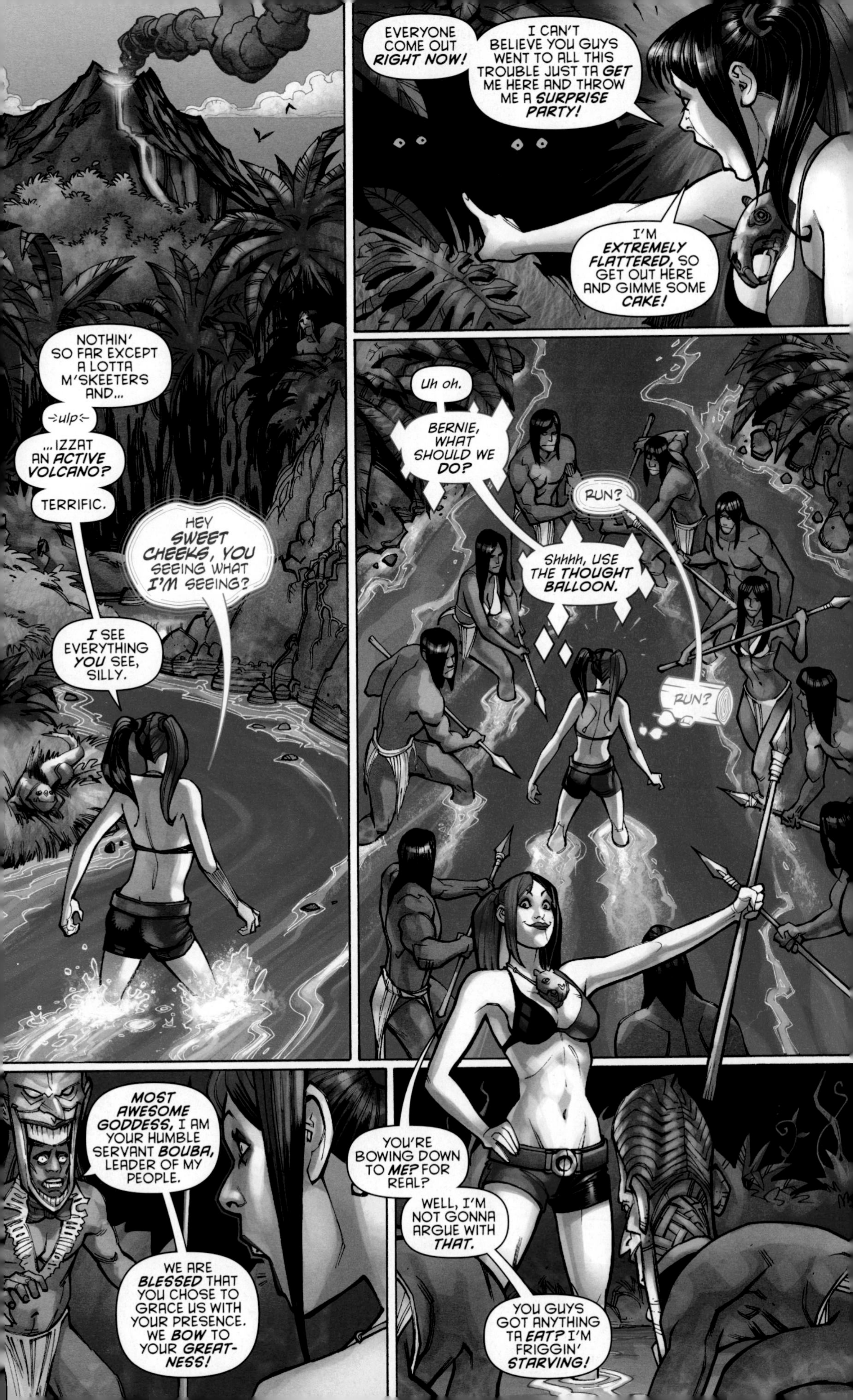
NOTHIN' SO FAR EXCEPT A LOTTA M'SKEETERS AND...
-ulp-
...IZZAT AN ACTIVE VOLCANO?
TERRIFIC.
HEY SWEET CHEEKS, YOU SEEING WHAT I'M SEEING?
I SEE EVERYTHING YOU SEE, SILLY.
EVERYONE COME OUT RIGHT NOW!
I CAN'T BELIEVE YOU GUYS WENT TO ALL THIS TROUBLE JUST TA GET ME HERE AND THROW ME A SURPRISE PARTY!
I'M EXTREMELY FLATTERED, SO GET OUT HERE AND GIMME SOME CAKE!
Uh oh.
BERNIE, WHAT SHOULD WE DO?
RUN?
Shhhh, USE THE THOUGHT BALLOON.
RUN?
MOST AWESOME GODDESS, I AM YOUR HUMBLE SERVANT BOUBA, LEADER OF MY PEOPLE.
WE ARE BLESSED THAT YOU CHOSE TO GRACE US WITH YOUR PRESENCE. WE BOW TO YOUR GREATNESS!
YOU'RE BOWING DOWN TO ME? FOR REAL?
WELL, I'M NOT GONNA ARGUE WITH THAT.
YOU GUYS GOT ANYTHING TA EAT? I'M FRIGGIN' STARVING!

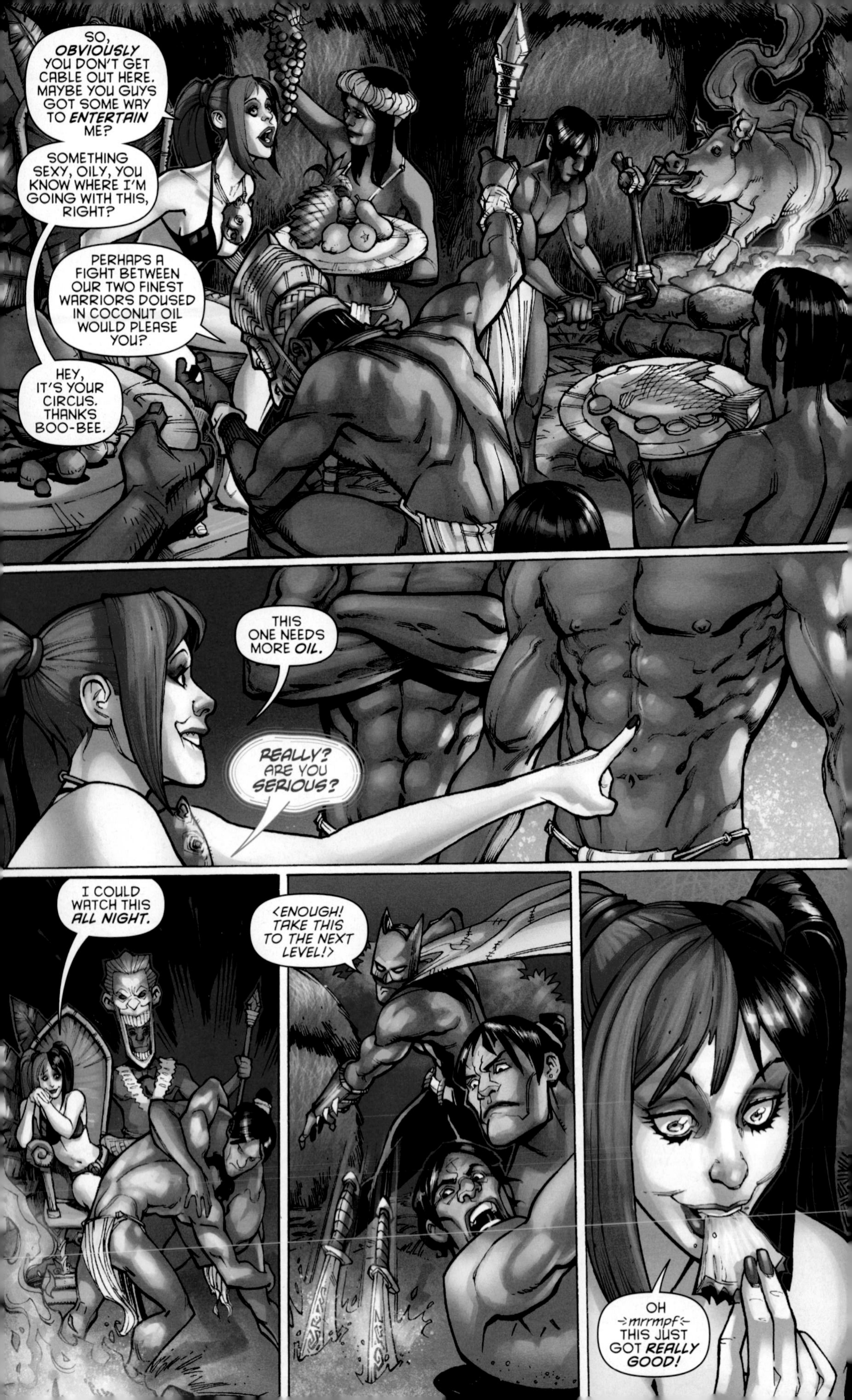

SO, OBVIOUSLY YOU DON'T GET CABLE OUT HERE. MAYBE YOU GUYS GOT SOME WAY TO ENTERTAIN ME?
SOMETHING SEXY, OILY, YOU KNOW WHERE I'M GOING WITH THIS, RIGHT?
PERHAPS A FIGHT BETWEEN OUR TWO FINEST WARRIORS DOUSED IN COCONUT OIL WOULD PLEASE YOU?
HEY, IT'S YOUR CIRCUS. THANKS BOO-BEE.
THIS ONE NEEDS MORE OIL.
REALLY? ARE YOU SERIOUS?
I COULD WATCH THIS ALL NIGHT.
<ENOUGH! TAKE THIS TO THE NEXT LEVEL!>
OH
-mrrmpf-
THIS JUST GOT REALLY GOOD!

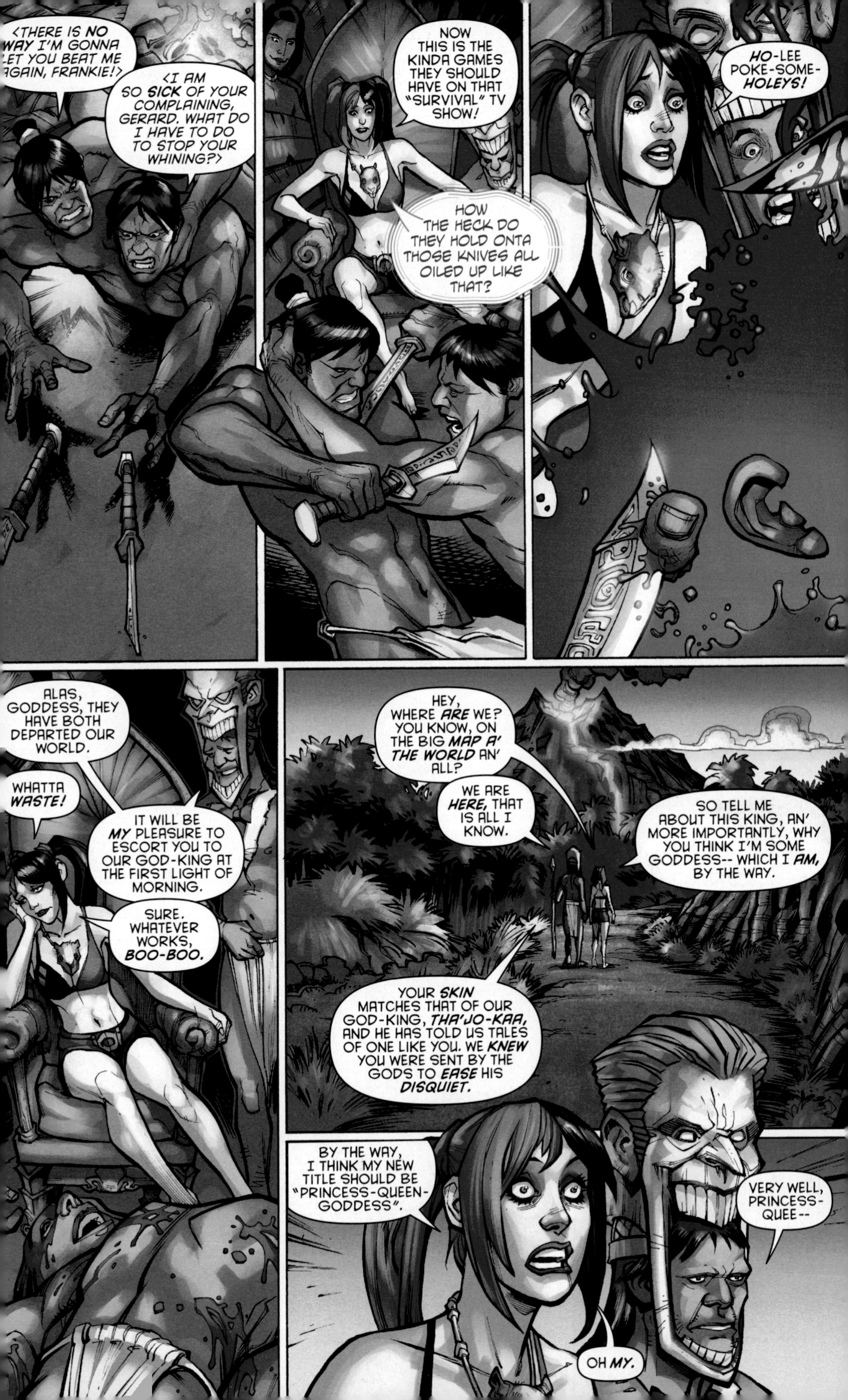
<THERE IS NO WAY I'M GONNA LET YOU BEAT ME AGAIN, FRANKIE!>
<I AM SO SICK OF YOUR COMPLAINING, GERARD. WHAT DO I HAVE TO DO TO STOP YOUR WHINING?>
NOW THIS IS THE KINDA GAMES THEY SHOULD HAVE ON THAT "SURVIVAL" TV SHOW!
HOW THE HECK DO THEY HOLD ONTA THOSE KNIVES ALL OILED UP LIKE THAT?
HO-LEE POKE-SOME-HOLEYS!
ALAS, GODDESS, THEY HAVE BOTH DEPARTED OUR WORLD.
WHATTA WASTE!
IT WILL BE MY PLEASURE TO ESCORT YOU TO OUR GOD-KING AT THE FIRST LIGHT OF MORNING.
SURE. WHATEVER WORKS, BOO-BOO.
HEY, WHERE ARE WE? YOU KNOW, ON THE BIG MAP A' THE WORLD AN' ALL?
WE ARE HERE, THAT IS ALL I KNOW.
SO TELL ME ABOUT THIS KING, AN' MORE IMPORTANTLY, WHY YOU THINK I'M SOME GODDESS-- WHICH I AM, BY THE WAY.
YOUR SKIN MATCHES THAT OF OUR GOD-KING, THA'JO-KAA, AND HE HAS TOLD US TALES OF ONE LIKE YOU. WE KNEW YOU WERE SENT BY THE GODS TO EASE HIS DISQUIET.
BY THE WAY, I THINK MY NEW TITLE SHOULD BE "PRINCESS-QUEEN-GODDESS".
VERY WELL, PRINCESS-QUEE--
OH MY.

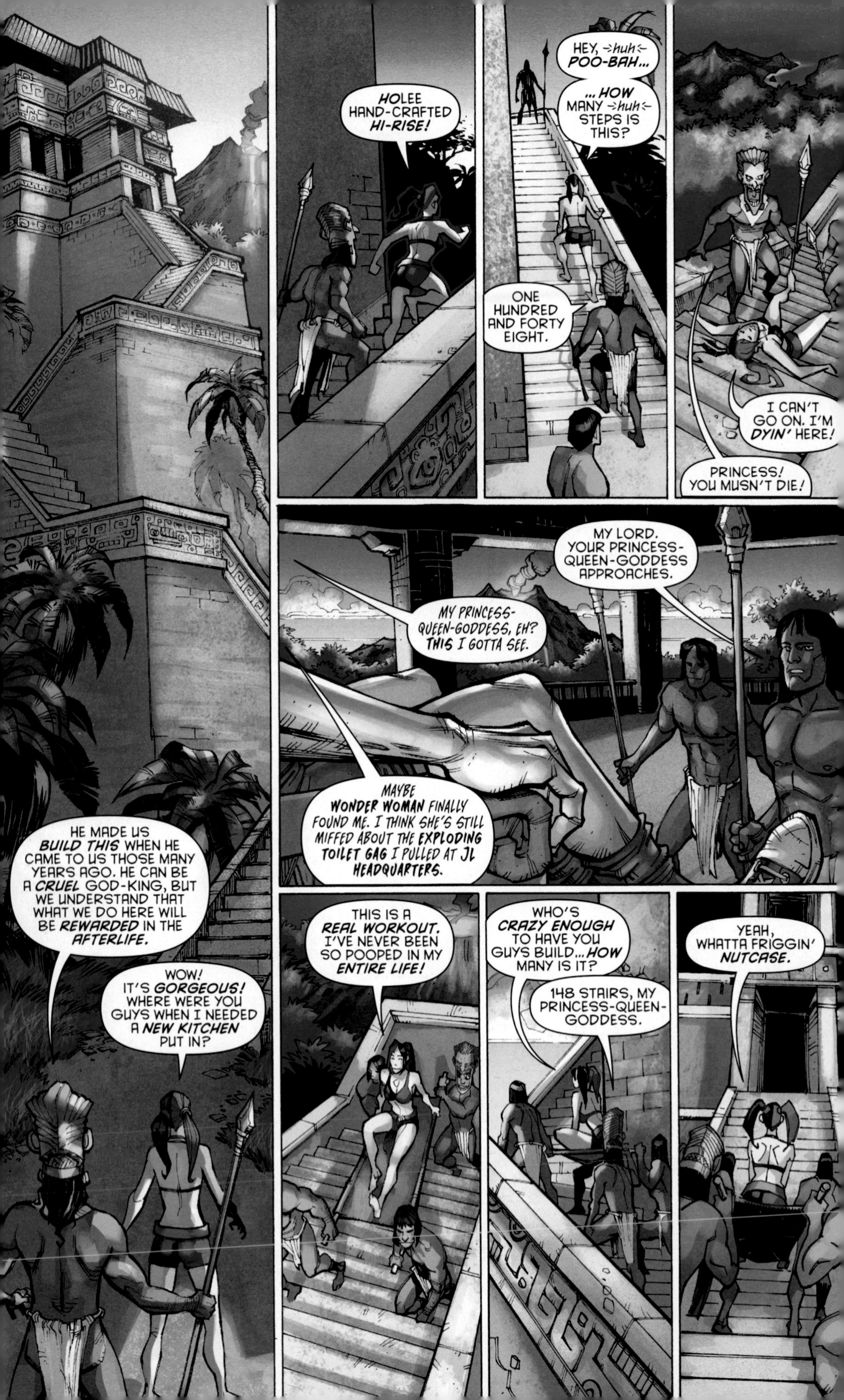
HOLEE HAND-CRAFTED HI-RISE!
HEY, ⇒huh⇐ POO-BAH...
...HOW MANY ⇒huh⇐ STEPS IS THIS?
ONE HUNDRED AND FORTY EIGHT.
I CAN'T GO ON. I'M DYIN' HERE!
PRINCESS! YOU MUSN'T DIE!
MY LORD. YOUR PRINCESS-QUEEN-GODDESS APPROACHES.
MY PRINCESS-QUEEN-GODDESS, EH? THIS I GOTTA SEE.
MAYBE WONDER WOMAN FINALLY FOUND ME. I THINK SHE'S STILL MIFFED ABOUT THE EXPLODING TOILET GAG I PULLED AT JL HEADQUARTERS.
HE MADE US BUILD THIS WHEN HE CAME TO US THOSE MANY YEARS AGO. HE CAN BE A CRUEL GOD-KING, BUT WE UNDERSTAND THAT WHAT WE DO HERE WILL BE REWARDED IN THE AFTERLIFE.
WOW! IT'S GORGEOUS! WHERE WERE YOU GUYS WHEN I NEEDED A NEW KITCHEN PUT IN?
THIS IS A REAL WORKOUT. I'VE NEVER BEEN SO POOPED IN MY ENTIRE LIFE!
WHO'S CRAZY ENOUGH TO HAVE YOU GUYS BUILD...HOW MANY IS IT?
148 STAIRS, MY PRINCESS-QUEEN-GODDESS.
YEAH, WHATTA FRIGGIN' NUTCASE.

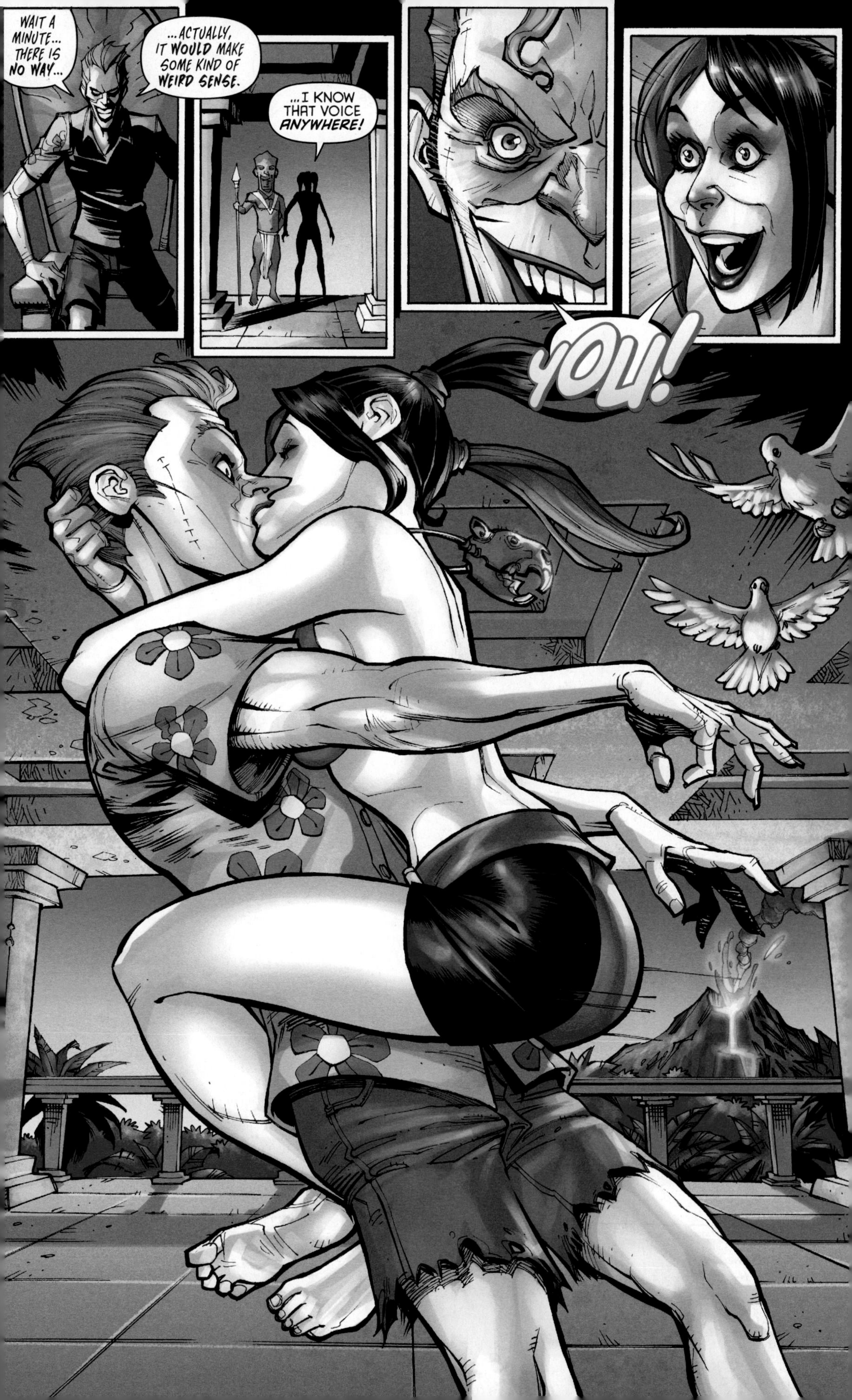
WAIT A MINUTE... THERE IS NO WAY...
...ACTUALLY, IT WOULD MAKE SOME KIND OF WEIRD SENSE.
...I KNOW THAT VOICE ANYWHERE!
YOU!

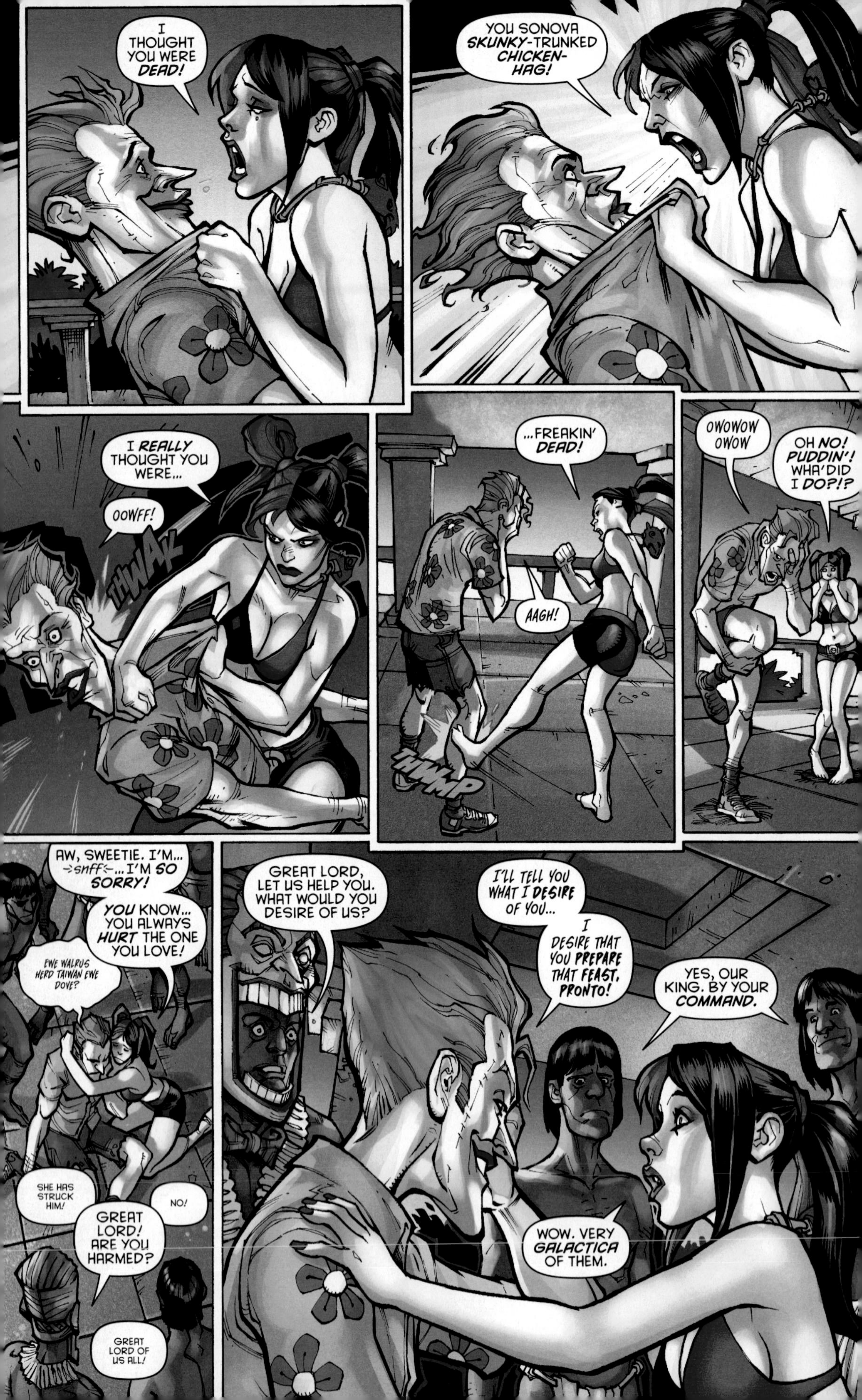
I THOUGHT YOU WERE DEAD!
YOU SONOVA SKUNKY-TRUNKED CHICKEN-HAG!
I REALLY THOUGHT YOU WERE...
OOWFF!
THWAK
...FREAKIN' DEAD!
AAGH!
THMP
OWOWOW OWOW
OH NO! PUDDIN'! WHA'DID I DO?!?
AW, SWEETIE. I'M... snff ...I'M SO SORRY!
YOU KNOW... YOU ALWAYS HURT THE ONE YOU LOVE!
EWE WALRUS HERD TAIWAN EWE DOVE?
SHE HAS STRUCK HIM!
NO!
GREAT LORD! ARE YOU HARMED?
GREAT LORD OF US ALL!
GREAT LORD, LET US HELP YOU. WHAT WOULD YOU DESIRE OF US?
I'LL TELL YOU WHAT I DESIRE OF YOU...
I DESIRE THAT YOU PREPARE THAT FEAST, PRONTO!
YES, OUR KING. BY YOUR COMMAND.
WOW. VERY GALACTICA OF THEM.

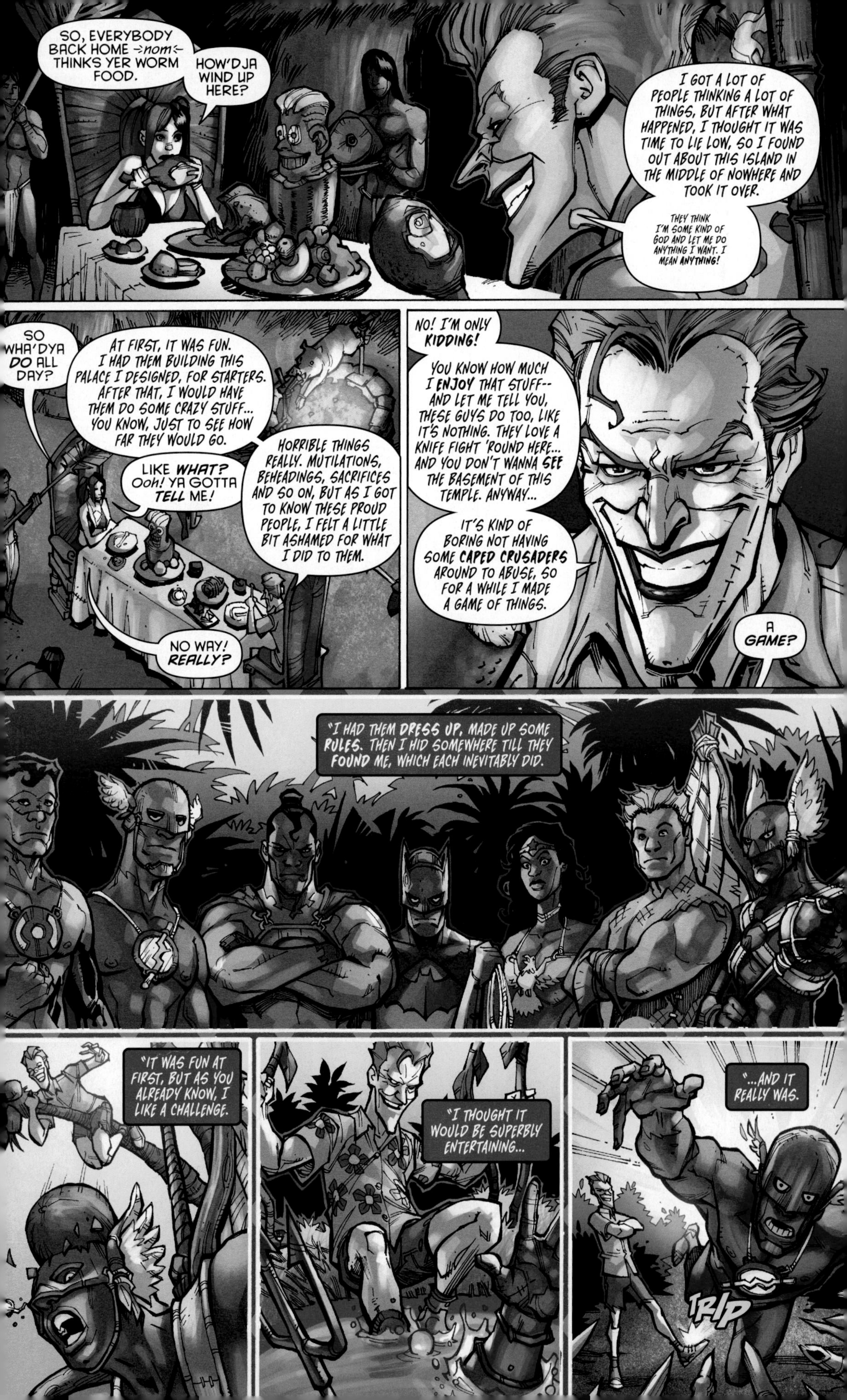
SO, EVERYBODY BACK HOME ⇒nom⇐ THINKS YER WORM FOOD.
HOW'DJA WIND UP HERE?
I GOT A LOT OF PEOPLE THINKING A LOT OF THINGS, BUT AFTER WHAT HAPPENED, I THOUGHT IT WAS TIME TO LIE LOW, SO I FOUND OUT ABOUT THIS ISLAND IN THE MIDDLE OF NOWHERE AND TOOK IT OVER.
THEY THINK I'M SOME KIND OF GOD AND LET ME DO ANYTHING I WANT. I MEAN ANYTHING!
SO WHA'DYA DO ALL DAY?
AT FIRST, IT WAS FUN. I HAD THEM BUILDING THIS PALACE I DESIGNED, FOR STARTERS. AFTER THAT, I WOULD HAVE THEM DO SOME CRAZY STUFF... YOU KNOW, JUST TO SEE HOW FAR THEY WOULD GO.
LIKE WHAT? Ooh! YA GOTTA TELL ME!
HORRIBLE THINGS REALLY. MUTILATIONS, BEHEADINGS, SACRIFICES AND SO ON, BUT AS I GOT TO KNOW THESE PROUD PEOPLE, I FELT A LITTLE BIT ASHAMED FOR WHAT I DID TO THEM.
NO WAY! REALLY?
NO! I'M ONLY KIDDING!
YOU KNOW HOW MUCH I ENJOY THAT STUFF-- AND LET ME TELL YOU, THESE GUYS DO TOO, LIKE IT'S NOTHING. THEY LOVE A KNIFE FIGHT 'ROUND HERE... AND YOU DON'T WANNA SEE THE BASEMENT OF THIS TEMPLE. ANYWAY...
IT'S KIND OF BORING NOT HAVING SOME CAPED CRUSADERS AROUND TO ABUSE, SO FOR A WHILE I MADE A GAME OF THINGS.
A GAME?
"I HAD THEM DRESS UP, MADE UP SOME RULES. THEN I HID SOMEWHERE TILL THEY FOUND ME, WHICH EACH INEVITABLY DID.
"IT WAS FUN AT FIRST, BUT AS YOU ALREADY KNOW, I LIKE A CHALLENGE.
"I THOUGHT IT WOULD BE SUPERBLY ENTERTAINING...
"...AND IT REALLY WAS.
TRIP

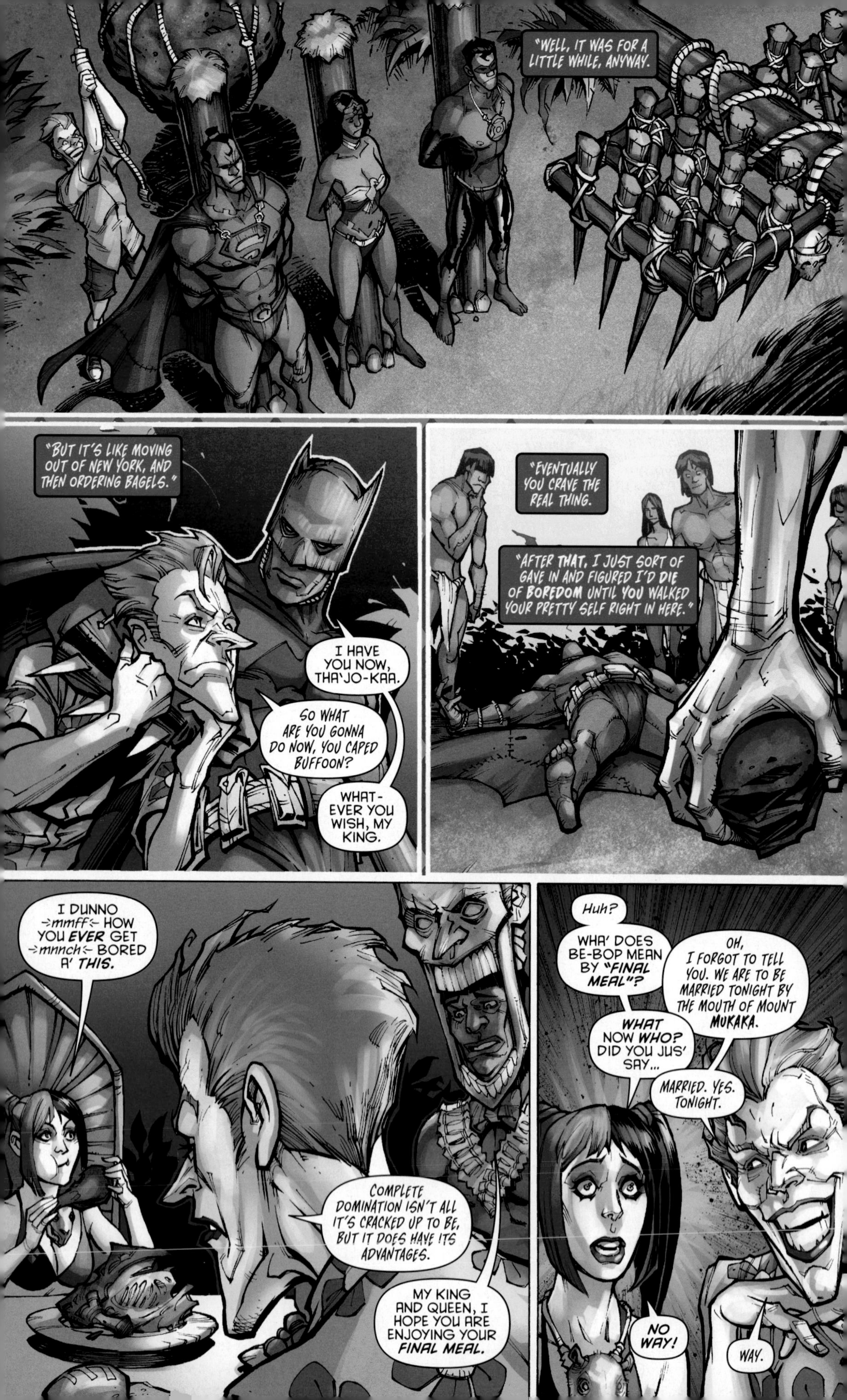
"WELL, IT WAS FOR A LITTLE WHILE, ANYWAY.
"BUT IT'S LIKE MOVING OUT OF NEW YORK, AND THEN ORDERING BAGELS."
I HAVE YOU NOW, THA'JO-KAA.
SO WHAT ARE YOU GONNA DO NOW, YOU CAPED BUFFOON?
WHAT-EVER YOU WISH, MY KING.
"EVENTUALLY YOU CRAVE THE REAL THING.
"AFTER THAT, I JUST SORT OF GAVE IN AND FIGURED I'D DIE OF BOREDOM UNTIL YOU WALKED YOUR PRETTY SELF RIGHT IN HERE."
I DUNNO -mmff- HOW YOU EVER GET -mnnch- BORED A' THIS.
COMPLETE DOMINATION ISN'T ALL IT'S CRACKED UP TO BE, BUT IT DOES HAVE ITS ADVANTAGES.
MY KING AND QUEEN, I HOPE YOU ARE ENJOYING YOUR FINAL MEAL.
Huh?
WHA' DOES BE-BOP MEAN BY "FINAL MEAL"?
OH, I FORGOT TO TELL YOU. WE ARE TO BE MARRIED TONIGHT BY THE MOUTH OF MOUNT MUKAKA.
WHAT NOW WHO? DID YOU JUS' SAY...
MARRIED. YES. TONIGHT.
NO WAY!
WAY.

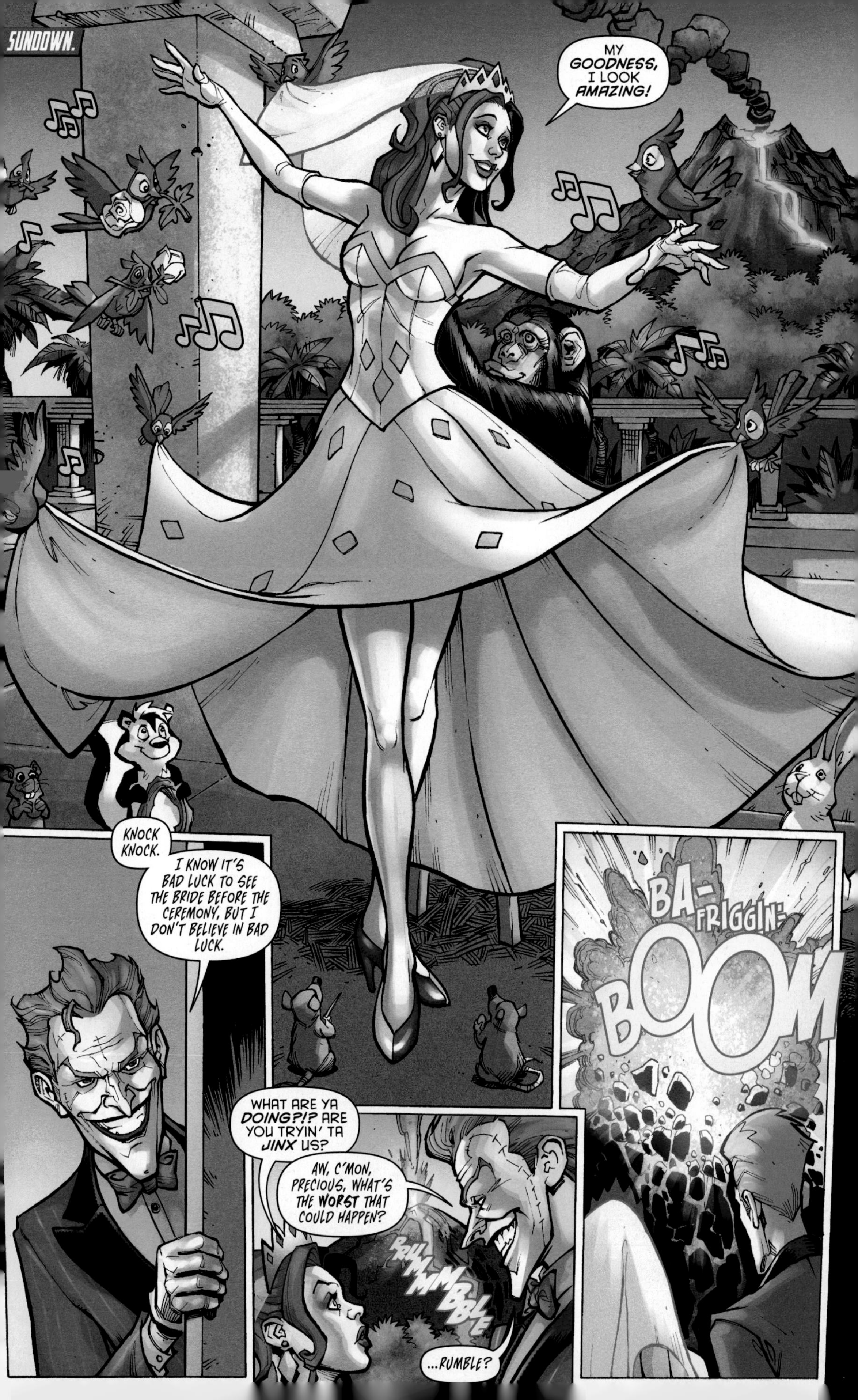
SUNDOWN.
MY GOODNESS, I LOOK AMAZING!
KNOCK KNOCK.
I KNOW IT'S BAD LUCK TO SEE THE BRIDE BEFORE THE CEREMONY, BUT I DON'T BELIEVE IN BAD LUCK.
WHAT ARE YA DOING?!? ARE YOU TRYIN' TA JINX US?
AW, C'MON, PRECIOUS, WHAT'S THE WORST THAT COULD HAPPEN?
RRUMMMBBLE
...RUMBLE?
BA-FRIGGIN'-BOOM

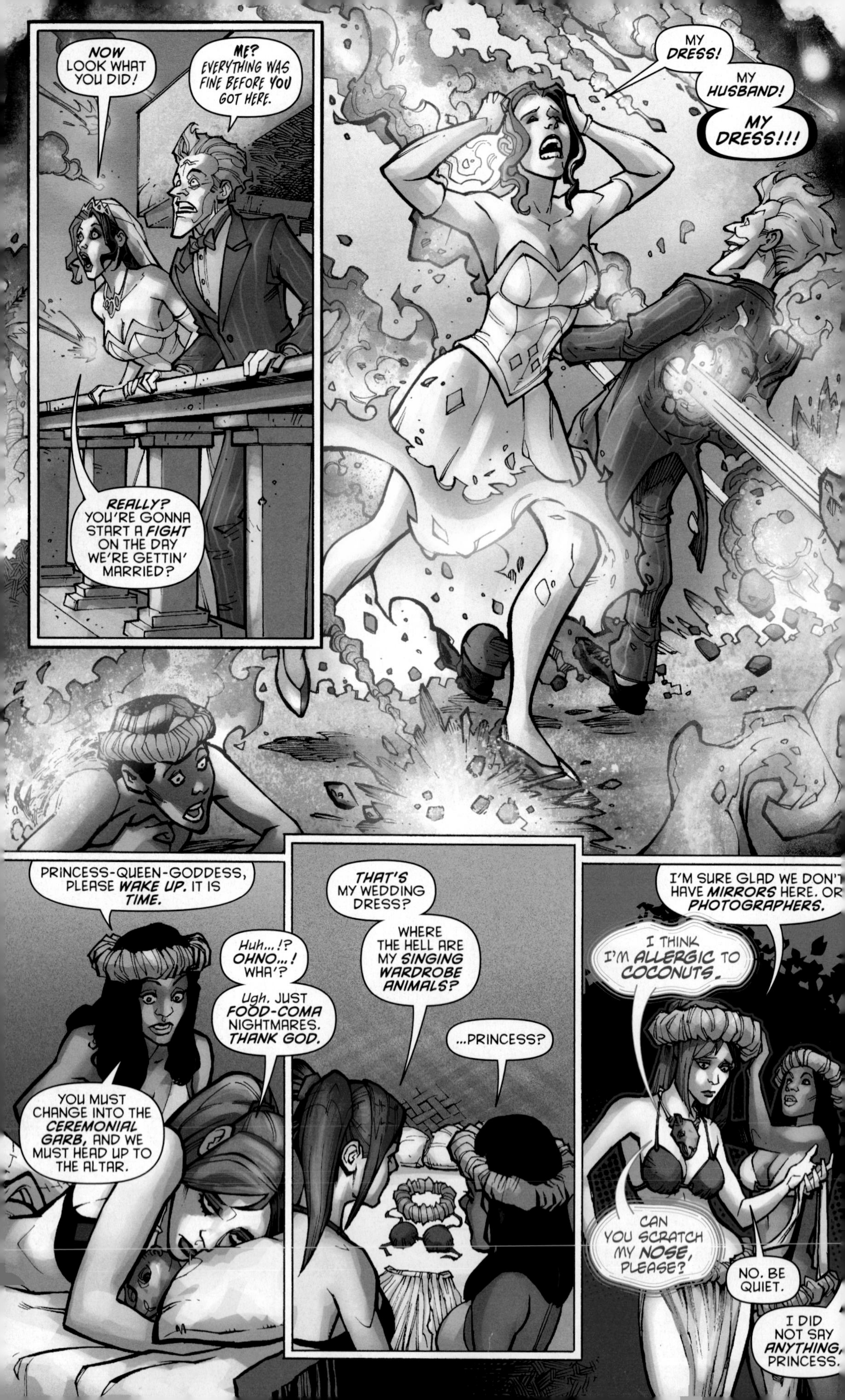
NOW LOOK WHAT YOU DID!
ME? EVERYTHING WAS FINE BEFORE YOU GOT HERE.
REALLY? YOU'RE GONNA START A FIGHT ON THE DAY WE'RE GETTIN' MARRIED?
MY DRESS!
MY HUSBAND!
MY DRESS!!!
PRINCESS-QUEEN-GODDESS, PLEASE WAKE UP. IT IS TIME.
Huh...!? OHNO...! WHA'?
Ugh. JUST FOOD-COMA NIGHTMARES. THANK GOD.
YOU MUST CHANGE INTO THE CEREMONIAL GARB, AND WE MUST HEAD UP TO THE ALTAR.
THAT'S MY WEDDING DRESS?
WHERE THE HELL ARE MY SINGING WARDROBE ANIMALS?
...PRINCESS?
I'M SURE GLAD WE DON'T HAVE MIRRORS HERE. OR PHOTOGRAPHERS.
I THINK I'M ALLERGIC TO COCONUTS.
CAN YOU SCRATCH MY NOSE, PLEASE?
NO. BE QUIET.
I DID NOT SAY ANYTHING, PRINCESS.

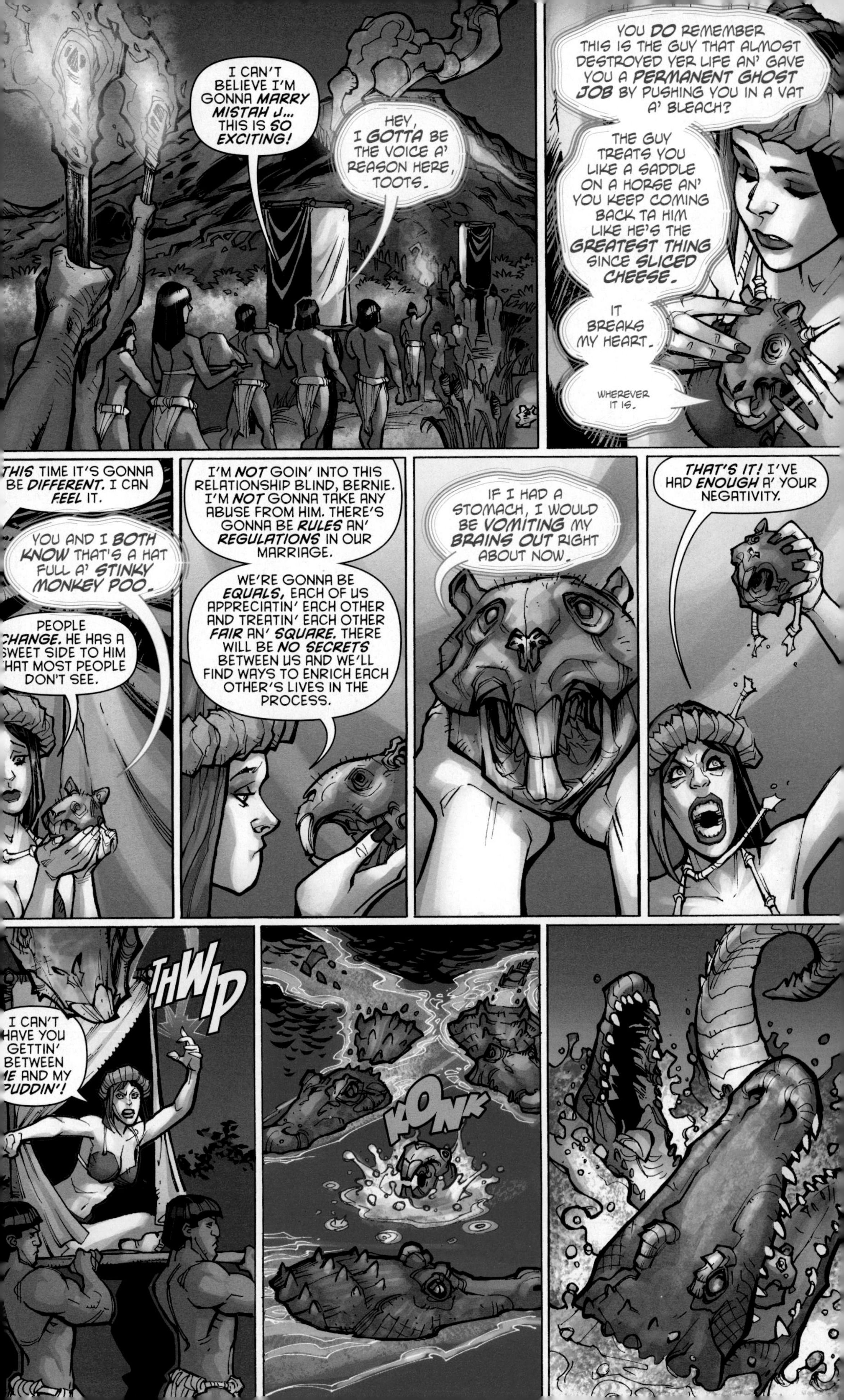

I CAN'T BELIEVE I'M GONNA MARRY MISTAH J... THIS IS SO EXCITING!
HEY, I GOTTA BE THE VOICE A' REASON HERE, TOOTS.
YOU DO REMEMBER THIS IS THE GUY THAT ALMOST DESTROYED YER LIFE AN' GAVE YOU A PERMANENT GHOST JOB BY PUSHING YOU IN A VAT A' BLEACH?
THE GUY TREATS YOU LIKE A SADDLE ON A HORSE AN' YOU KEEP COMING BACK TA HIM LIKE HE'S THE GREATEST THING SINCE SLICED CHEESE.
IT BREAKS MY HEART.
WHEREVER IT IS.
THIS TIME IT'S GONNA BE DIFFERENT. I CAN FEEL IT.
YOU AND I BOTH KNOW THAT'S A HAT FULL A' STINKY MONKEY POO.
PEOPLE CHANGE. HE HAS A SWEET SIDE TO HIM THAT MOST PEOPLE DON'T SEE.
I'M NOT GOIN' INTO THIS RELATIONSHIP BLIND, BERNIE. I'M NOT GONNA TAKE ANY ABUSE FROM HIM. THERE'S GONNA BE RULES AN' REGULATIONS IN OUR MARRIAGE.
WE'RE GONNA BE EQUALS, EACH OF US APPRECIATIN' EACH OTHER AND TREATIN' EACH OTHER FAIR AN' SQUARE. THERE WILL BE NO SECRETS BETWEEN US AND WE'LL FIND WAYS TO ENRICH EACH OTHER'S LIVES IN THE PROCESS.
IF I HAD A STOMACH, I WOULD BE VOMITING MY BRAINS OUT RIGHT ABOUT NOW.
THAT'S IT! I'VE HAD ENOUGH A' YOUR NEGATIVITY.
THWIP
I CAN'T HAVE YOU GETTIN' BETWEEN ME AND MY PUDDIN'!
KONK

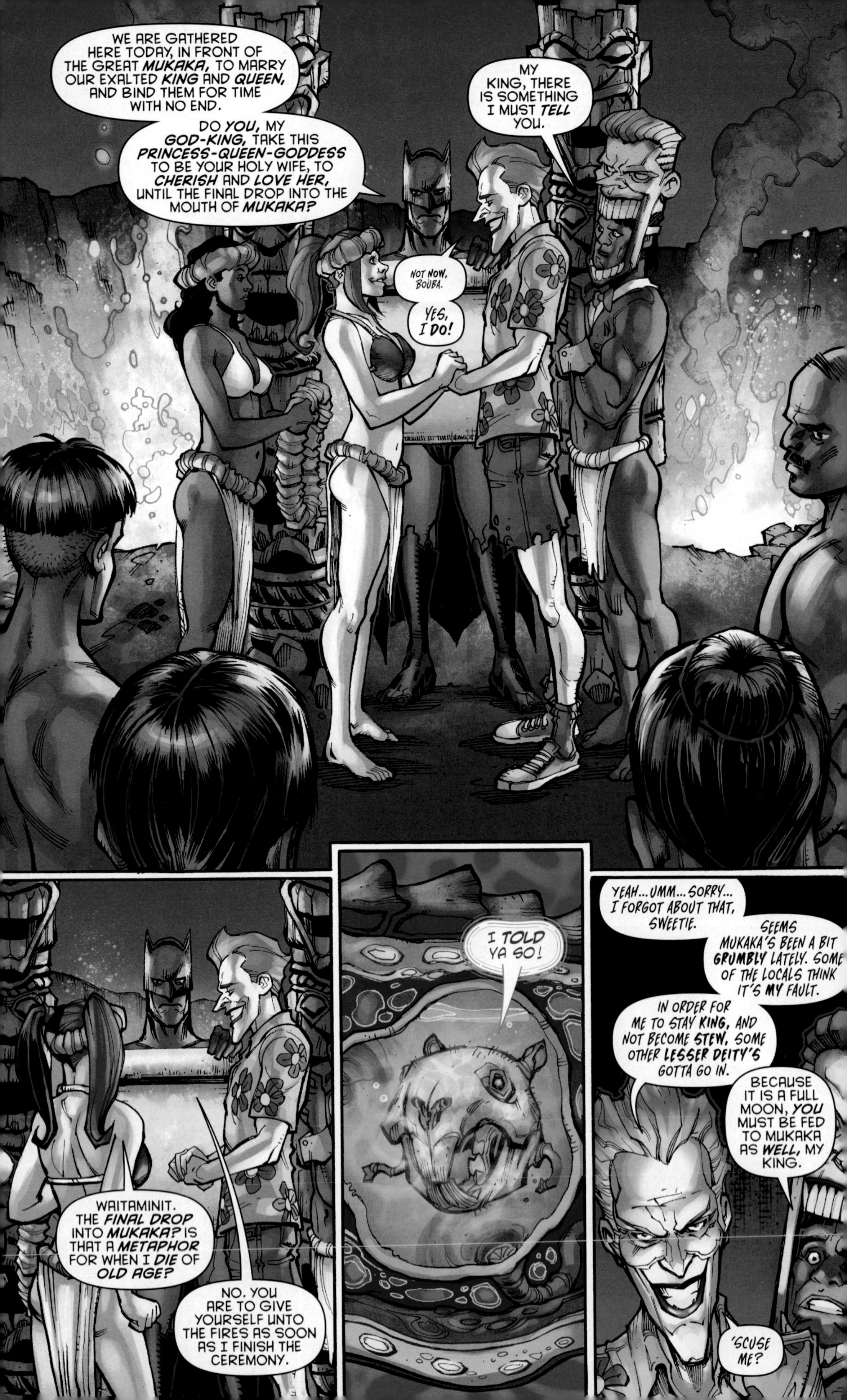
WE ARE GATHERED HERE TODAY, IN FRONT OF THE GREAT MUKAKA, TO MARRY OUR EXALTED KING AND QUEEN, AND BIND THEM FOR TIME WITH NO END.
DO YOU, MY GOD-KING, TAKE THIS PRINCESS-QUEEN-GODDESS TO BE YOUR HOLY WIFE, TO CHERISH AND LOVE HER, UNTIL THE FINAL DROP INTO THE MOUTH OF MUKAKA?
MY KING, THERE IS SOMETHING I MUST TELL YOU.
NOT NOW, BOUBA.
YES, I DO!
WAITAMINIT. THE FINAL DROP INTO MUKAKA? IS THAT A METAPHOR FOR WHEN I DIE OF OLD AGE?
NO. YOU ARE TO GIVE YOURSELF UNTO THE FIRES AS SOON AS I FINISH THE CEREMONY.
I TOLD YA SO!
YEAH...UMM...SORRY... I FORGOT ABOUT THAT, SWEETIE.
SEEMS MUKAKA'S BEEN A BIT GRUMBLY LATELY. SOME OF THE LOCALS THINK IT'S MY FAULT.
IN ORDER FOR ME TO STAY KING, AND NOT BECOME STEW, SOME OTHER LESSER DEITY'S GOTTA GO IN.
BECAUSE IT IS A FULL MOON, YOU MUST BE FED TO MUKAKA AS WELL, MY KING.
'SCUSE ME?

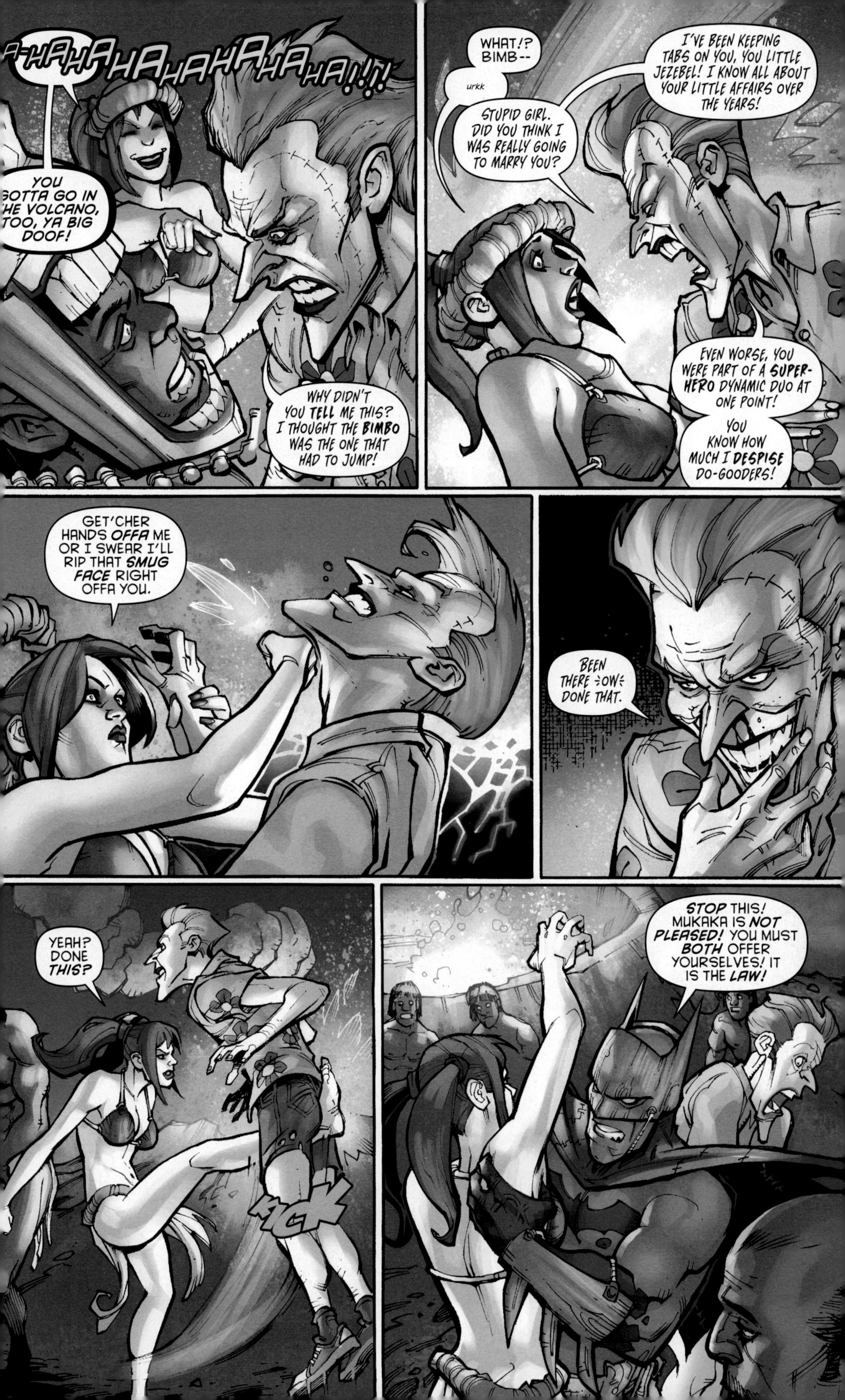

A-HAHAHAHAHAHAHAHAHA!!!!
YOU GOTTA GO IN THE VOLCANO, TOO, YA BIG DOOF!
WHY DIDN'T YOU TELL ME THIS? I THOUGHT THE BIMBO WAS THE ONE THAT HAD TO JUMP!
WHAT!? BIMB--
urkk
STUPID GIRL. DID YOU THINK I WAS REALLY GOING TO MARRY YOU?
I'VE BEEN KEEPING TABS ON YOU, YOU LITTLE JEZEBEL! I KNOW ALL ABOUT YOUR LITTLE AFFAIRS OVER THE YEARS!
EVEN WORSE, YOU WERE PART OF A SUPER-HERO DYNAMIC DUO AT ONE POINT!
YOU KNOW HOW MUCH I DESPISE DO-GOODERS!
GET'CHER HANDS OFFA ME OR I SWEAR I'LL RIP THAT SMUG FACE RIGHT OFFA YOU.
BEEN THERE ~OW~ DONE THAT.
YEAH? DONE THIS?
KICK
STOP THIS! MUKAKA IS NOT PLEASED! YOU MUST BOTH OFFER YOURSELVES! IT IS THE LAW!

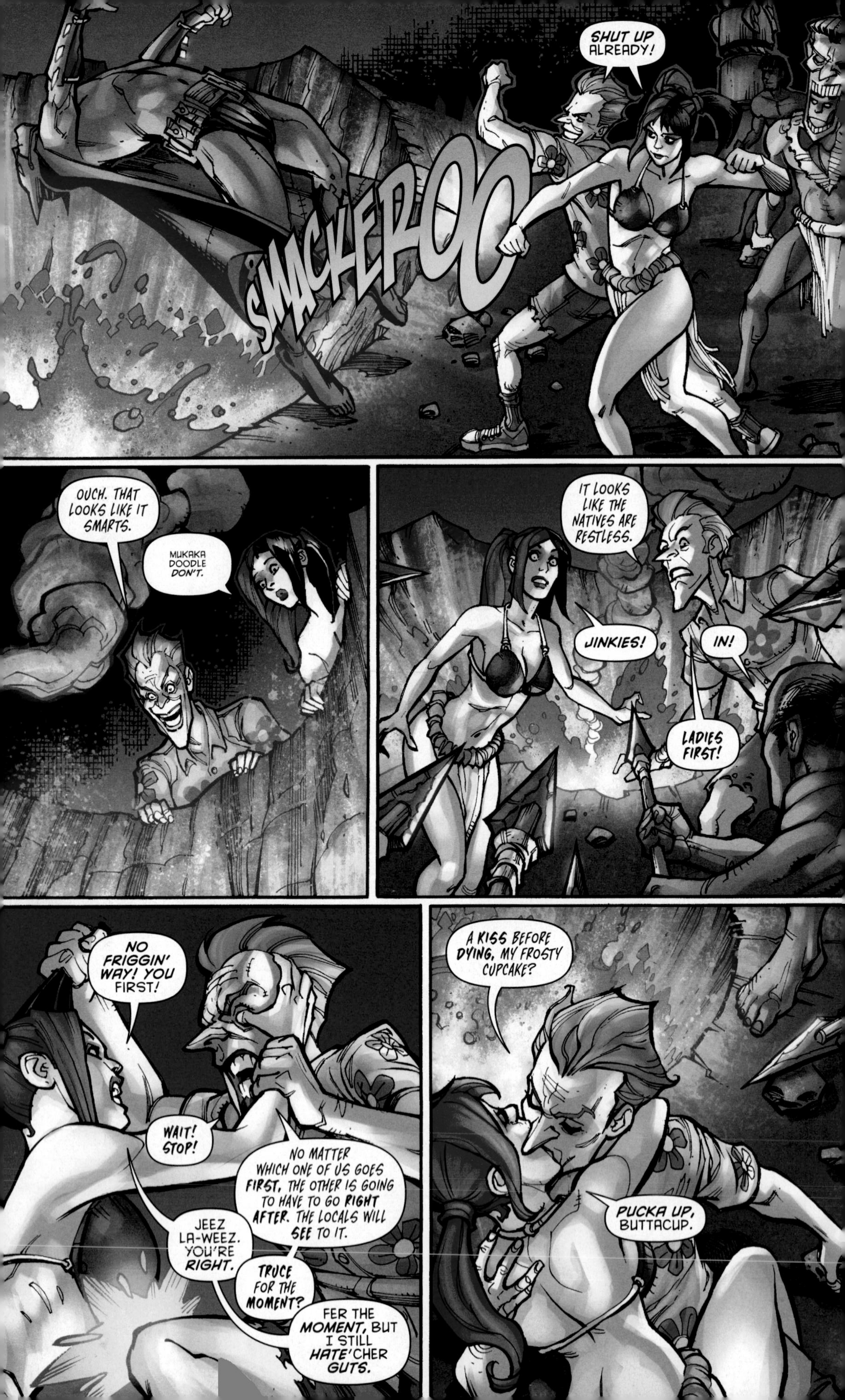
SHUT UP ALREADY!
SMACKEROO
OUCH. THAT LOOKS LIKE IT SMARTS.
MUKAKA DOODLE DON'T.
IT LOOKS LIKE THE NATIVES ARE RESTLESS.
JINKIES!
IN!
LADIES FIRST!
NO FRIGGIN' WAY! YOU FIRST!
WAIT! STOP!
NO MATTER WHICH ONE OF US GOES FIRST, THE OTHER IS GOING TO HAVE TO GO RIGHT AFTER. THE LOCALS WILL SEE TO IT.
JEEZ LA-WEEZ. YOU'RE RIGHT.
TRUCE FOR THE MOMENT?
FER THE MOMENT, BUT I STILL HATE'CHER GUTS.
A KISS BEFORE DYING, MY FROSTY CUPCAKE?
PUCKA UP, BUTTACUP.

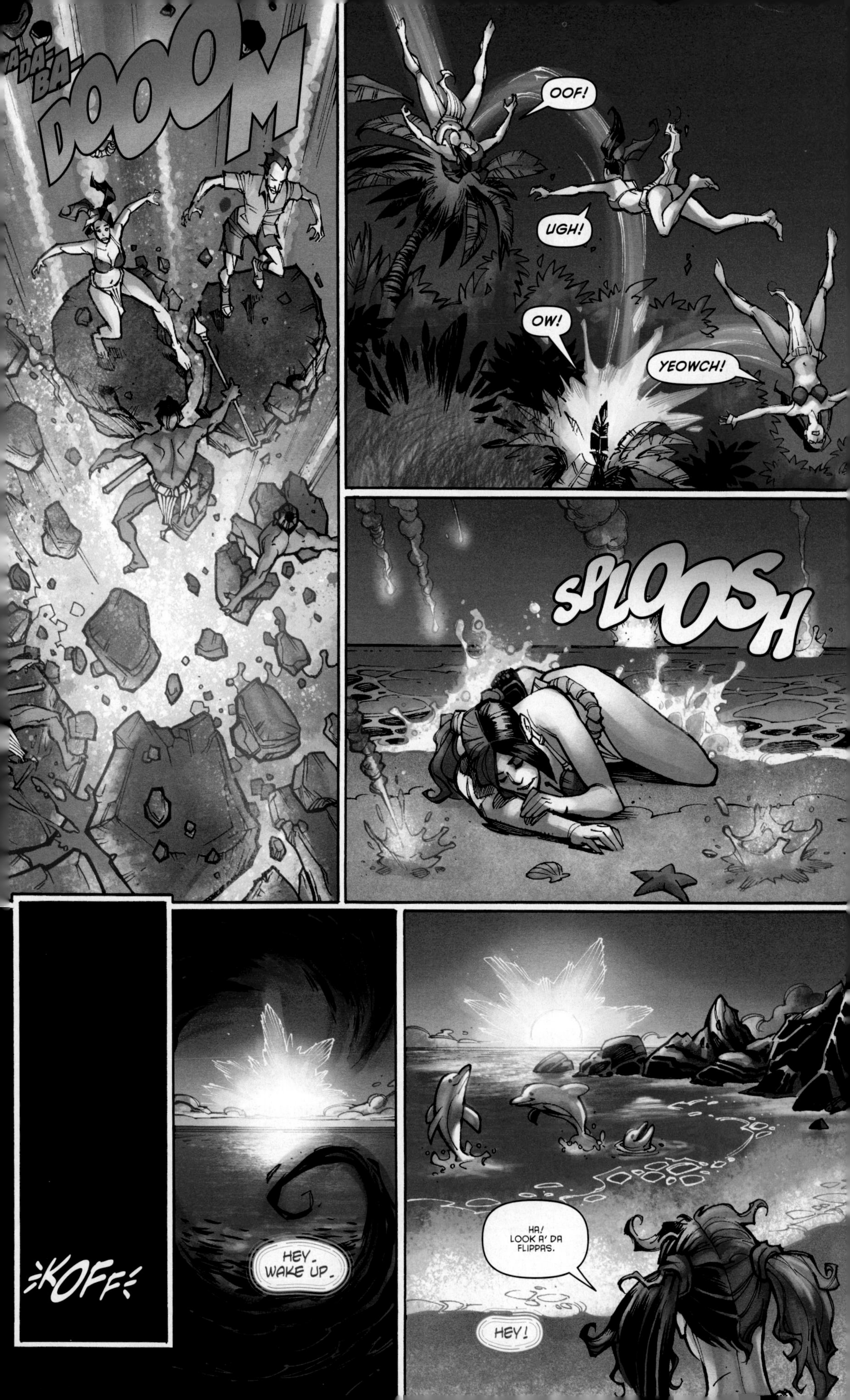
A-DA-BA-DOOOM
OOF!
UGH!
OW!
YEOWCH!
SPLOOSH
KOFF
HEY. WAKE UP.
HA! LOOK A' DA FLIPPAS.
HEY!

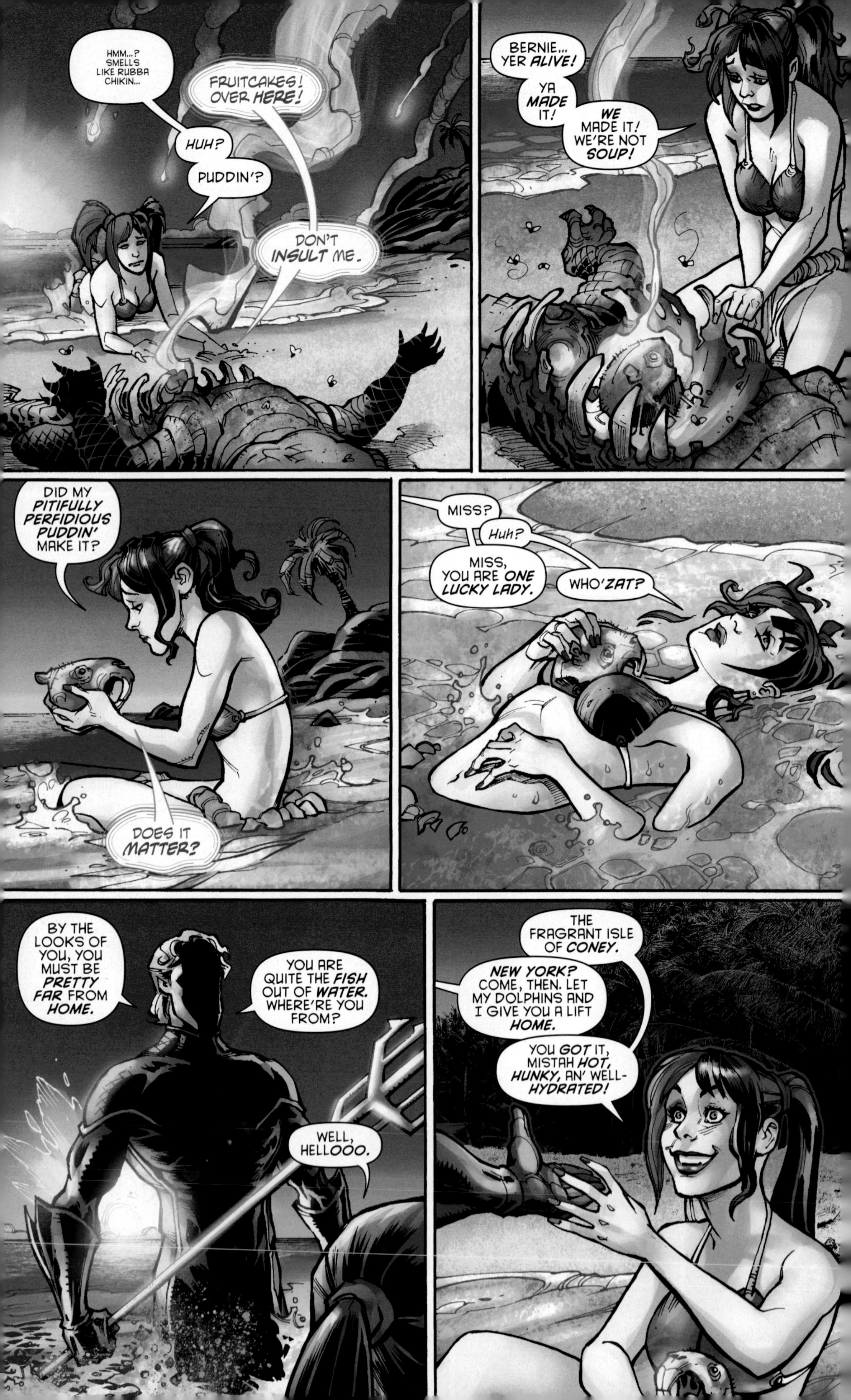

HMM...? SMELLS LIKE RUBBA CHIKIN...
FRUITCAKES! OVER HERE!
HUH?
PUDDIN'?
DON'T INSULT ME.
BERNIE... YER ALIVE!
YA MADE IT!
WE MADE IT! WE'RE NOT SOUP!
DID MY PITIFULLY PERFIDIOUS PUDDIN' MAKE IT?
DOES IT MATTER?
MISS?
Huh?
MISS, YOU ARE ONE LUCKY LADY.
WHO'ZAT?
BY THE LOOKS OF YOU, YOU MUST BE PRETTY FAR FROM HOME.
YOU ARE QUITE THE FISH OUT OF WATER. WHERE'RE YOU FROM?
WELL, HELLOOO.
THE FRAGRANT ISLE OF CONEY.
NEW YORK? COME, THEN. LET MY DOLPHINS AND I GIVE YOU A LIFT HOME.
YOU GOT IT, MISTAH HOT, HUNKY, AN' WELL-HYDRATED!

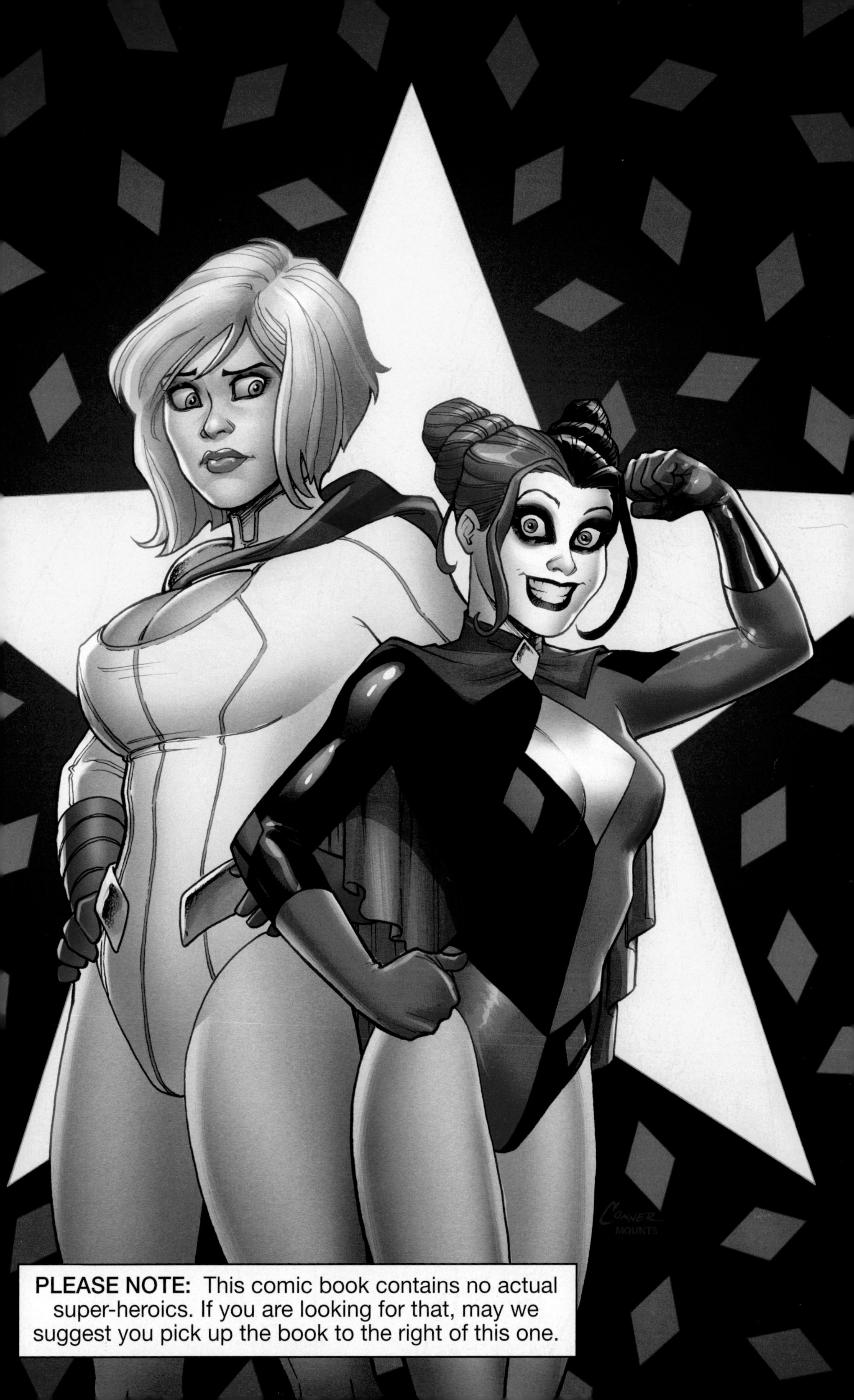
CONNER
MOUNTS
PLEASE NOTE: This comic book contains no actual super-heroics. If you are looking for that, may we suggest you pick up the book to the right of this one.

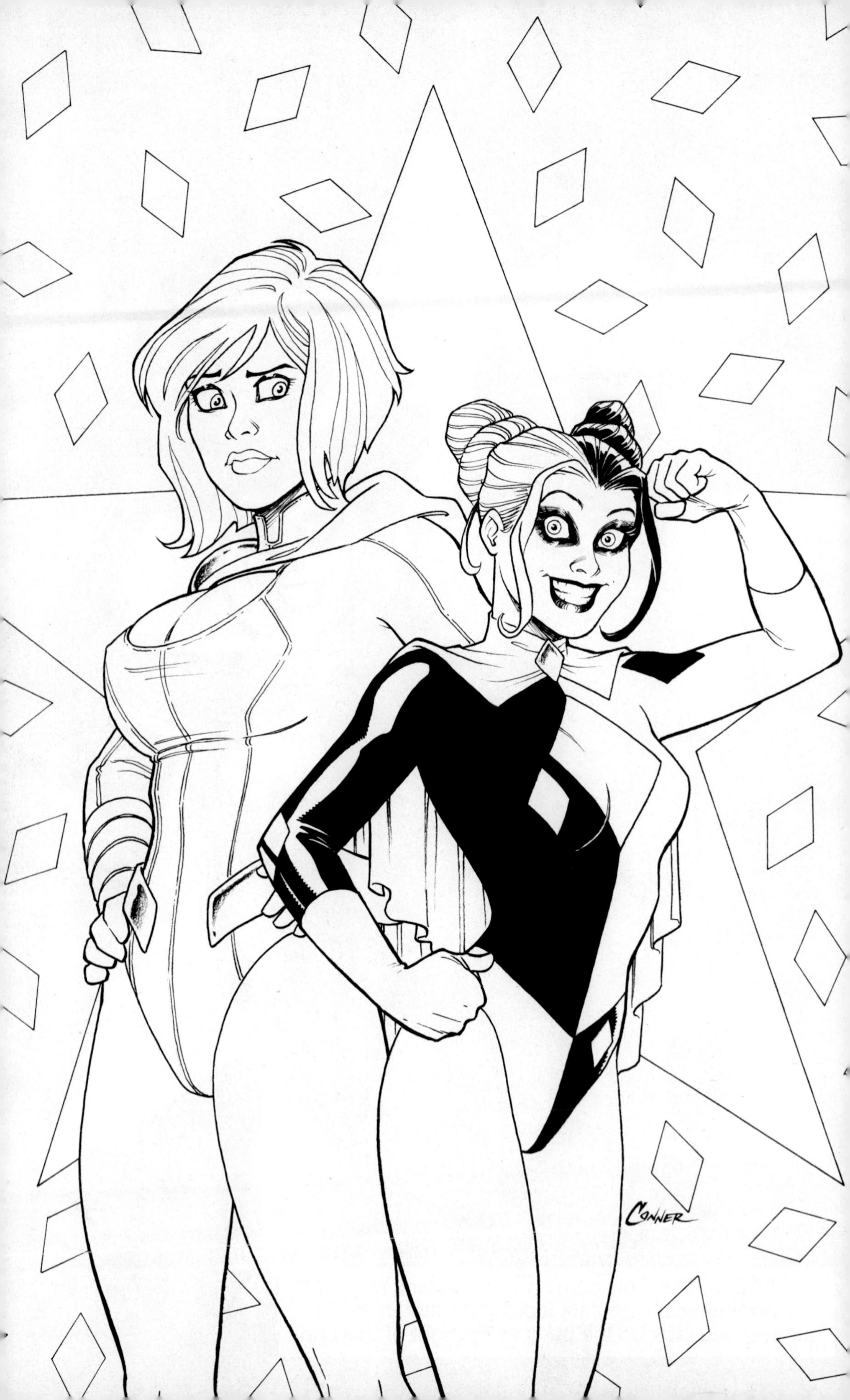
CONNER

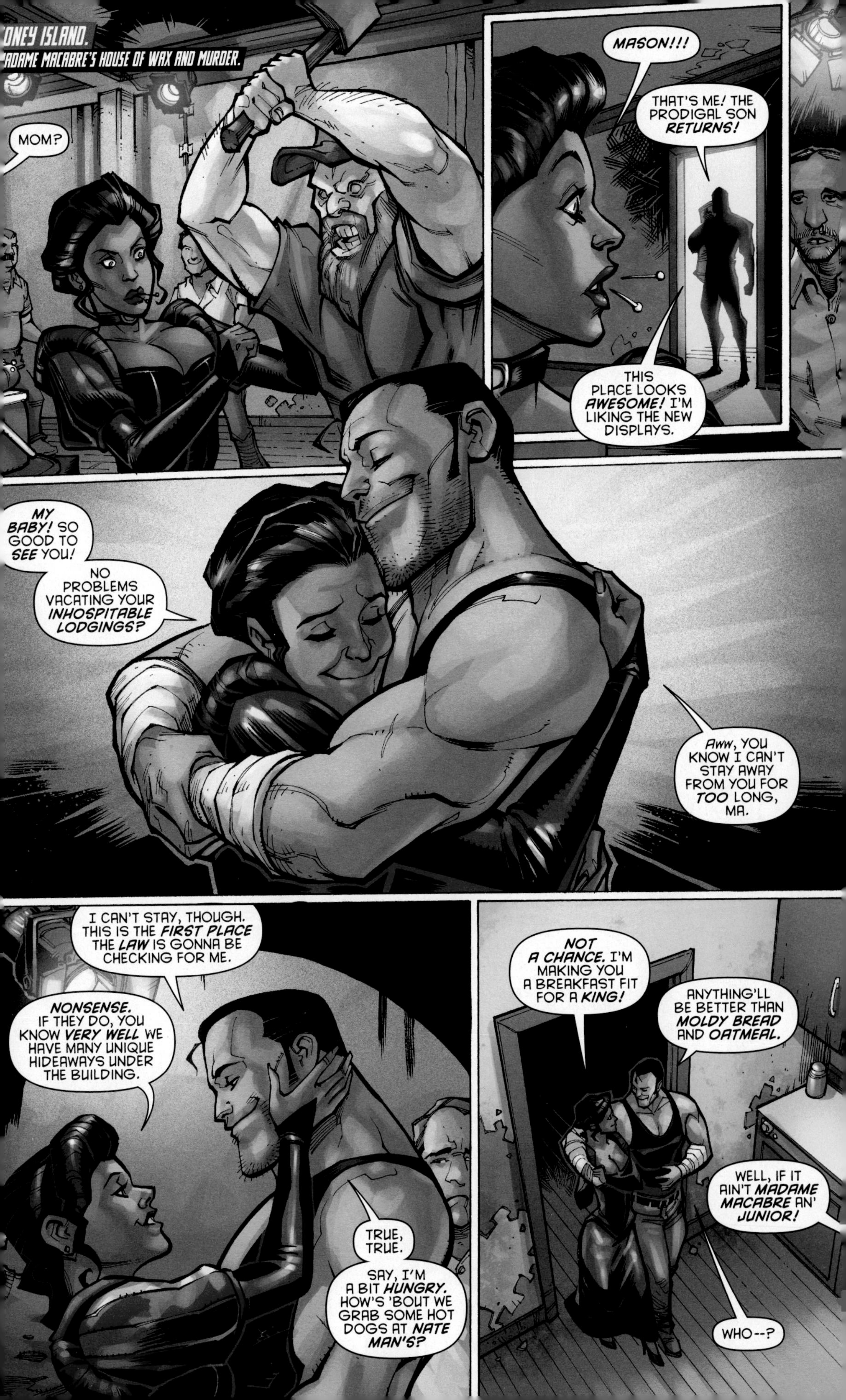
ONEY ISLAND.
ADAME MACABRE'S HOUSE OF WAX AND MURDER.
MOM?
MASON!!!
THAT'S ME! THE PRODIGAL SON RETURNS!
THIS PLACE LOOKS AWESOME! I'M LIKING THE NEW DISPLAYS.
MY BABY! SO GOOD TO SEE YOU!
NO PROBLEMS VACATING YOUR INHOSPITABLE LODGINGS?
AWW, YOU KNOW I CAN'T STAY AWAY FROM YOU FOR TOO LONG, MA.
I CAN'T STAY, THOUGH. THIS IS THE FIRST PLACE THE LAW IS GONNA BE CHECKING FOR ME.
NONSENSE. IF THEY DO, YOU KNOW VERY WELL WE HAVE MANY UNIQUE HIDEAWAYS UNDER THE BUILDING.
TRUE, TRUE.
SAY, I'M A BIT HUNGRY. HOW'S 'BOUT WE GRAB SOME HOT DOGS AT NATE MAN'S?
NOT A CHANCE. I'M MAKING YOU A BREAKFAST FIT FOR A KING!
ANYTHING'LL BE BETTER THAN MOLDY BREAD AND OATMEAL.
WELL, IF IT AIN'T MADAME MACABRE AN' JUNIOR!
WHO--?

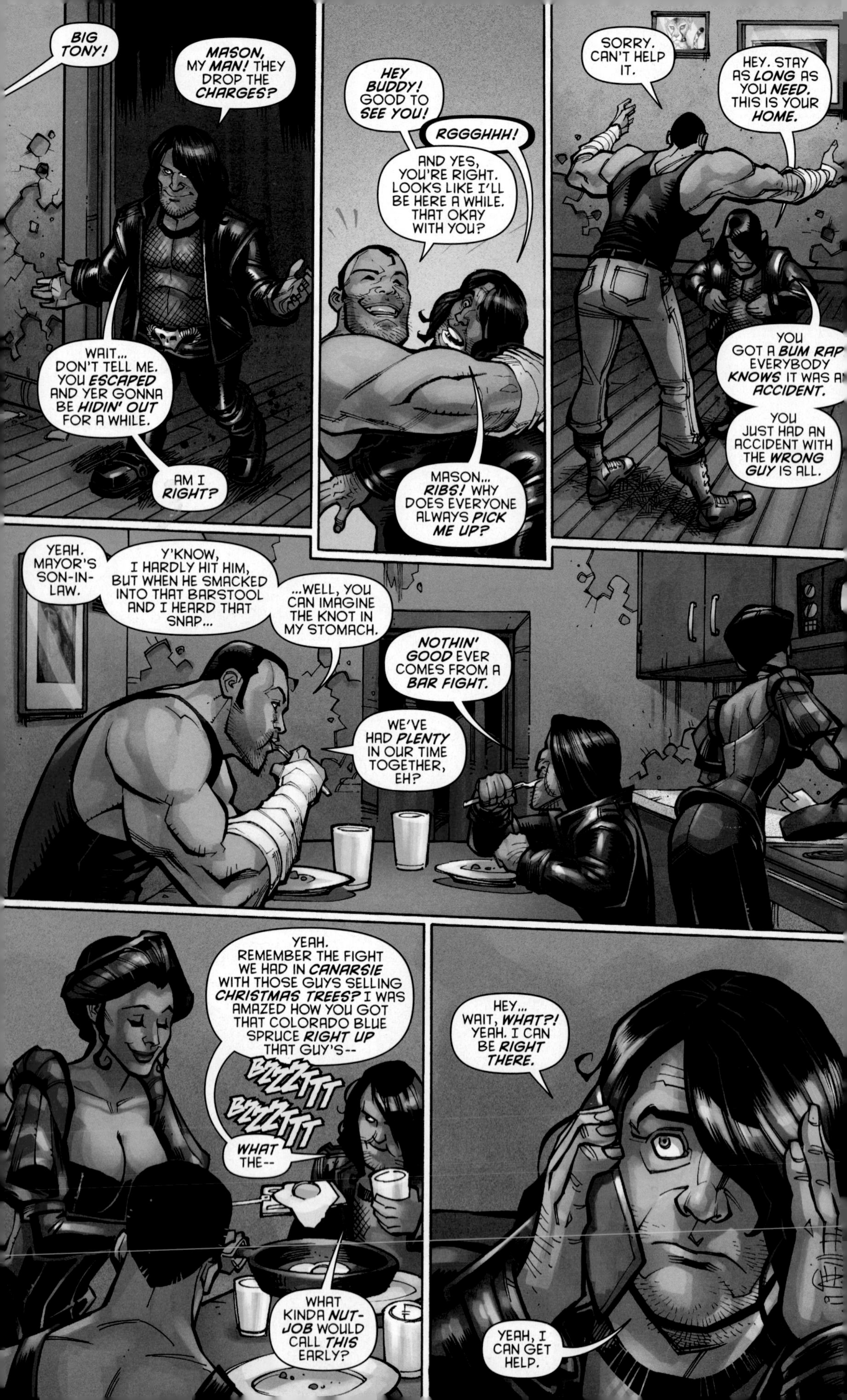
BIG TONY!
MASON, MY MAN! THEY DROP THE CHARGES?
WAIT... DON'T TELL ME. YOU ESCAPED AND YER GONNA BE HIDIN' OUT FOR A WHILE.
AM I RIGHT?
HEY BUDDY! GOOD TO SEE YOU!
RGGGHHH!
AND YES, YOU'RE RIGHT. LOOKS LIKE I'LL BE HERE A WHILE. THAT OKAY WITH YOU?
MASON... RIBS! WHY DOES EVERYONE ALWAYS PICK ME UP?
SORRY. CAN'T HELP IT.
HEY. STAY AS LONG AS YOU NEED. THIS IS YOUR HOME.
YOU GOT A BUM RAP EVERYBODY KNOWS IT WAS AN ACCIDENT.
YOU JUST HAD AN ACCIDENT WITH THE WRONG GUY IS ALL.
YEAH. MAYOR'S SON-IN-LAW.
Y'KNOW, I HARDLY HIT HIM, BUT WHEN HE SMACKED INTO THAT BARSTOOL AND I HEARD THAT SNAP...
...WELL, YOU CAN IMAGINE THE KNOT IN MY STOMACH.
NOTHIN' GOOD EVER COMES FROM A BAR FIGHT.
WE'VE HAD PLENTY IN OUR TIME TOGETHER, EH?
YEAH. REMEMBER THE FIGHT WE HAD IN CANARSIE WITH THOSE GUYS SELLING CHRISTMAS TREES? I WAS AMAZED HOW YOU GOT THAT COLORADO BLUE SPRUCE RIGHT UP THAT GUY'S--
BZZZZTTT
BZZZZTTT
WHAT THE--
WHAT KINDA NUT-JOB WOULD CALL THIS EARLY?
HEY... WAIT, WHAT?! YEAH. I CAN BE RIGHT THERE.
YEAH, I CAN GET HELP.

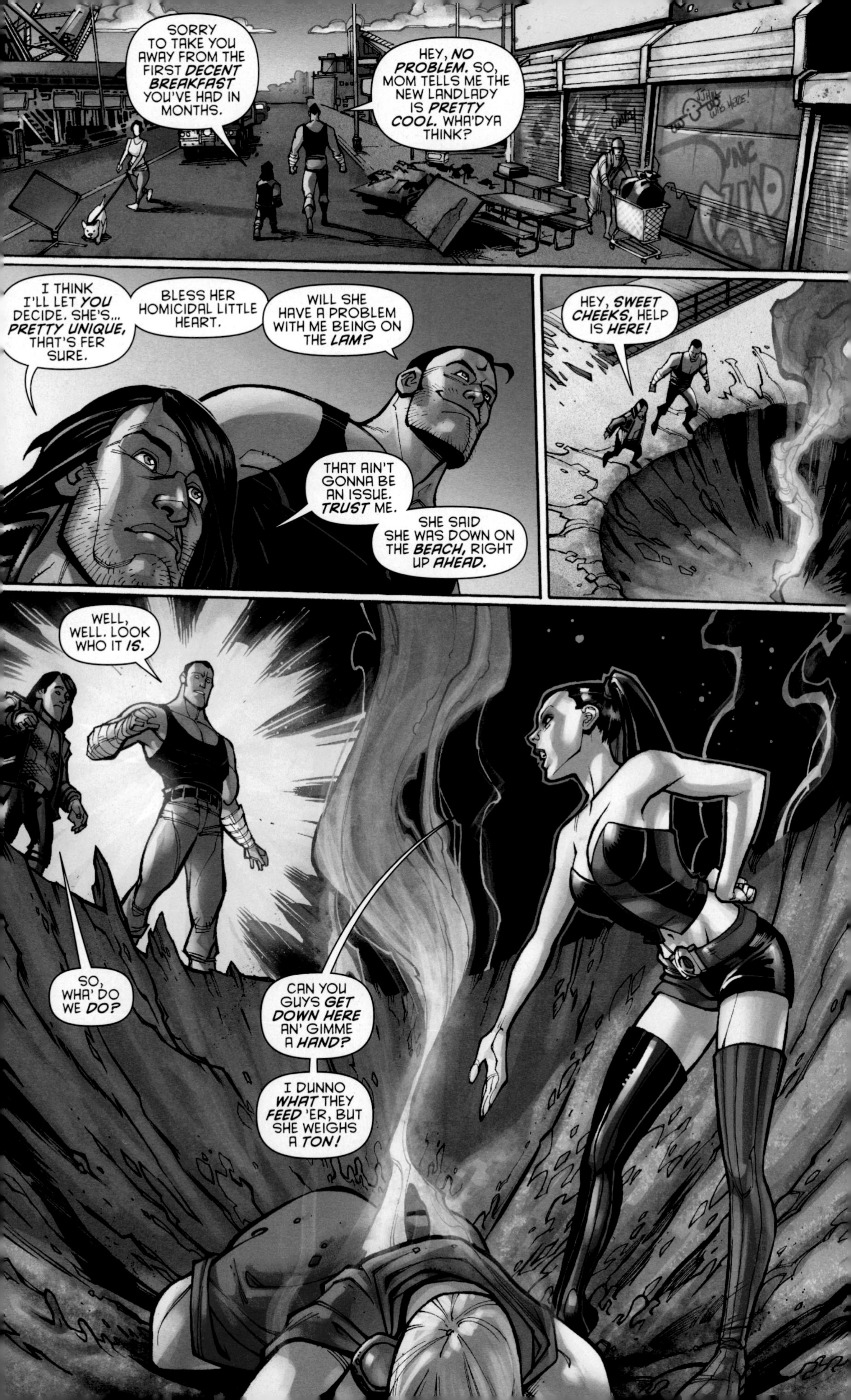

SORRY TO TAKE YOU AWAY FROM THE FIRST *DECENT BREAKFAST* YOU'VE HAD IN MONTHS.
HEY, *NO PROBLEM.* SO, MOM TELLS ME THE NEW LANDLADY IS *PRETTY COOL.* WHA'DYA THINK?
I THINK I'LL LET *YOU* DECIDE. SHE'S... *PRETTY UNIQUE,* THAT'S FER SURE.
BLESS HER HOMICIDAL LITTLE HEART.
WILL SHE HAVE A PROBLEM WITH ME BEING ON THE *LAM?*
THAT AIN'T GONNA BE AN ISSUE. *TRUST* ME.
SHE SAID SHE WAS DOWN ON THE *BEACH,* RIGHT UP *AHEAD.*
HEY, *SWEET CHEEKS,* HELP IS *HERE!*
WELL, WELL. LOOK WHO IT *IS.*
SO, WHA' DO WE *DO?*
CAN YOU GUYS *GET DOWN HERE* AN' GIMME A *HAND?*
I DUNNO *WHAT* THEY *FEED* 'ER, BUT SHE WEIGHS A *TON!*

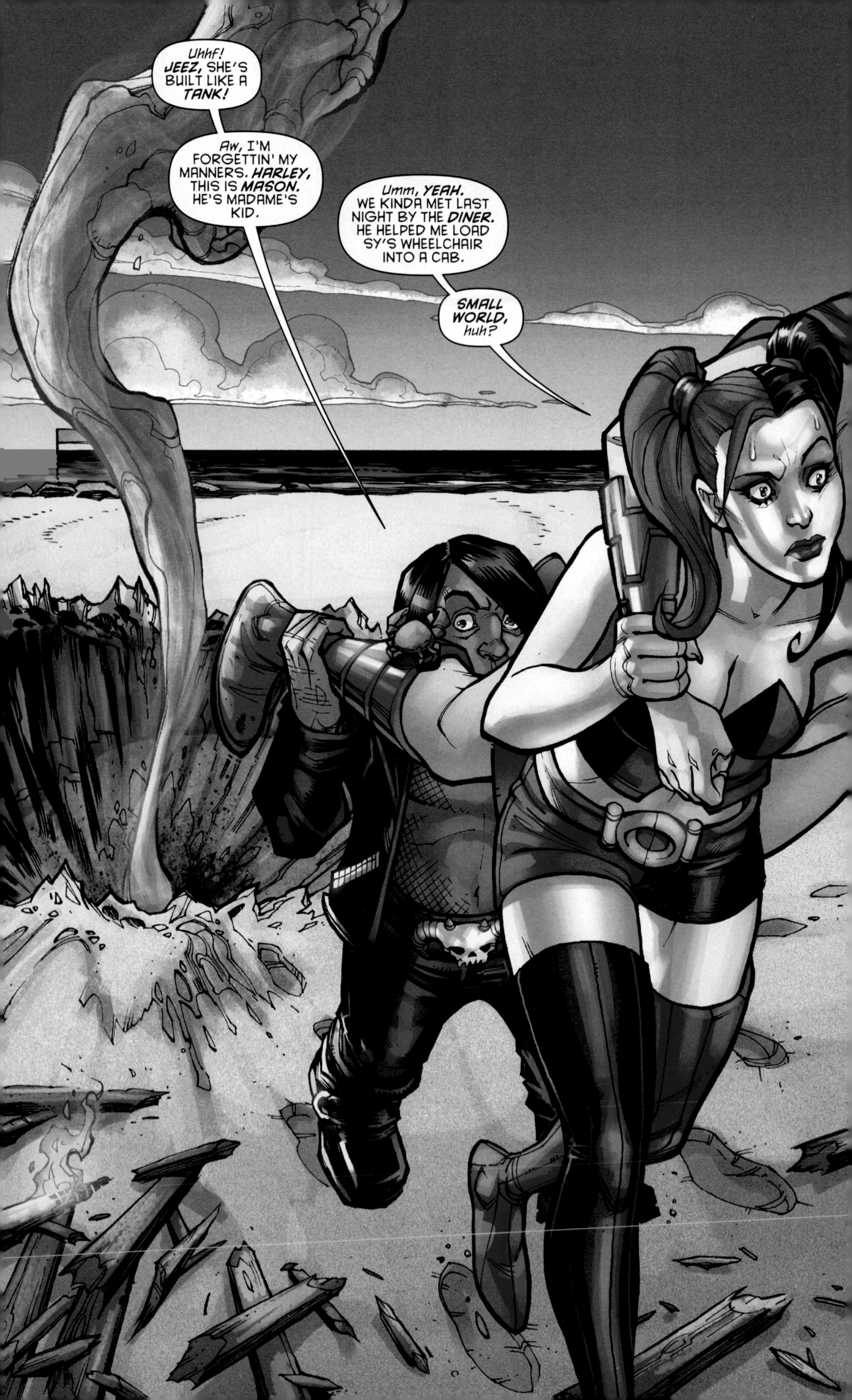
Uhhf! JEEZ, SHE'S BUILT LIKE A TANK!
Aw, I'M FORGETTIN' MY MANNERS. HARLEY, THIS IS MASON. HE'S MADAME'S KID.
Umm, YEAH. WE KINDA MET LAST NIGHT BY THE DINER. HE HELPED ME LOAD SY'S WHEELCHAIR INTO A CAB.
SMALL WORLD, huh?

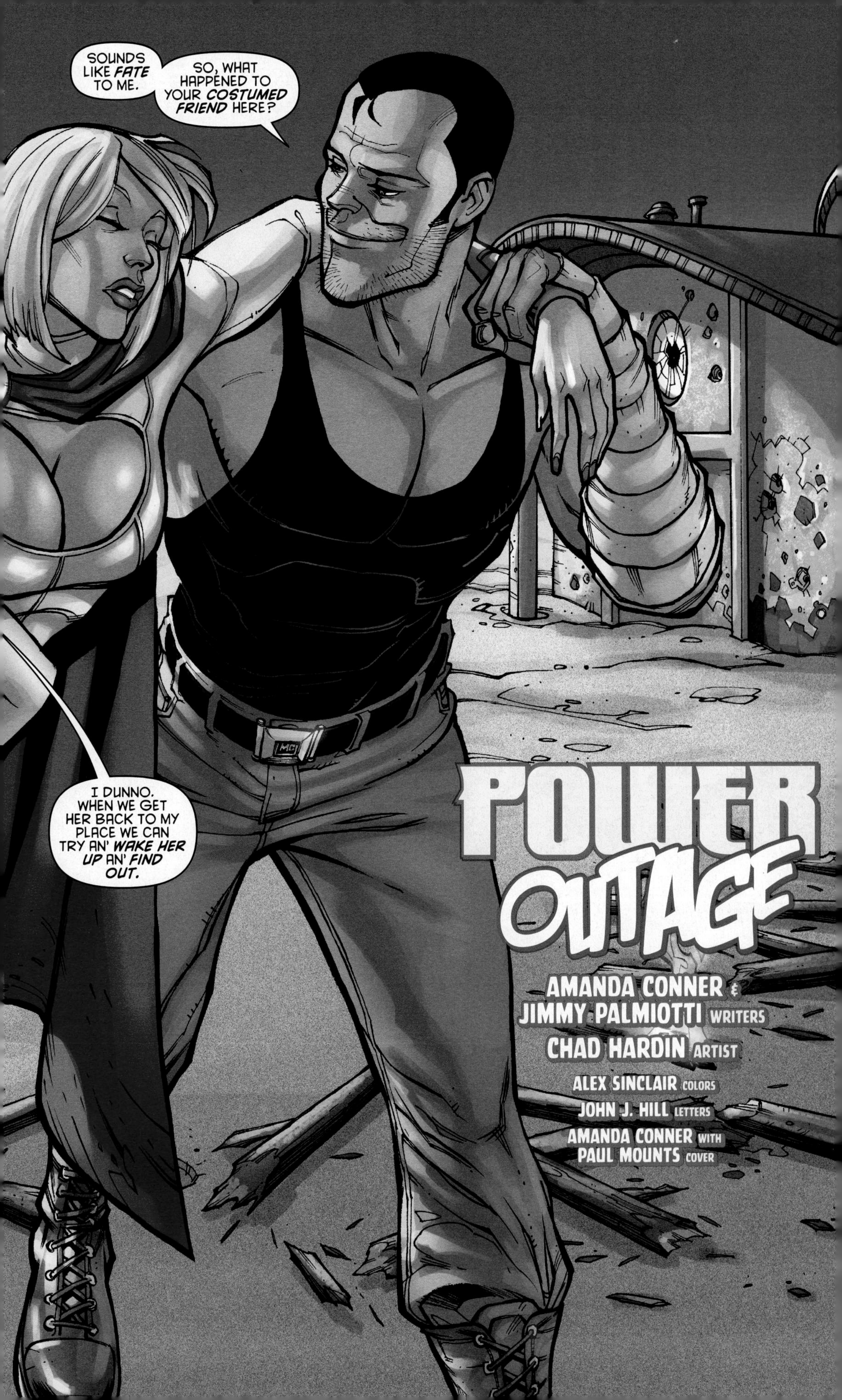
SOUNDS LIKE FATE TO ME.
SO, WHAT HAPPENED TO YOUR COSTUMED FRIEND HERE?
I DUNNO. WHEN WE GET HER BACK TO MY PLACE WE CAN TRY AN' WAKE HER UP AN' FIND OUT.
POWER OUTAGE
AMANDA CONNER & JIMMY PALMIOTTI WRITERS
CHAD HARDIN ARTIST
ALEX SINCLAIR COLORS
JOHN J. HILL LETTERS
AMANDA CONNER WITH PAUL MOUNTS COVER

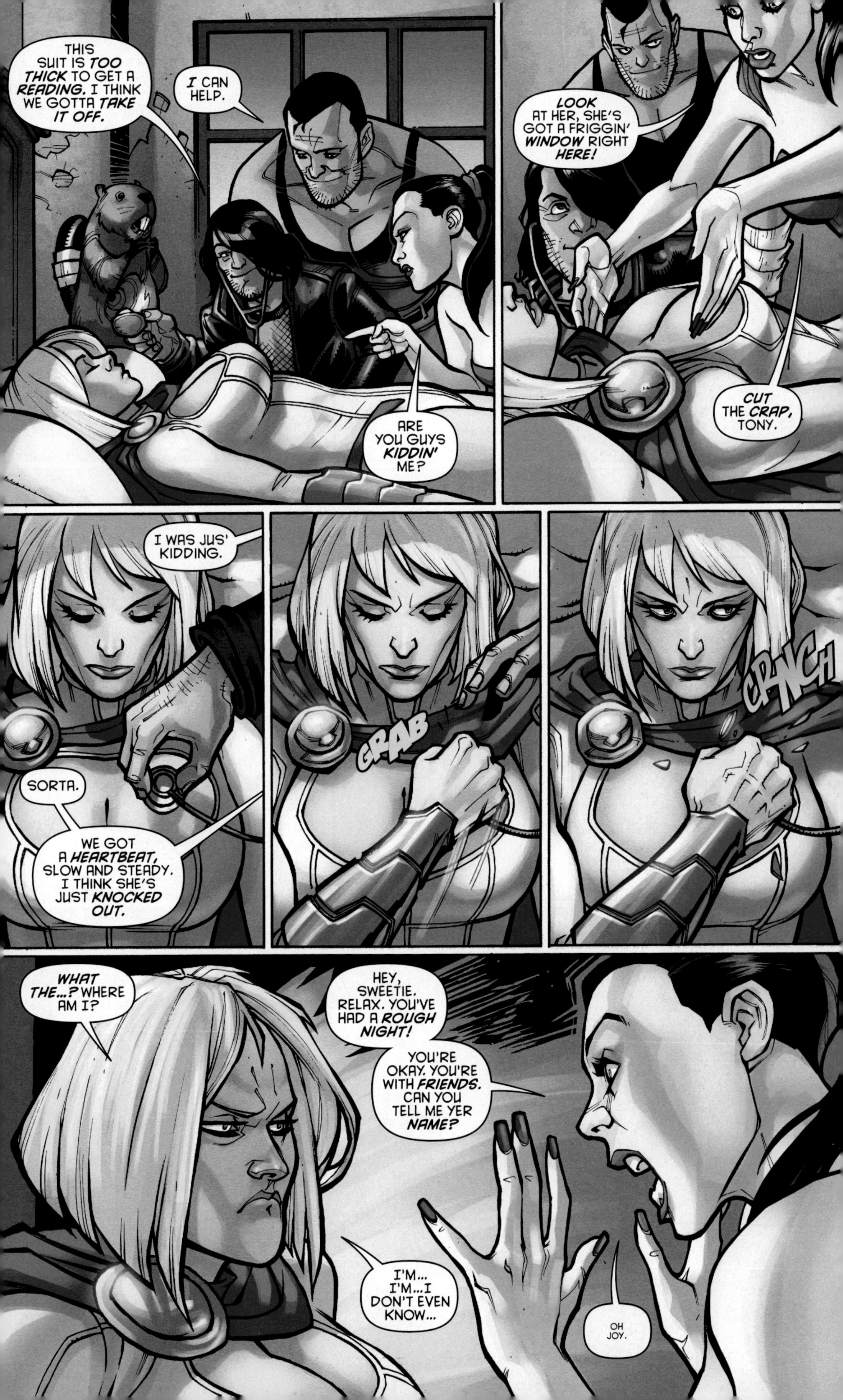
THIS SUIT IS TOO THICK TO GET A READING. I THINK WE GOTTA TAKE IT OFF.
I CAN HELP.
ARE YOU GUYS KIDDIN' ME?
LOOK AT HER, SHE'S GOT A FRIGGIN' WINDOW RIGHT HERE!
CUT THE CRAP, TONY.
I WAS JUS' KIDDING.
SORTA.
WE GOT A HEARTBEAT, SLOW AND STEADY. I THINK SHE'S JUST KNOCKED OUT.
GRAB
CRNCH
WHAT THE...? WHERE AM I?
HEY, SWEETIE. RELAX. YOU'VE HAD A ROUGH NIGHT!
YOU'RE OKAY. YOU'RE WITH FRIENDS. CAN YOU TELL ME YER NAME?
I'M... I'M...I DON'T EVEN KNOW...
OH JOY.

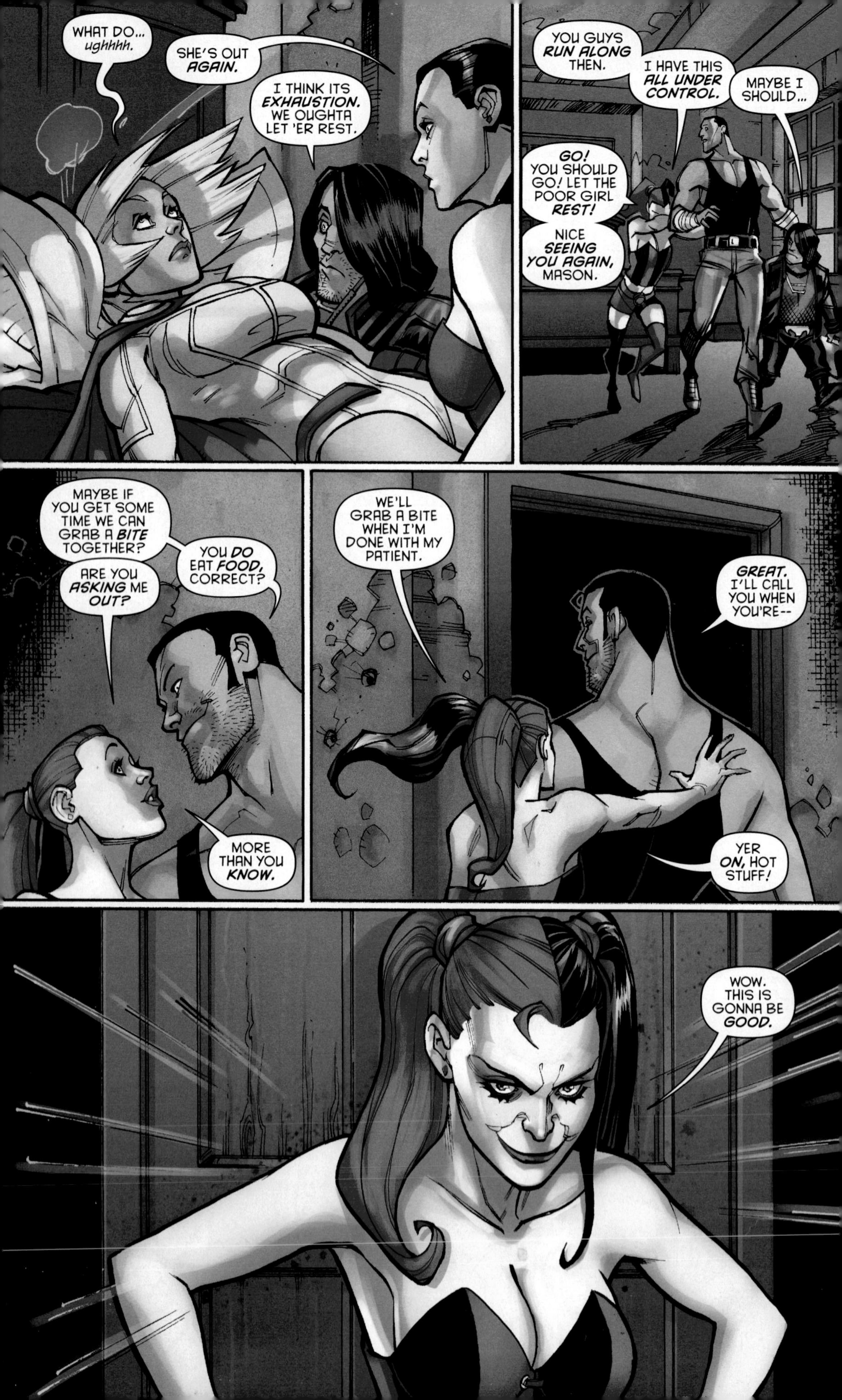
WHAT DO... ughhhh.
SHE'S OUT AGAIN.
I THINK ITS EXHAUSTION. WE OUGHTA LET 'ER REST.
YOU GUYS RUN ALONG THEN.
I HAVE THIS ALL UNDER CONTROL.
MAYBE I SHOULD...
GO! YOU SHOULD GO! LET THE POOR GIRL REST!
NICE SEEING YOU AGAIN, MASON.
MAYBE IF YOU GET SOME TIME WE CAN GRAB A BITE TOGETHER?
ARE YOU ASKING ME OUT?
YOU DO EAT FOOD, CORRECT?
MORE THAN YOU KNOW.
WE'LL GRAB A BITE WHEN I'M DONE WITH MY PATIENT.
GREAT. I'LL CALL YOU WHEN YOU'RE--
YER ON, HOT STUFF!
WOW. THIS IS GONNA BE GOOD.

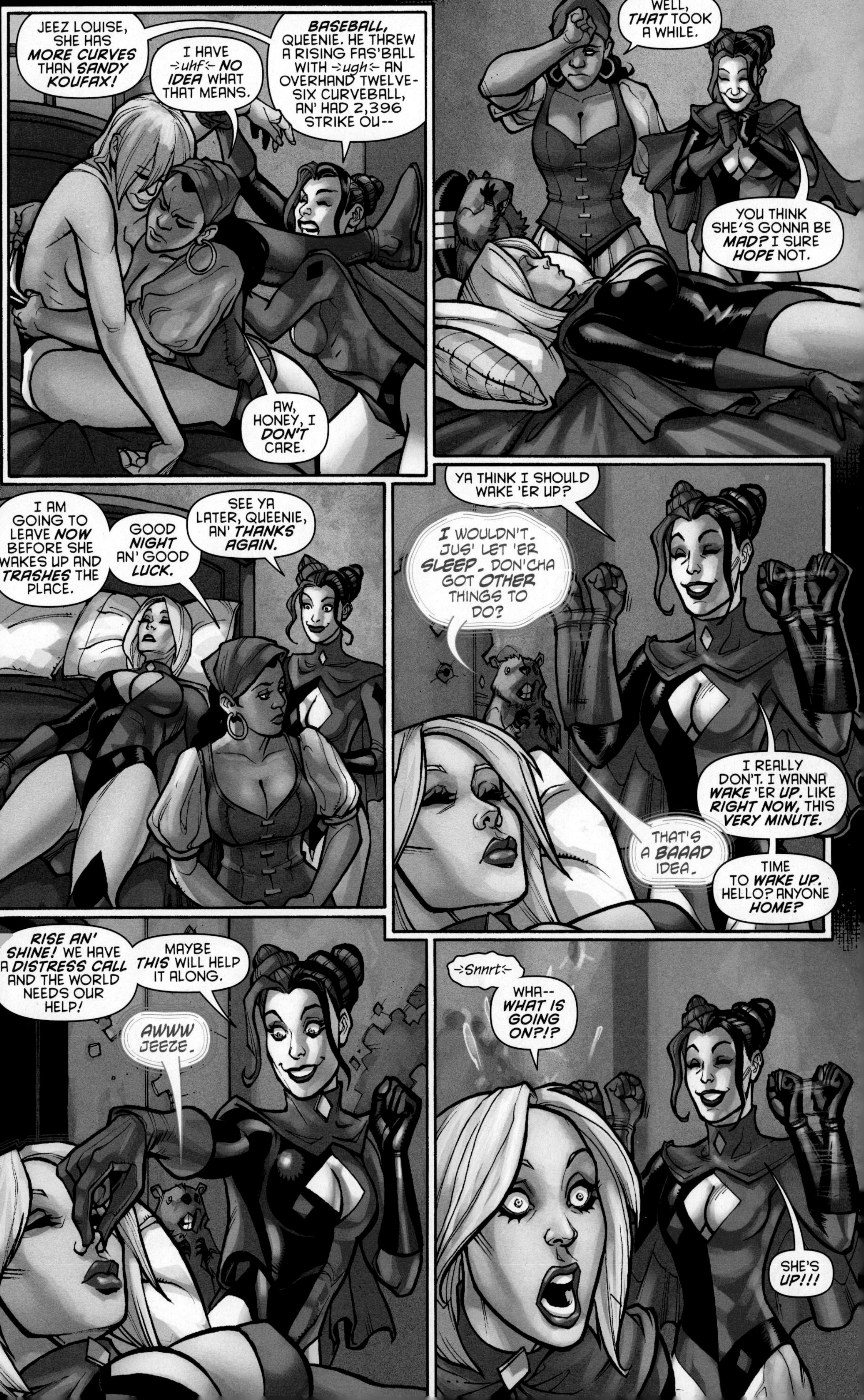

JEEZ LOUISE, SHE HAS MORE CURVES THAN SANDY KOUFAX!
I HAVE ⇢uhf⇠ NO IDEA WHAT THAT MEANS.
BASEBALL, QUEENIE. HE THREW A RISING FAS'BALL WITH ⇢ugh⇠ AN OVERHAND TWELVE-SIX CURVEBALL, AN' HAD 2,396 STRIKE OU--
AW, HONEY, I DON'T CARE.
WELL, THAT TOOK A WHILE.
YOU THINK SHE'S GONNA BE MAD? I SURE HOPE NOT.
I AM GOING TO LEAVE NOW BEFORE SHE WAKES UP AND TRASHES THE PLACE.
GOOD NIGHT AN' GOOD LUCK.
SEE YA LATER, QUEENIE, AN' THANKS AGAIN.
YA THINK I SHOULD WAKE 'ER UP?
I WOULDN'T. JUS' LET 'ER SLEEP. DON'CHA GOT OTHER THINGS TO DO?
I REALLY DON'T. I WANNA WAKE 'ER UP. LIKE RIGHT NOW, THIS VERY MINUTE.
THAT'S A BAAAD IDEA.
TIME TO WAKE UP. HELLO? ANYONE HOME?
RISE AN' SHINE! WE HAVE A DISTRESS CALL AND THE WORLD NEEDS OUR HELP!
MAYBE THIS WILL HELP IT ALONG.
AWWW JEEZE.
⇢Snnrt⇠
WHA-- WHAT IS GOING ON?!?
SHE'S UP!!!

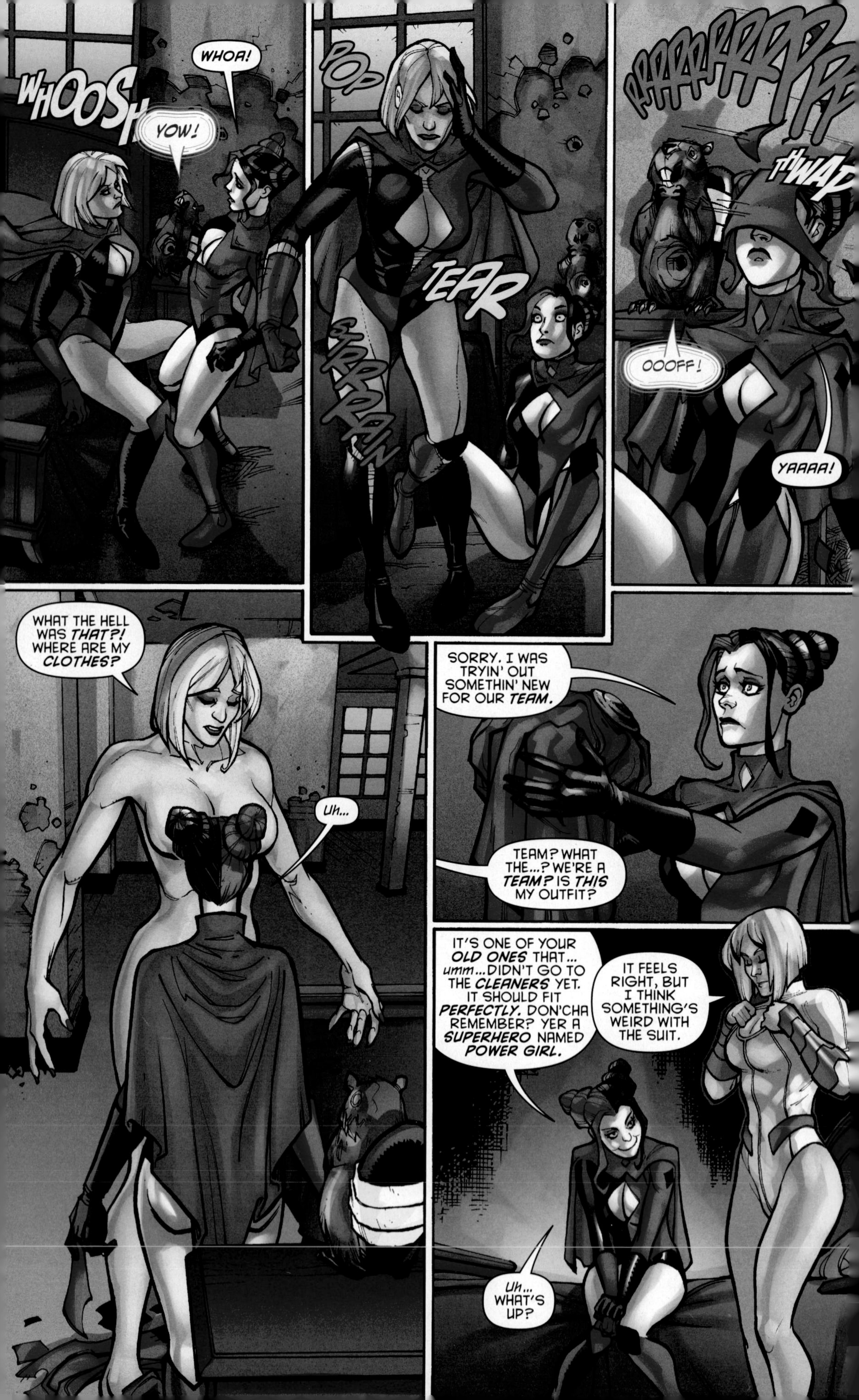
WHOOSH
WHOA!
YOW!
POP
TEAR
SKRRRAAAN
RRRRRRRRRRRRIP
THWAP
OOOFF!
YAAAA!
WHAT THE HELL WAS THAT?! WHERE ARE MY CLOTHES?
Uh...
SORRY. I WAS TRYIN' OUT SOMETHIN' NEW FOR OUR TEAM.
TEAM? WHAT THE...? WE'RE A TEAM? IS THIS MY OUTFIT?
IT'S ONE OF YOUR OLD ONES THAT... umm...DIDN'T GO TO THE CLEANERS YET. IT SHOULD FIT PERFECTLY. DON'CHA REMEMBER? YER A SUPERHERO NAMED POWER GIRL.
IT FEELS RIGHT, BUT I THINK SOMETHING'S WEIRD WITH THE SUIT.
Uh... WHAT'S UP?

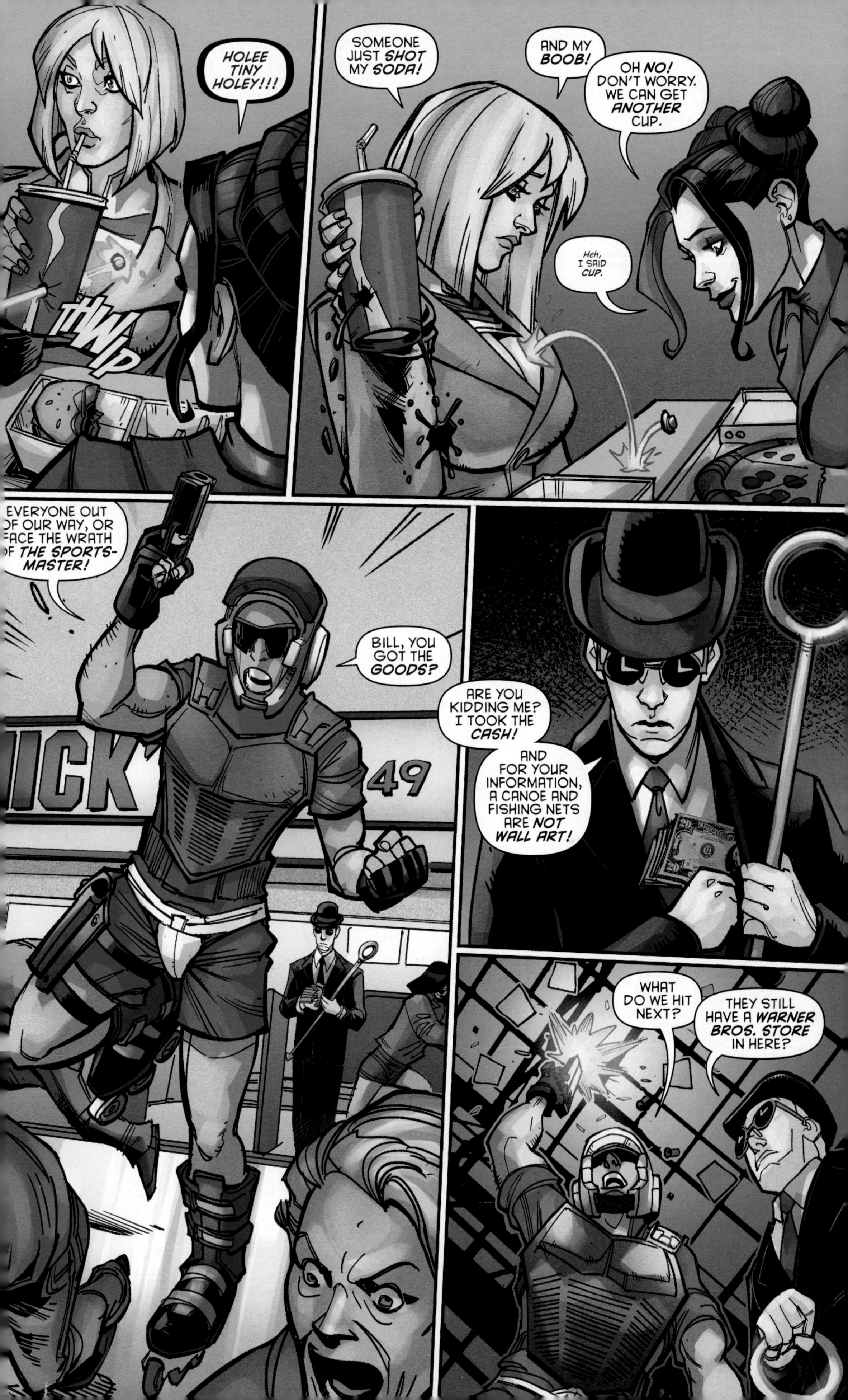
HOLEE TINY HOLEY!!!
THWIP
SOMEONE JUST SHOT MY SODA!
AND MY BOOB!
OH NO! DON'T WORRY. WE CAN GET ANOTHER CUP.
Heh, I SAID CUP.
EVERYONE OUT OF OUR WAY, OR FACE THE WRATH OF THE SPORTS-MASTER!
BILL, YOU GOT THE GOODS?
ARE YOU KIDDING ME? I TOOK THE CASH!
AND FOR YOUR INFORMATION, A CANOE AND FISHING NETS ARE NOT WALL ART!
WHAT DO WE HIT NEXT?
THEY STILL HAVE A WARNER BROS. STORE IN HERE?

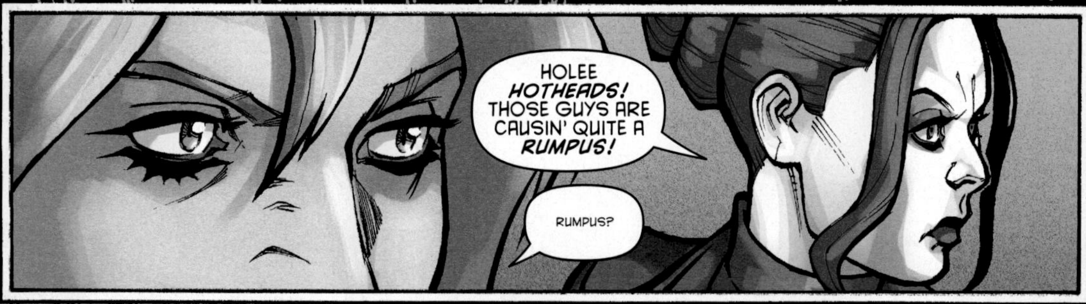
HOLEE HOTHEADS! THOSE GUYS ARE CAUSIN' QUITE A RUMPUS!
RUMPUS?

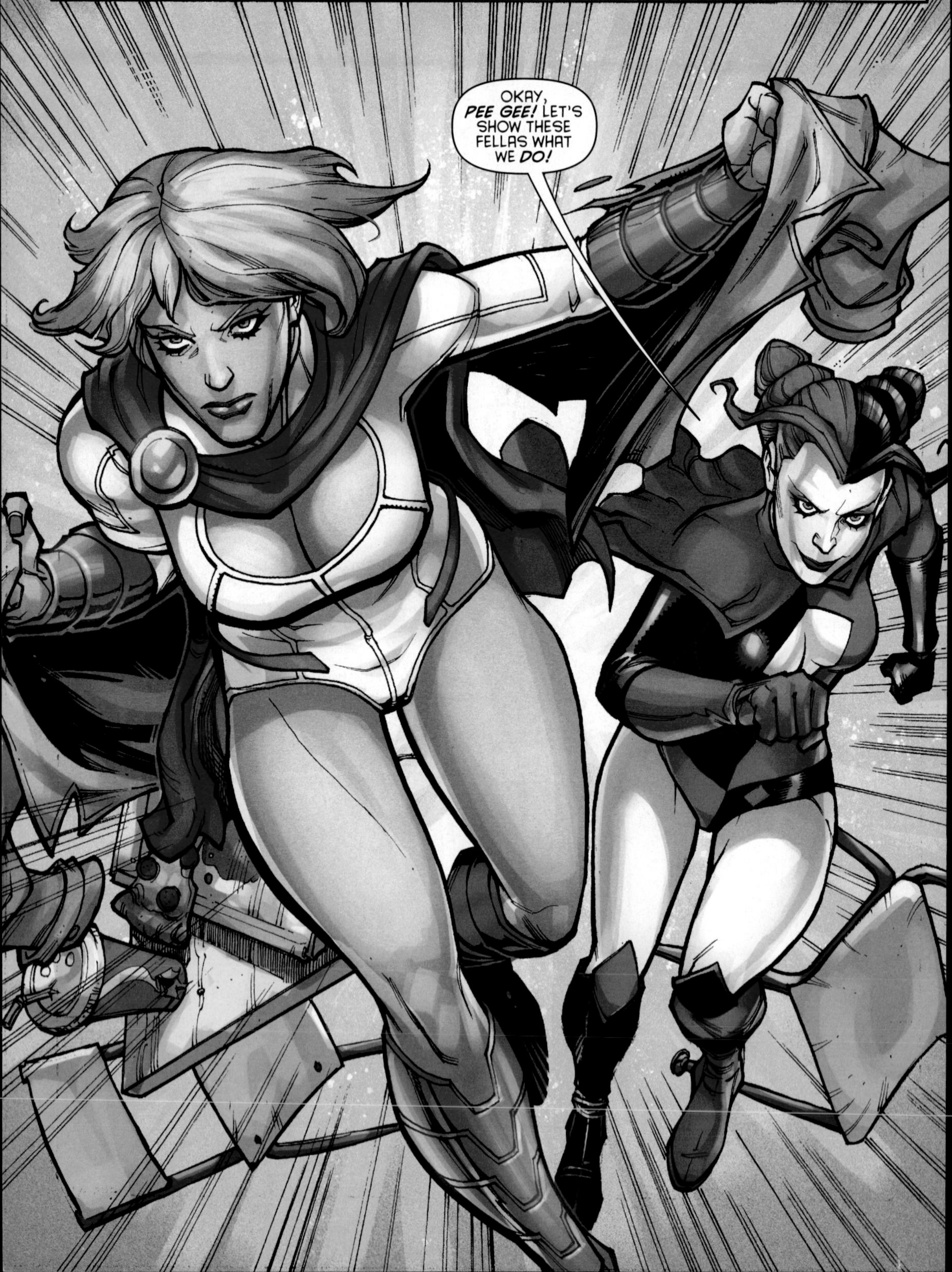
OKAY, PEE GEE! LET'S SHOW THESE FELLAS WHAT WE DO!

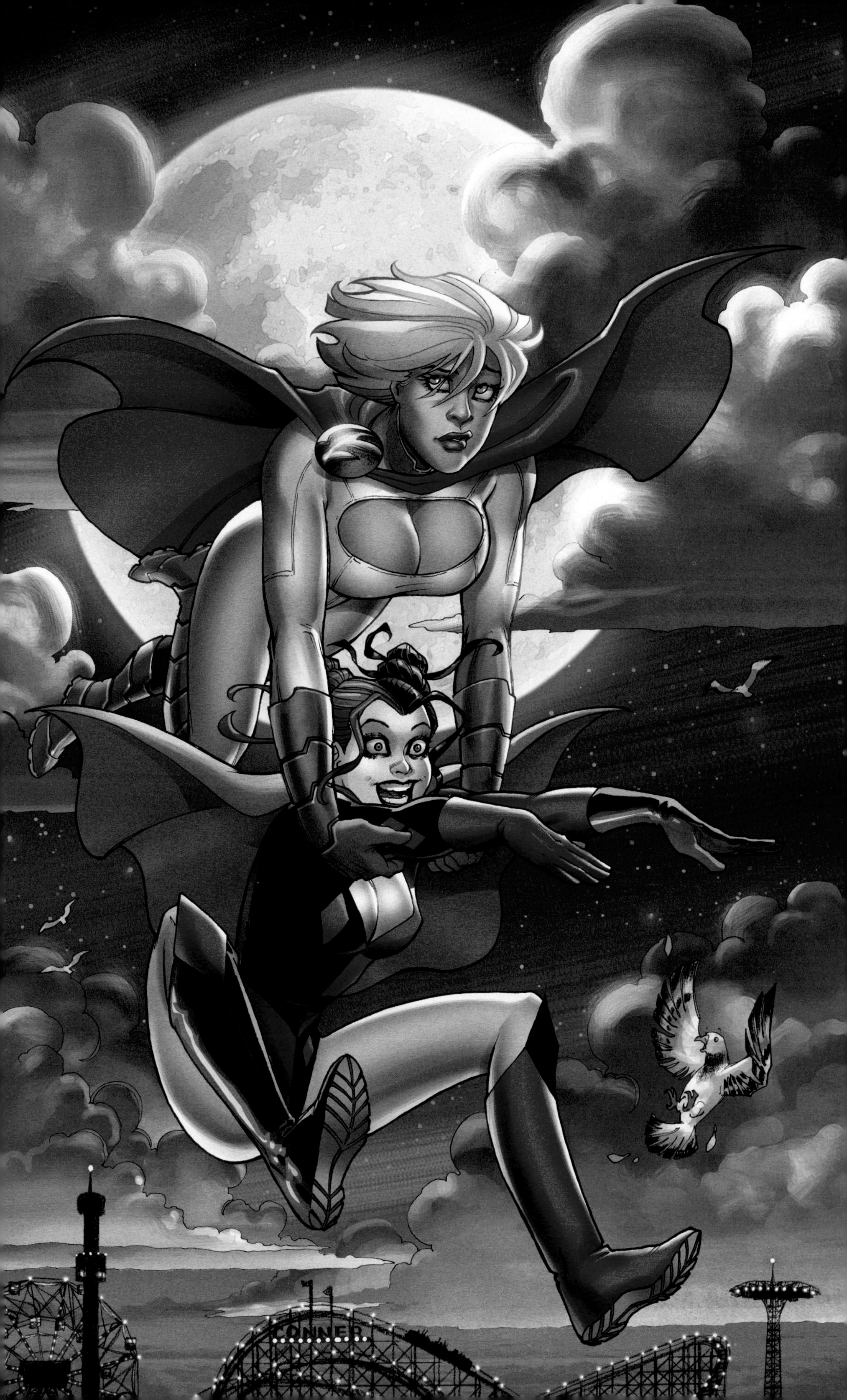
CONNER

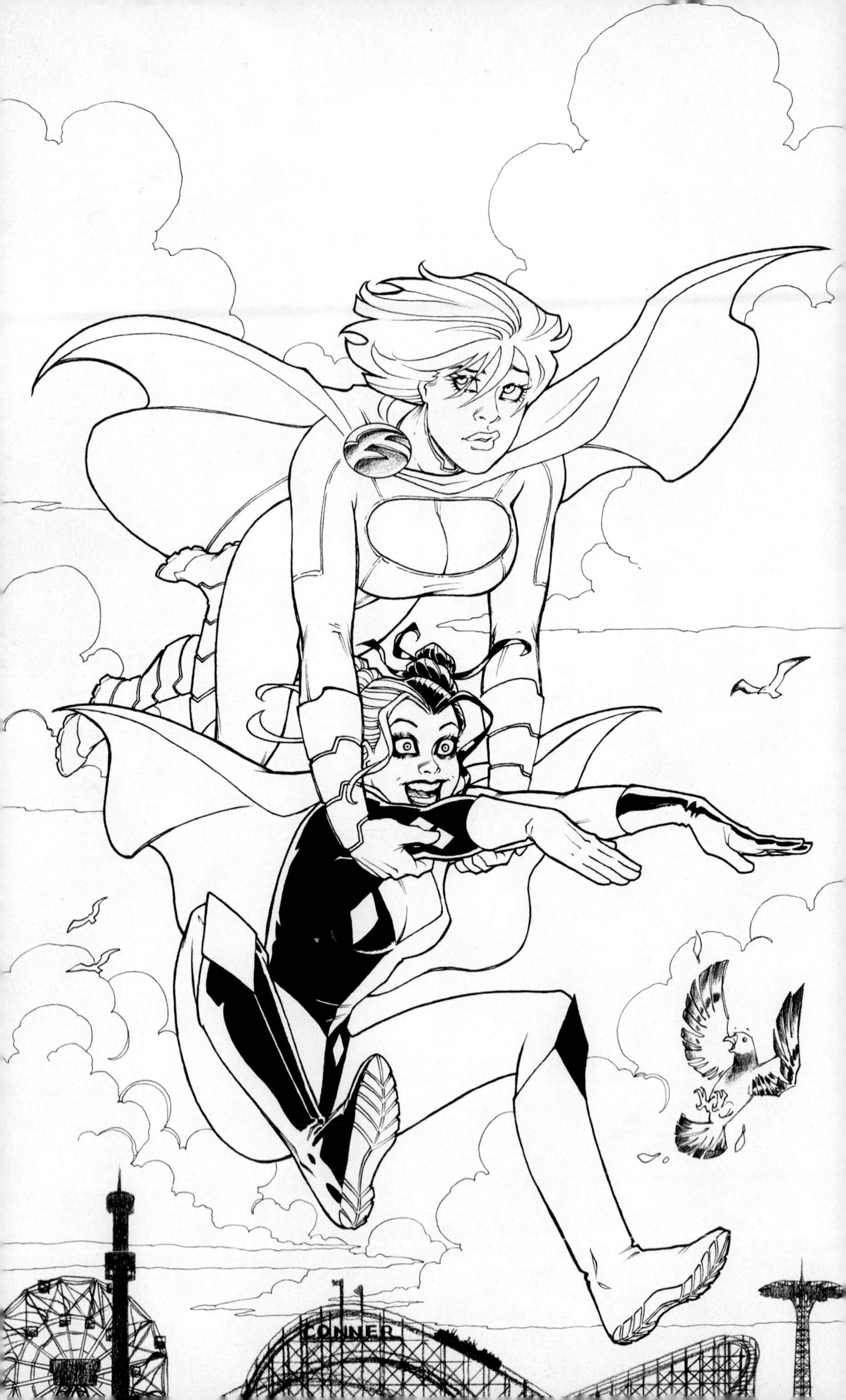
CONNER

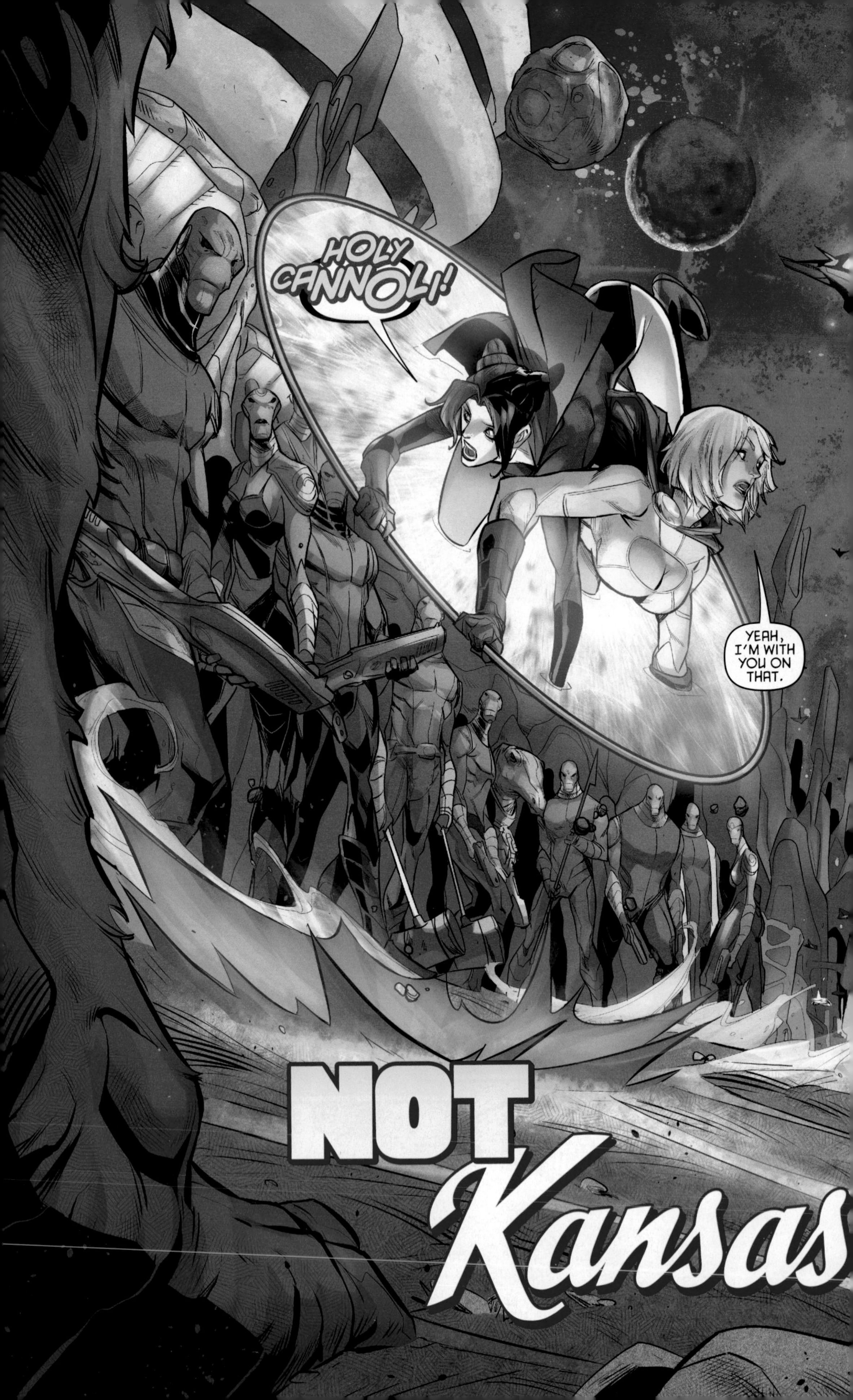
HOLY CANNOLI!
YEAH, I'M WITH YOU ON THAT.
NOT Kansas

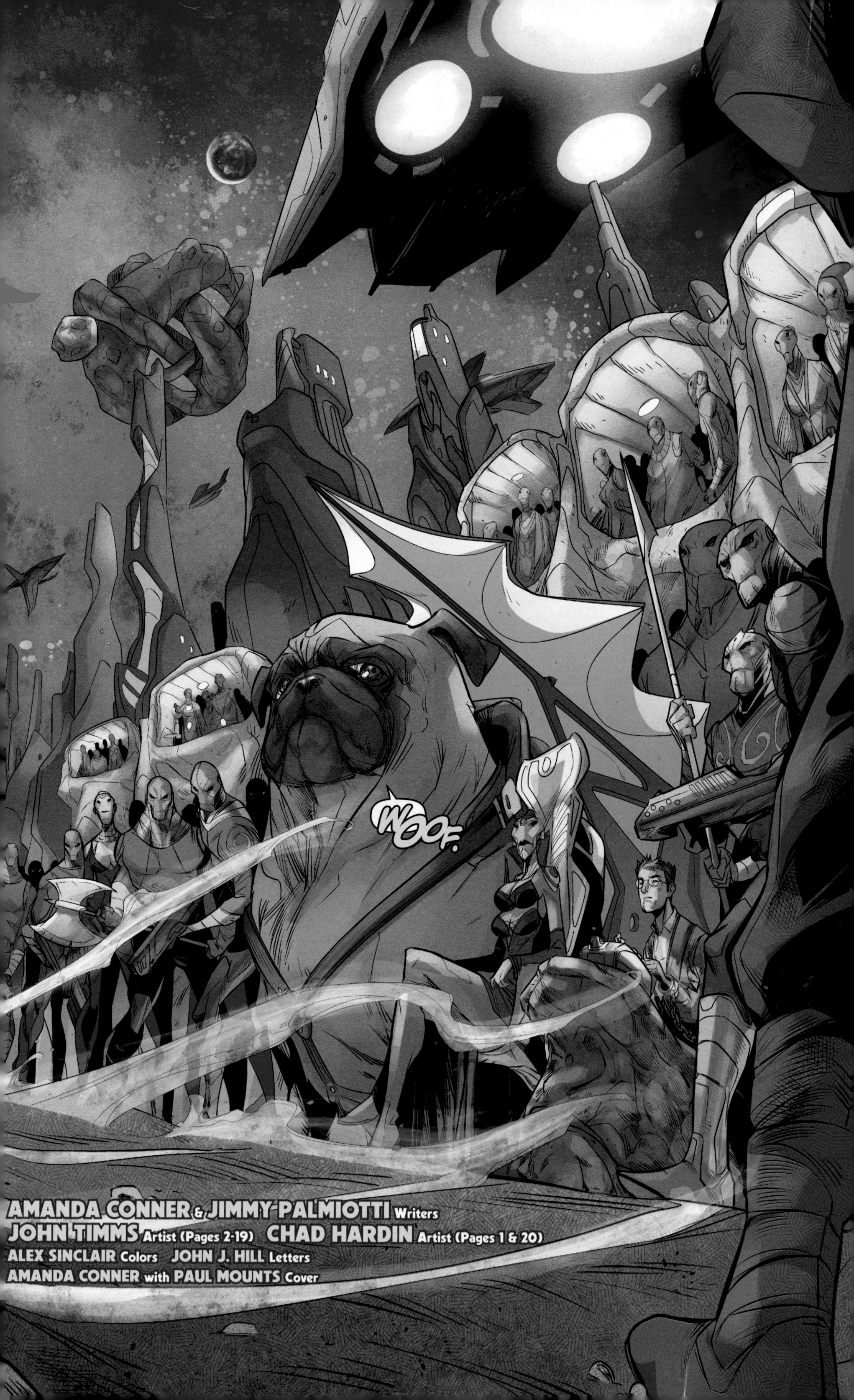

WOOF.
AMANDA CONNER & JIMMY PALMIOTTI Writers
JOHN TIMMS Artist (Pages 2-19) CHAD HARDIN Artist (Pages 1 & 20)
ALEX SINCLAIR Colors JOHN J. HILL Letters
AMANDA CONNER with PAUL MOUNTS Cover

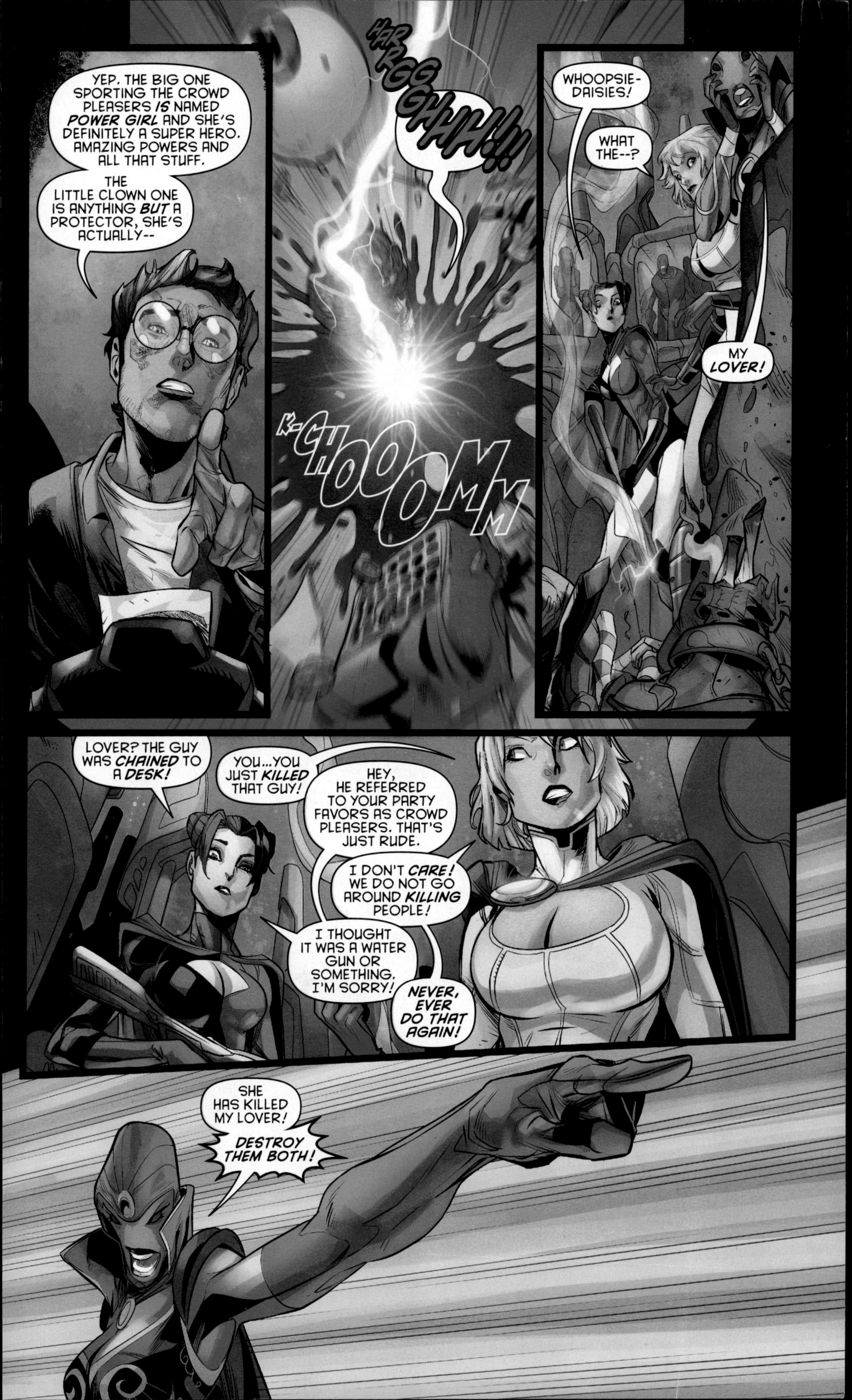
YEP. THE BIG ONE SPORTING THE CROWD PLEASERS *IS* NAMED **POWER GIRL** AND SHE'S DEFINITELY A SUPER HERO. AMAZING POWERS AND ALL THAT STUFF.
THE LITTLE CLOWN ONE IS ANYTHING *BUT* A PROTECTOR, SHE'S ACTUALLY--
HARRGGGHHH!!!
K-CHOOOOMM
WHOOPSIE-DAISIES!
WHAT THE--?
MY **LOVER!**
LOVER? THE GUY WAS *CHAINED* TO A *DESK!*
YOU...YOU JUST *KILLED* THAT GUY!
HEY, HE REFERRED TO YOUR PARTY FAVORS AS CROWD PLEASERS. THAT'S JUST RUDE.
I DON'T *CARE!* WE DO NOT GO AROUND *KILLING* PEOPLE!
I THOUGHT IT WAS A WATER GUN OR SOMETHING. I'M SORRY!
NEVER, EVER DO THAT AGAIN!
SHE HAS KILLED MY LOVER!
DESTROY THEM BOTH!

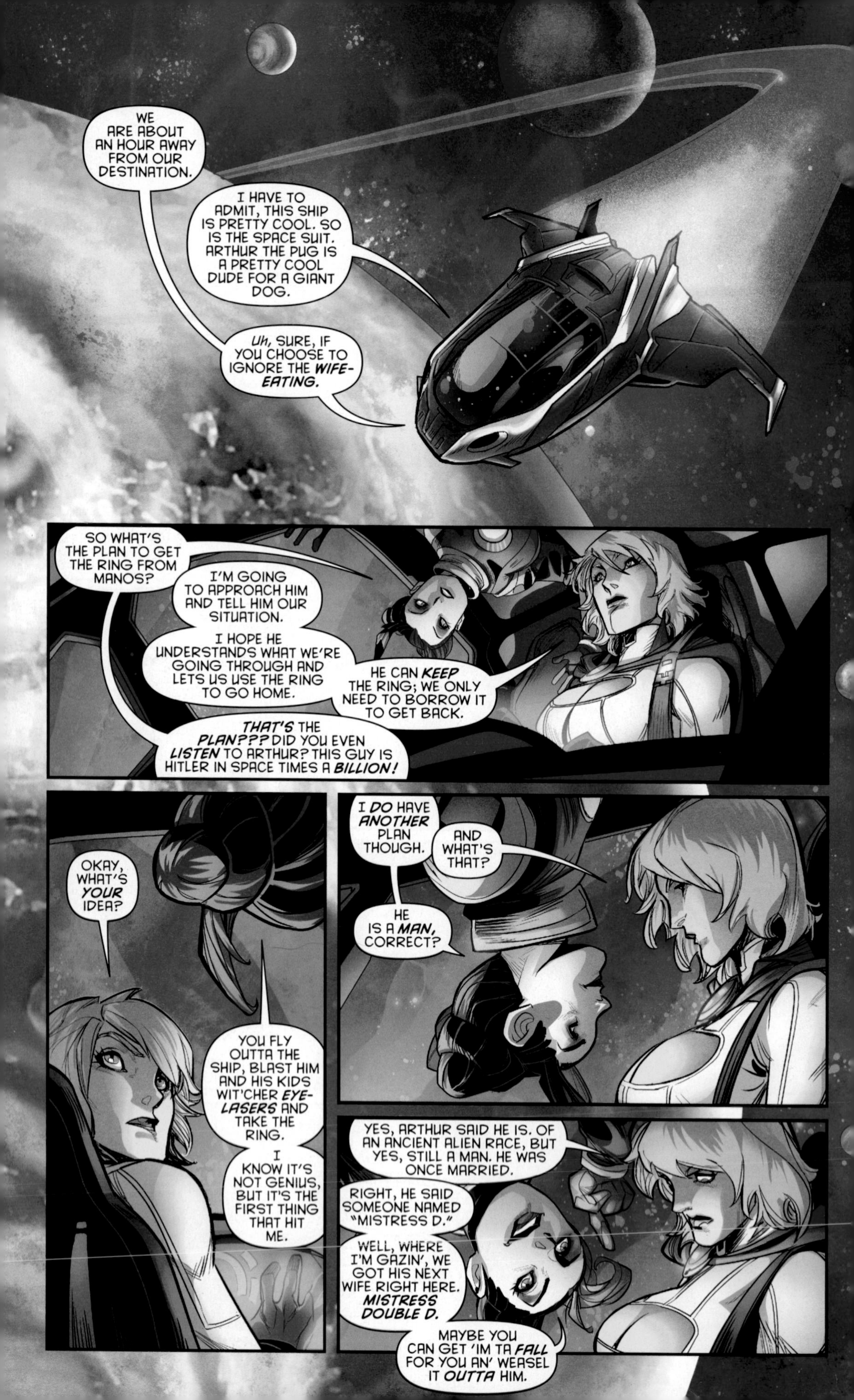
WE ARE ABOUT AN HOUR AWAY FROM OUR DESTINATION.
I HAVE TO ADMIT, THIS SHIP IS PRETTY COOL. SO IS THE SPACE SUIT. ARTHUR THE PUG IS A PRETTY COOL DUDE FOR A GIANT DOG.
UH, SURE, IF YOU CHOOSE TO IGNORE THE ***WIFE-EATING.***
SO WHAT'S THE PLAN TO GET THE RING FROM MANOS?
I'M GOING TO APPROACH HIM AND TELL HIM OUR SITUATION.
I HOPE HE UNDERSTANDS WHAT WE'RE GOING THROUGH AND LETS US USE THE RING TO GO HOME.
HE CAN ***KEEP*** THE RING; WE ONLY NEED TO BORROW IT TO GET BACK.
THAT'S THE ***PLAN???*** DID YOU EVEN ***LISTEN*** TO ARTHUR? THIS GUY IS HITLER IN SPACE TIMES A ***BILLION!***
OKAY, WHAT'S ***YOUR*** IDEA?
YOU FLY OUTTA THE SHIP, BLAST HIM AND HIS KIDS WIT'CHER ***EYE-LASERS*** AND TAKE THE RING.
I KNOW IT'S NOT GENIUS, BUT IT'S THE FIRST THING THAT HIT ME.
I ***DO*** HAVE ***ANOTHER*** PLAN THOUGH.
AND WHAT'S THAT?
HE IS A ***MAN,*** CORRECT?
YES, ARTHUR SAID HE IS. OF AN ANCIENT ALIEN RACE, BUT YES, STILL A MAN. HE WAS ONCE MARRIED.
RIGHT, HE SAID SOMEONE NAMED "MISTRESS D."
WELL, WHERE I'M GAZIN', WE GOT HIS NEXT WIFE RIGHT HERE. ***MISTRESS DOUBLE D.***
MAYBE YOU CAN GET 'IM TA ***FALL*** FOR YOU AN' WEASEL IT ***OUTTA*** HIM.

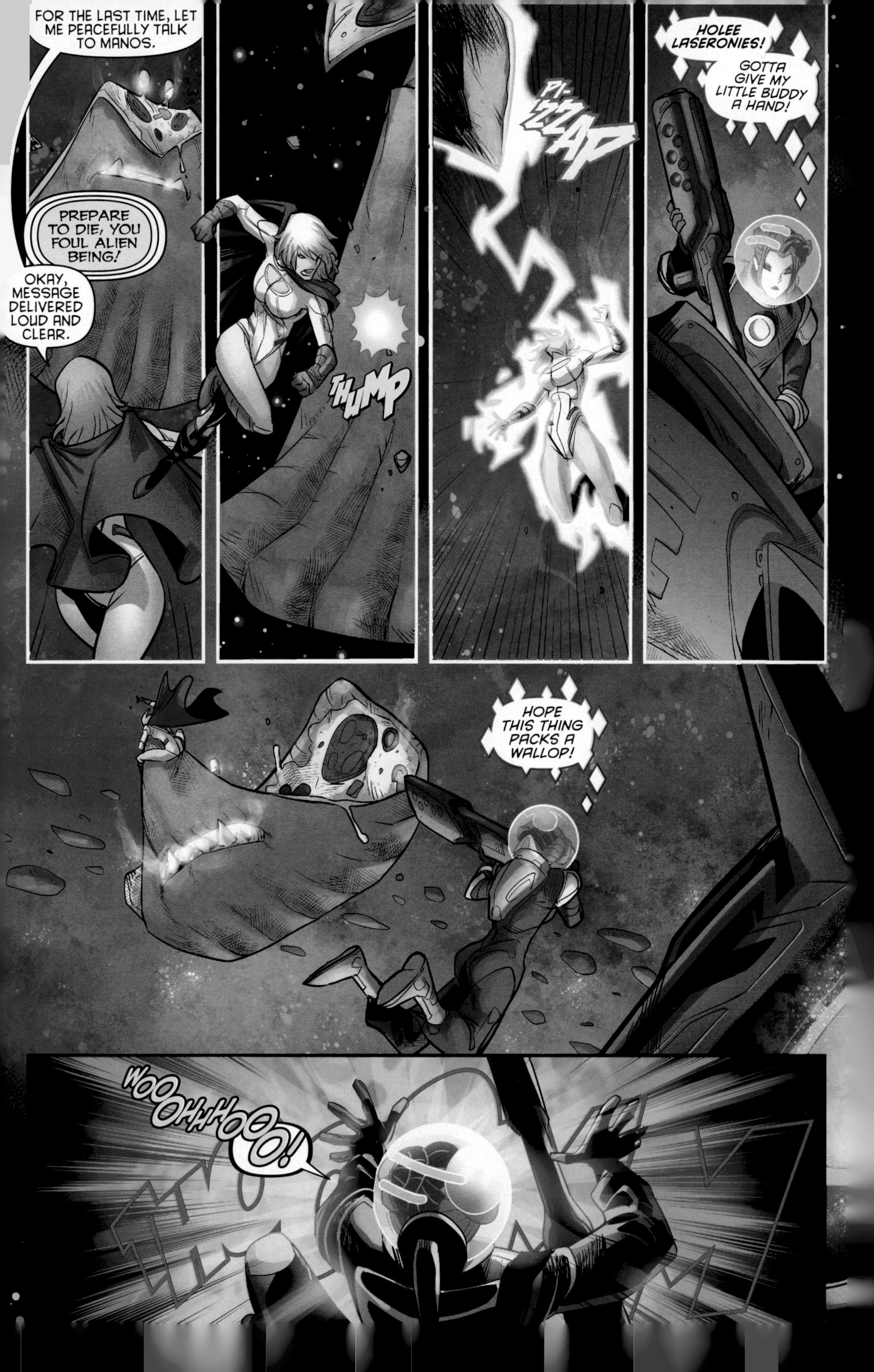
FOR THE LAST TIME, LET ME PEACEFULLY TALK TO MANOS.
PREPARE TO DIE, YOU FOUL ALIEN BEING!
OKAY, MESSAGE DELIVERED LOUD AND CLEAR.
THUMP
PI-ZZZAP
HOLEE LASERONIES!
GOTTA GIVE MY LITTLE BUDDY A HAND!
HOPE THIS THING PACKS A WALLOP!
WOOOHHHOOOO!

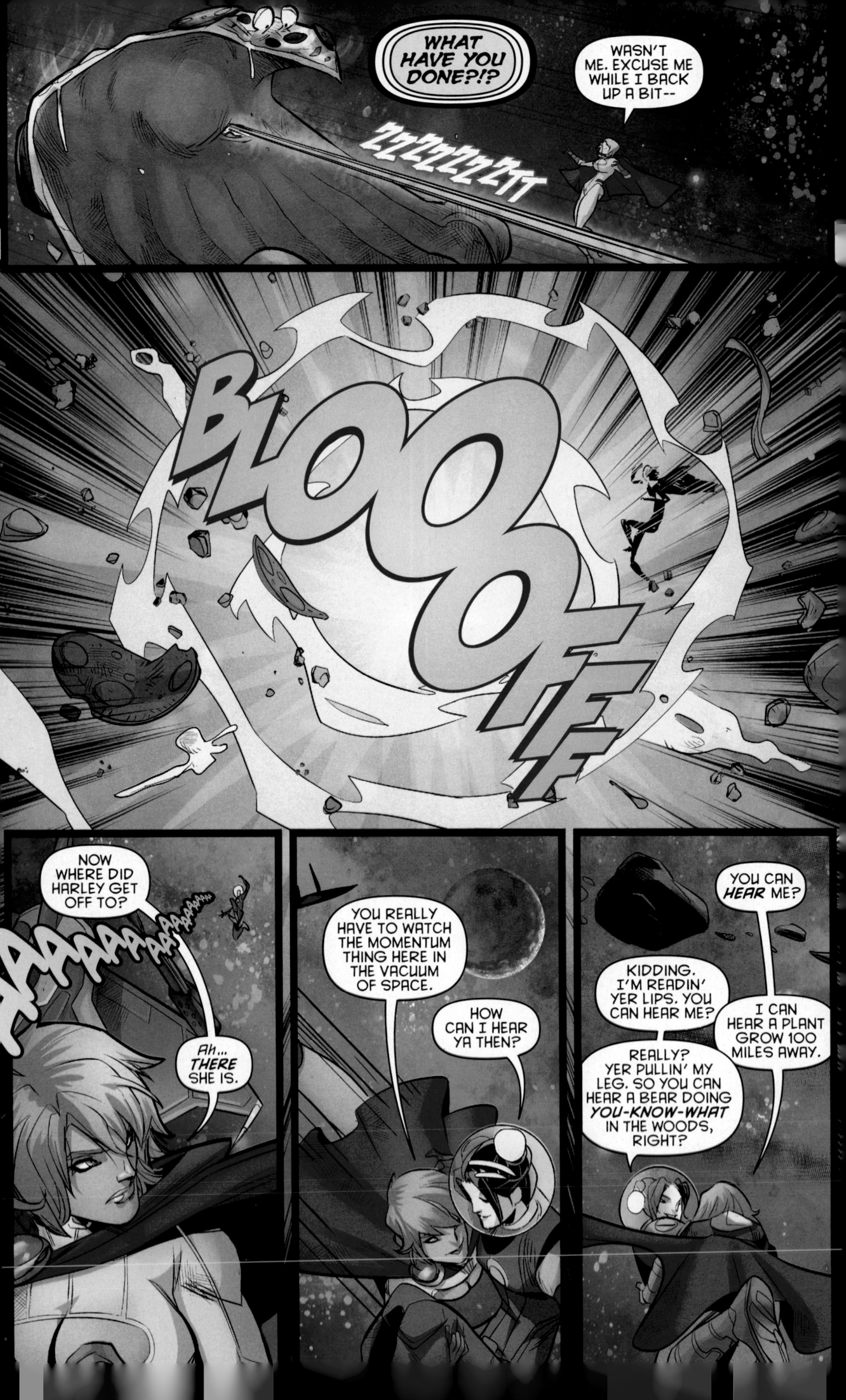

WHAT HAVE YOU DONE?!?
WASN'T ME. EXCUSE ME WHILE I BACK UP A BIT--
ZZZZZZZZZTT
BLOOOOFFF
NOW WHERE DID HARLEY GET OFF TO?
AAAAAAAAAAAAA
Ah... THERE SHE IS.
YOU REALLY HAVE TO WATCH THE MOMENTUM THING HERE IN THE VACUUM OF SPACE.
HOW CAN I HEAR YA THEN?
YOU CAN HEAR ME?
KIDDING. I'M READIN' YER LIPS. YOU CAN HEAR ME?
I CAN HEAR A PLANT GROW 100 MILES AWAY.
REALLY? YER PULLIN' MY LEG. SO YOU CAN HEAR A BEAR DOING YOU-KNOW-WHAT IN THE WOODS, RIGHT?

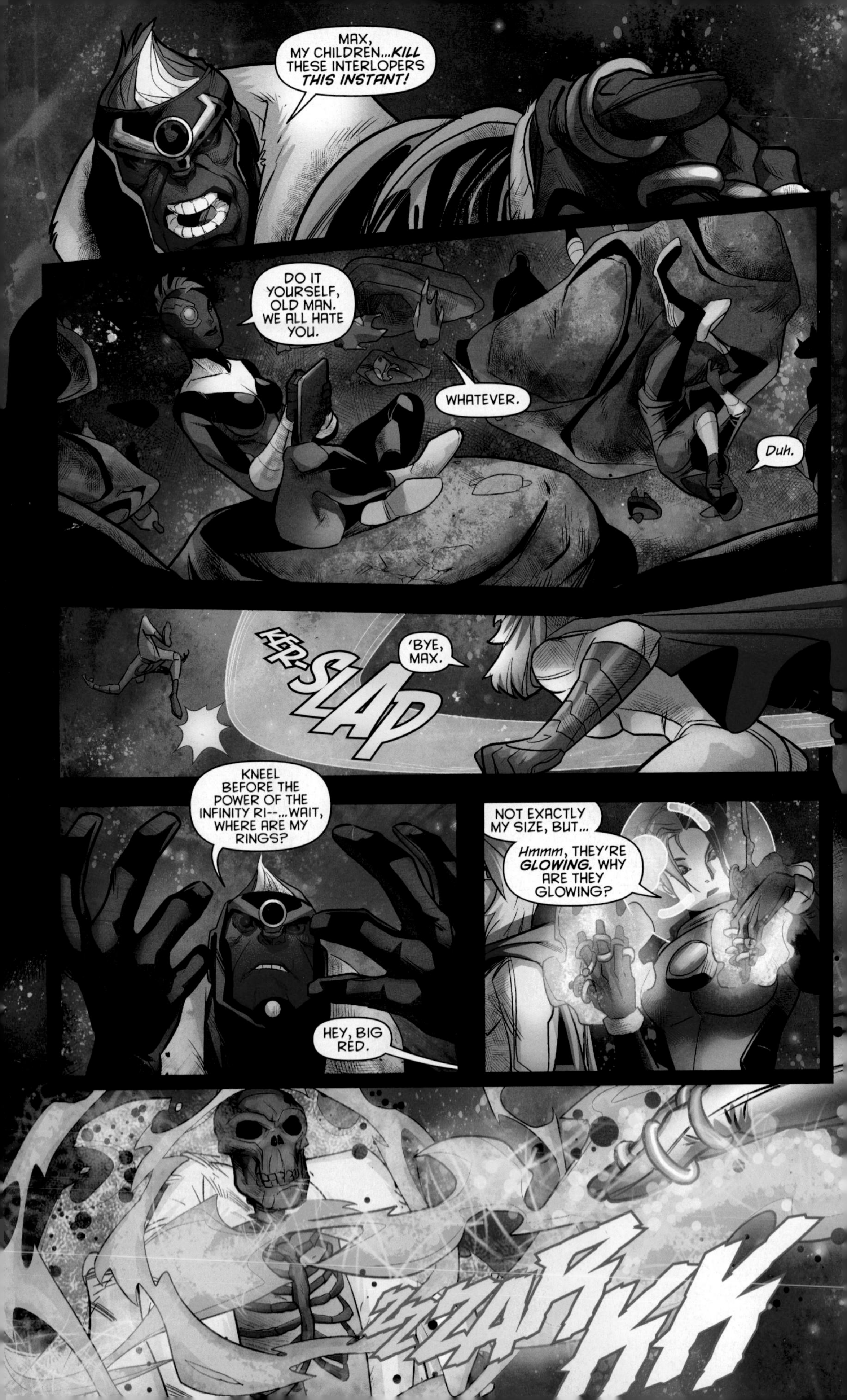
MAX, MY CHILDREN...KILL THESE INTERLOPERS THIS INSTANT!
DO IT YOURSELF, OLD MAN. WE ALL HATE YOU.
WHATEVER.
Duh.
KER-SLAP
'BYE, MAX.
KNEEL BEFORE THE POWER OF THE INFINITY RI--...WAIT, WHERE ARE MY RINGS?
HEY, BIG RED.
NOT EXACTLY MY SIZE, BUT...
Hmmm, THEY'RE GLOWING. WHY ARE THEY GLOWING?

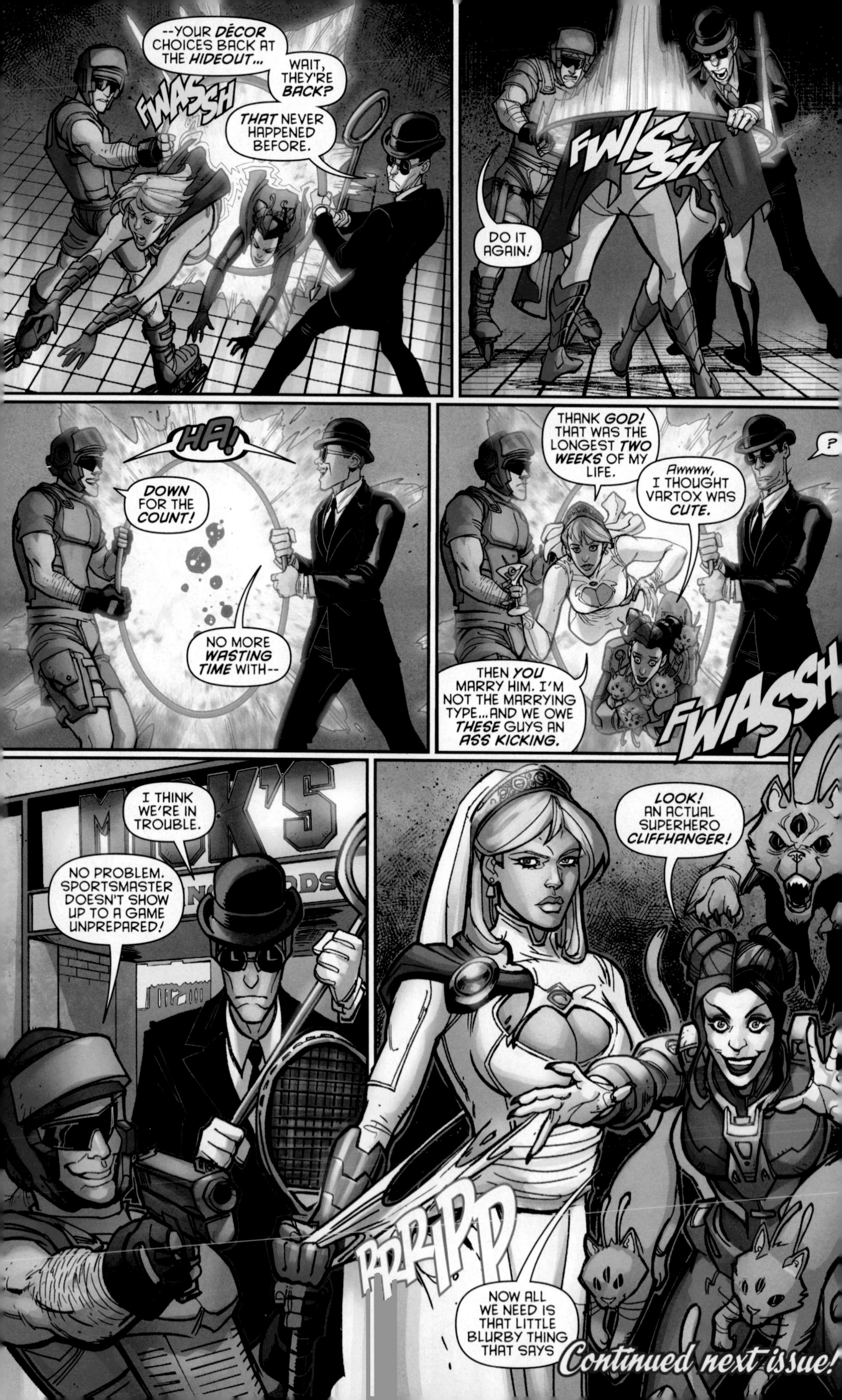

--YOUR DÉCOR CHOICES BACK AT THE HIDEOUT...
FWASSH
WAIT, THEY'RE BACK?
THAT NEVER HAPPENED BEFORE.
FWISSH
DO IT AGAIN!
HA!
DOWN FOR THE COUNT!
NO MORE WASTING TIME WITH--
THANK GOD! THAT WAS THE LONGEST TWO WEEKS OF MY LIFE.
?
Awwww, I THOUGHT VARTOX WAS CUTE.
THEN YOU MARRY HIM. I'M NOT THE MARRYING TYPE...AND WE OWE THESE GUYS AN ASS KICKING.
FWASSH
I THINK WE'RE IN TROUBLE.
NO PROBLEM. SPORTSMASTER DOESN'T SHOW UP TO A GAME UNPREPARED!
LOOK! AN ACTUAL SUPERHERO CLIFFHANGER!
RRRIPP
NOW ALL WE NEED IS THAT LITTLE BLURBY THING THAT SAYS
Continued next issue!

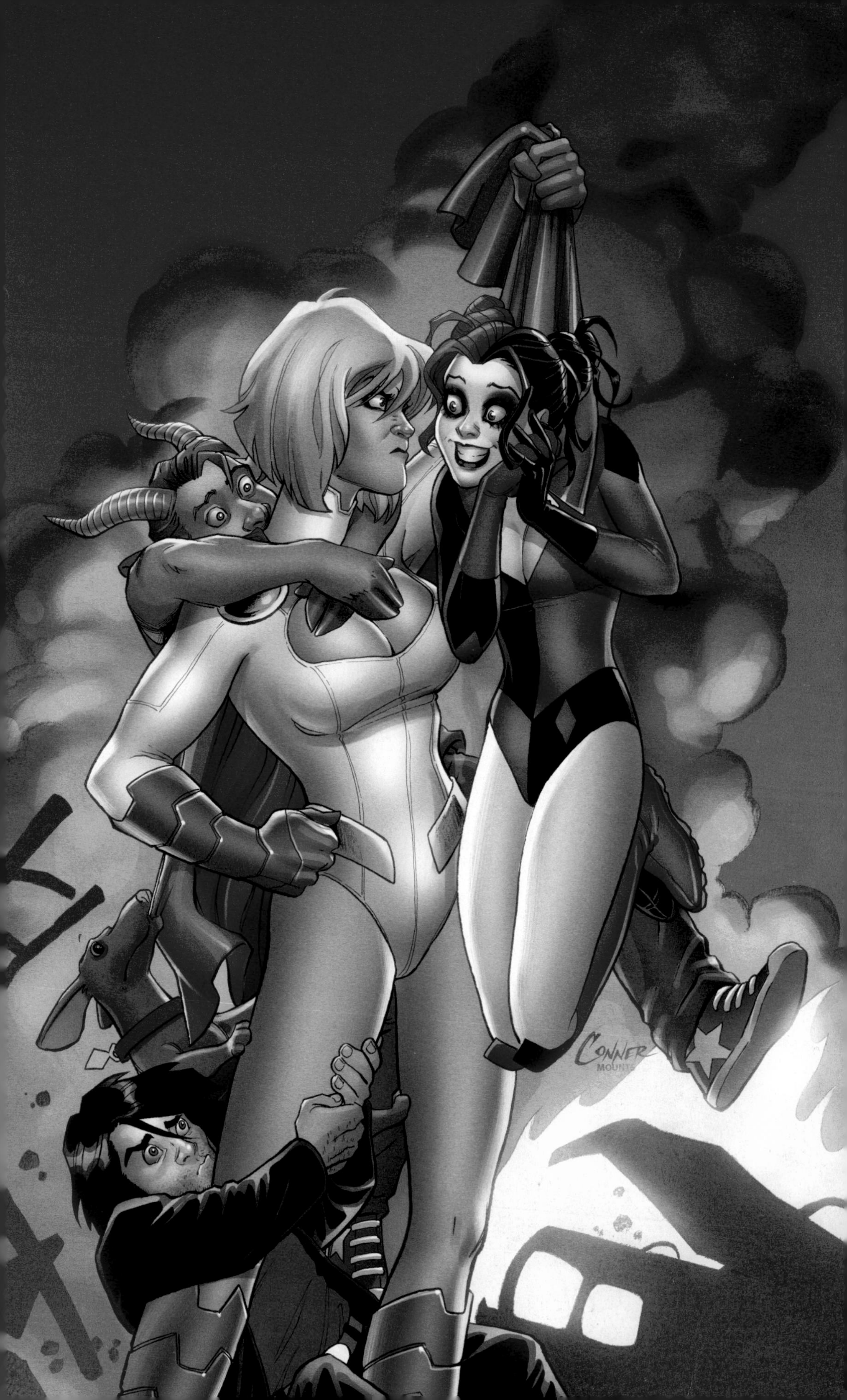
CONNER
MOUNTS

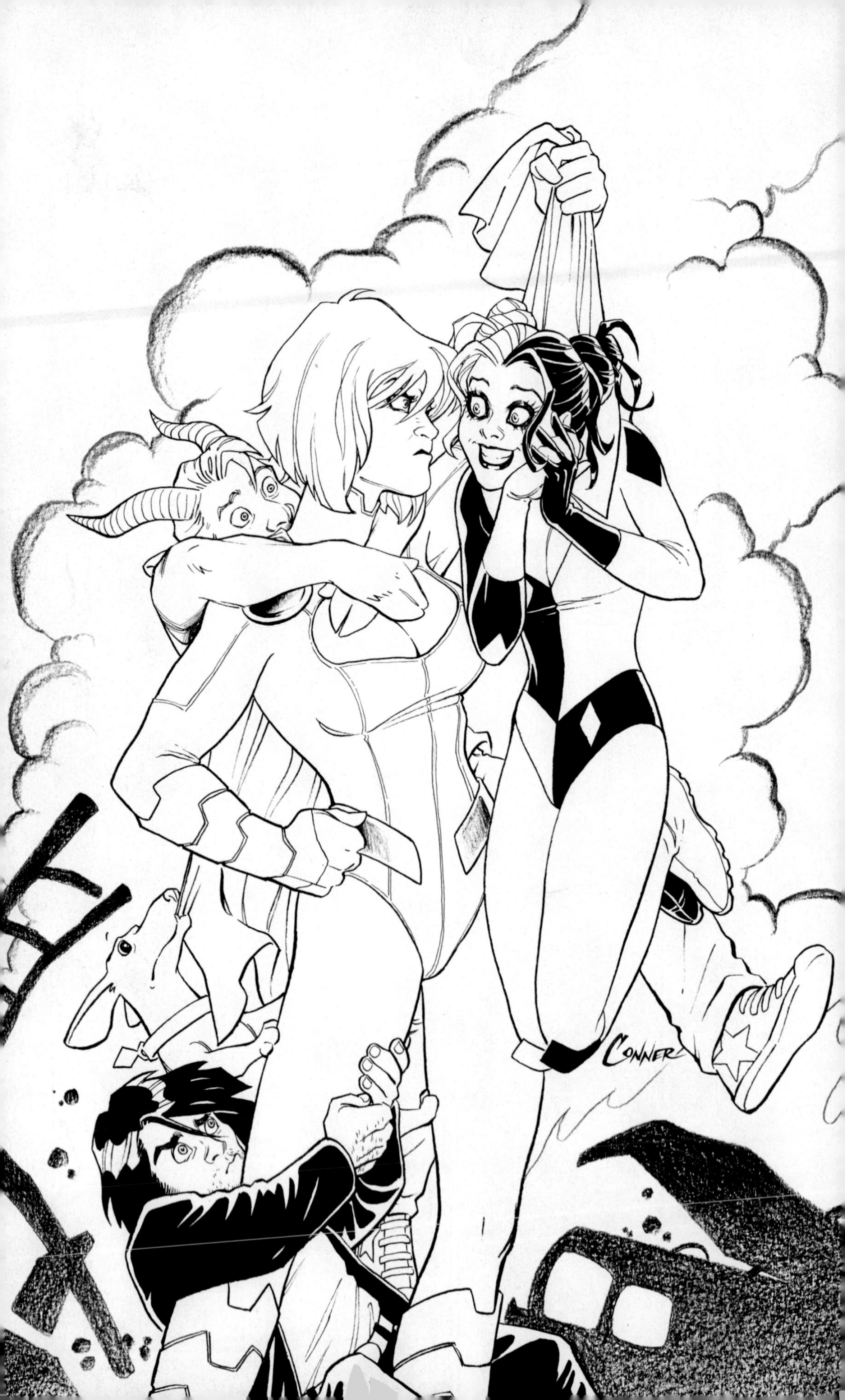
CONNER

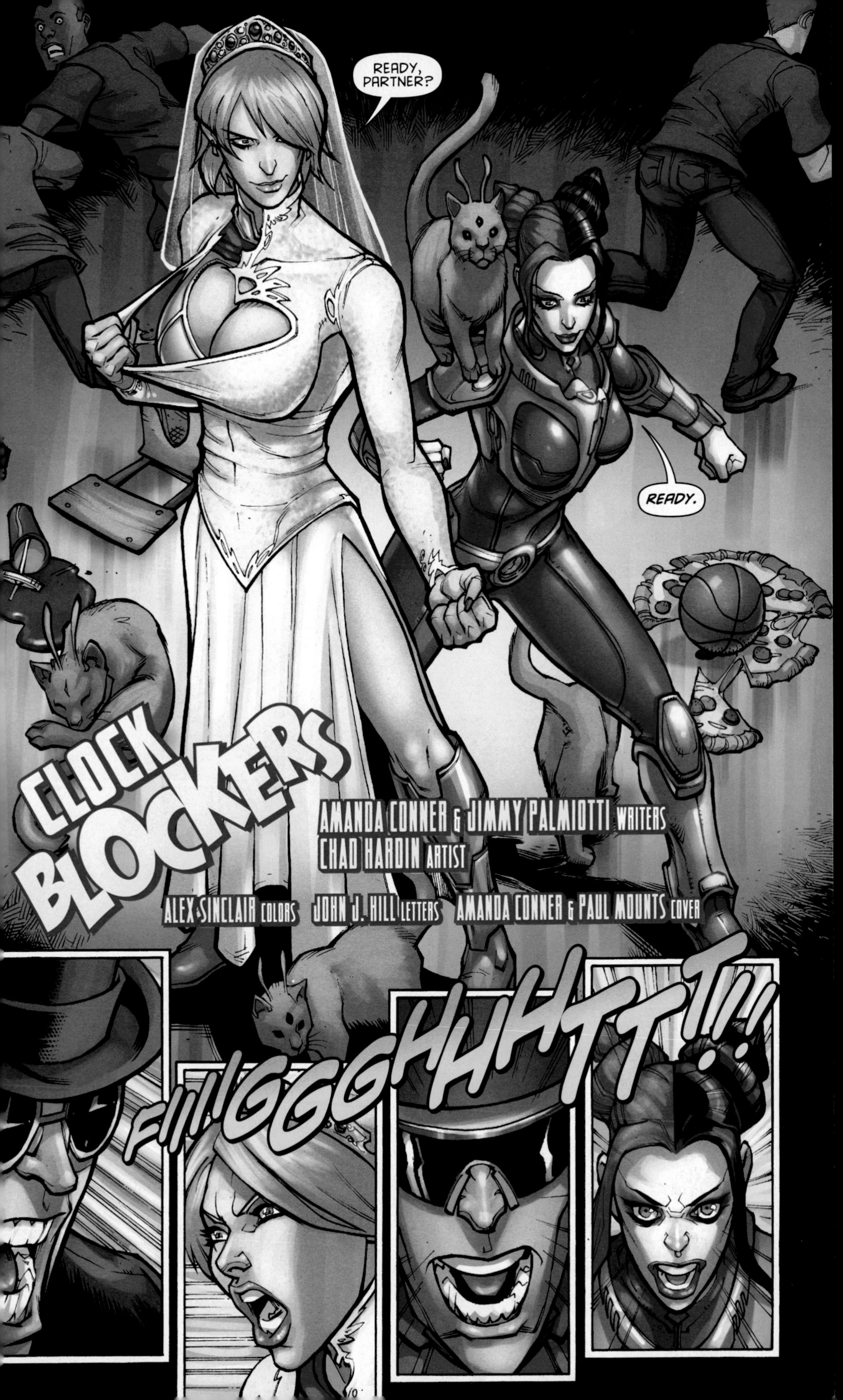
READY, PARTNER?
READY.
CLOCK BLOCKERS
AMANDA CONNER & JIMMY PALMIOTTI WRITERS
CHAD HARDIN ARTIST
ALEX SINCLAIR COLORS JOHN J. HILL LETTERS AMANDA CONNER & PAUL MOUNTS COVER
FIIIGGGHHHTTT!!!

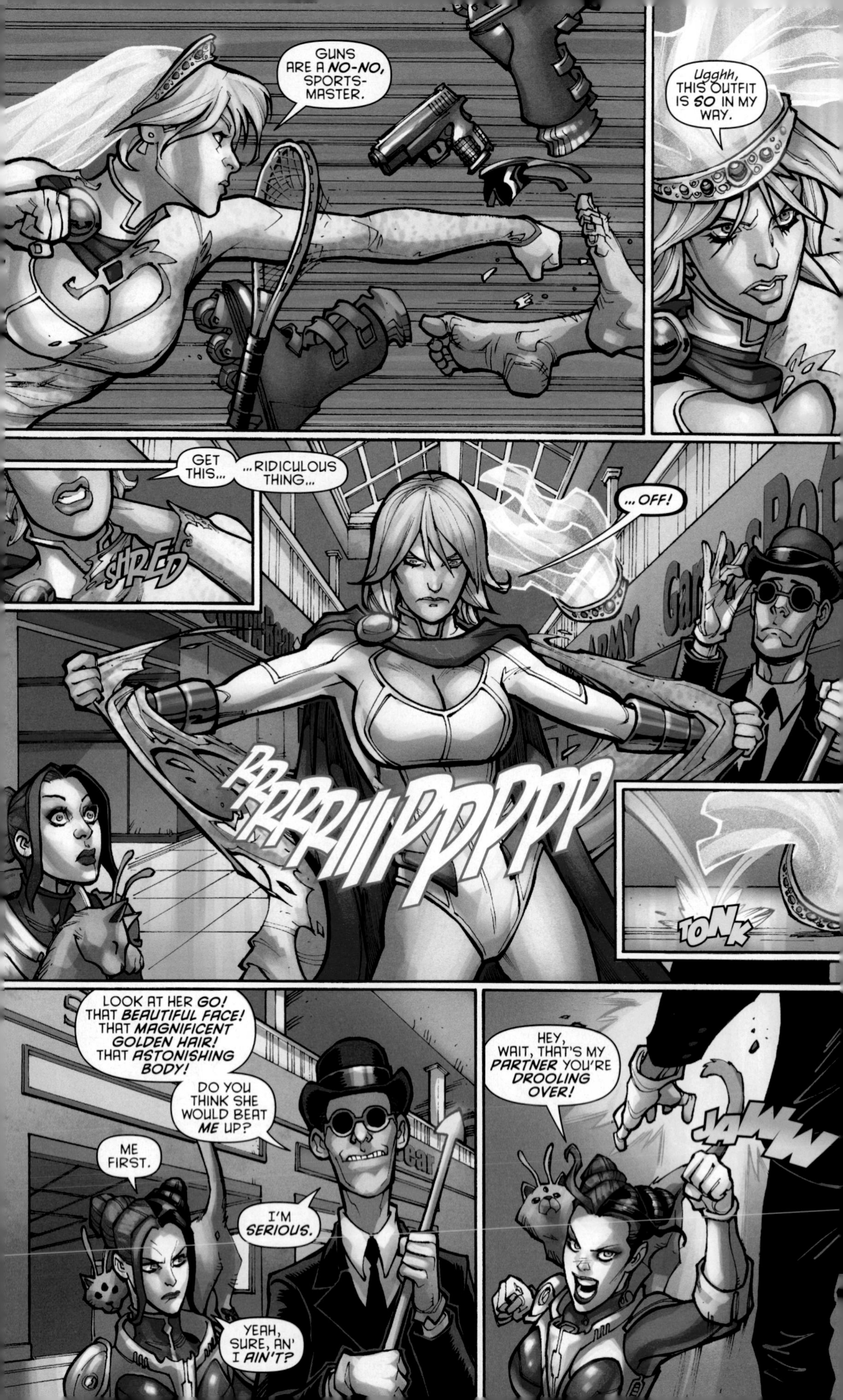
GUNS ARE A *NO-NO,* SPORTS-MASTER.
Ugghh, THIS OUTFIT IS *SO* IN MY WAY.
GET THIS...
...RIDICULOUS THING...
...*OFF!*
SHRED
RRRRIIIPPPPPP
TONK
LOOK AT HER *GO!* THAT *BEAUTIFUL FACE!* THAT *MAGNIFICENT GOLDEN HAIR!* THAT *ASTONISHING BODY!*
DO YOU THINK SHE WOULD BEAT *ME* UP?
ME FIRST.
I'M *SERIOUS.*
YEAH, SURE, AN' I *AIN'T?*
HEY, WAIT, THAT'S MY *PARTNER* YOU'RE *DROOLING OVER!*
JAWW

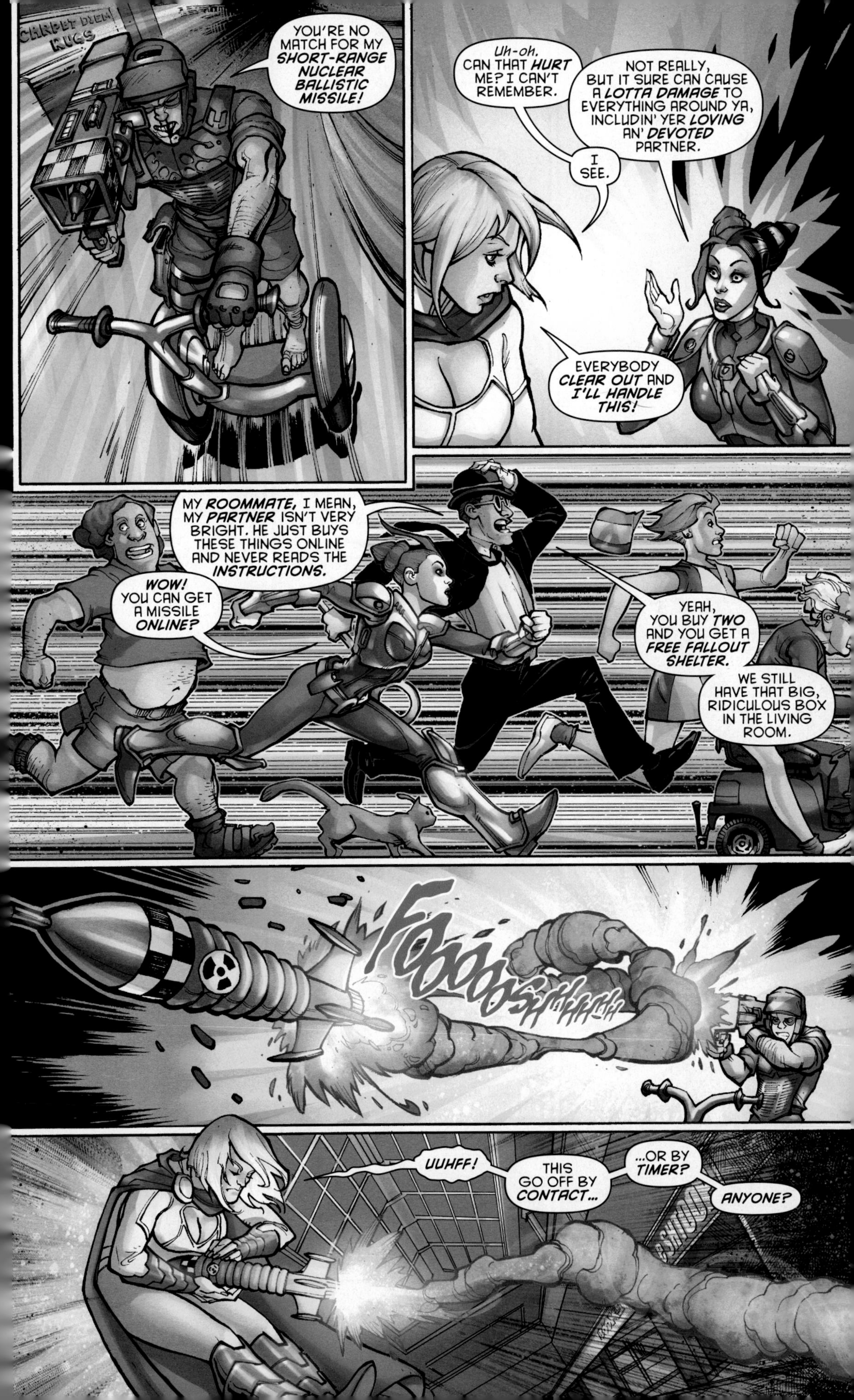
CARPET DIEM RUGS
YOU'RE NO MATCH FOR MY SHORT-RANGE NUCLEAR BALLISTIC MISSILE!
Uh-oh. CAN THAT HURT ME? I CAN'T REMEMBER.
NOT REALLY, BUT IT SURE CAN CAUSE A LOTTA DAMAGE TO EVERYTHING AROUND YA, INCLUDIN' YER LOVING AN' DEVOTED PARTNER.
I SEE.
EVERYBODY CLEAR OUT AND I'LL HANDLE THIS!
MY ROOMMATE, I MEAN, MY PARTNER ISN'T VERY BRIGHT. HE JUST BUYS THESE THINGS ONLINE AND NEVER READS THE INSTRUCTIONS.
WOW! YOU CAN GET A MISSILE ONLINE?
YEAH, YOU BUY TWO AND YOU GET A FREE FALLOUT SHELTER.
WE STILL HAVE THAT BIG, RIDICULOUS BOX IN THE LIVING ROOM.
FOOOOOSHHHHH
UUHFF!
THIS GO OFF BY CONTACT...
...OR BY TIMER?
ANYONE?

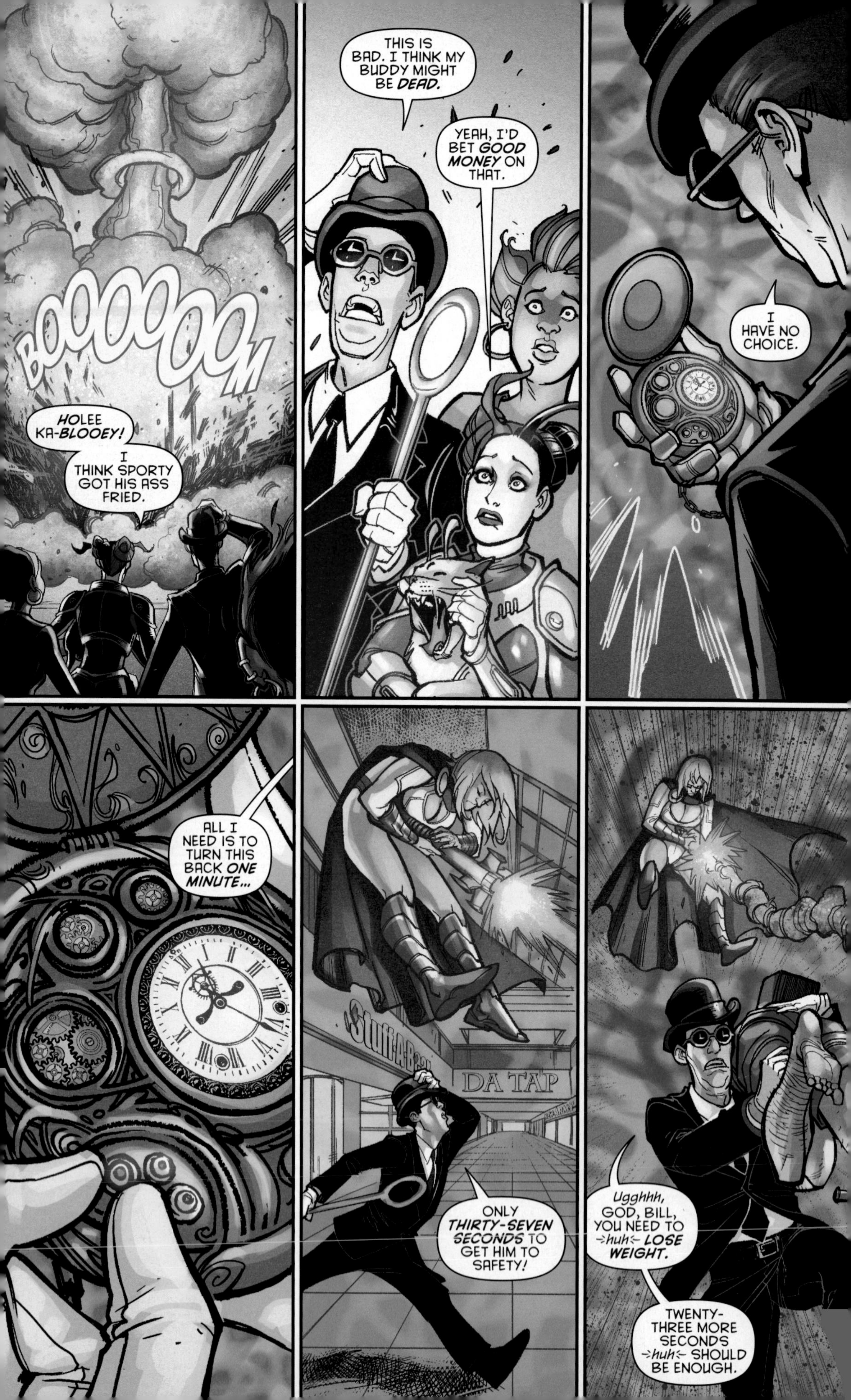
BOOOOOOOM
HOLEE KA-BLOOEY!
I THINK SPORTY GOT HIS ASS FRIED.
THIS IS BAD. I THINK MY BUDDY MIGHT BE DEAD.
YEAH, I'D BET GOOD MONEY ON THAT.
I HAVE NO CHOICE.
ALL I NEED IS TO TURN THIS BACK ONE MINUTE...
Stuff-A-Bear
DA TAP
ONLY THIRTY-SEVEN SECONDS TO GET HIM TO SAFETY!
Ugghhh, GOD, BILL, YOU NEED TO -huh- LOSE WEIGHT.
TWENTY-THREE MORE SECONDS -huh- SHOULD BE ENOUGH.

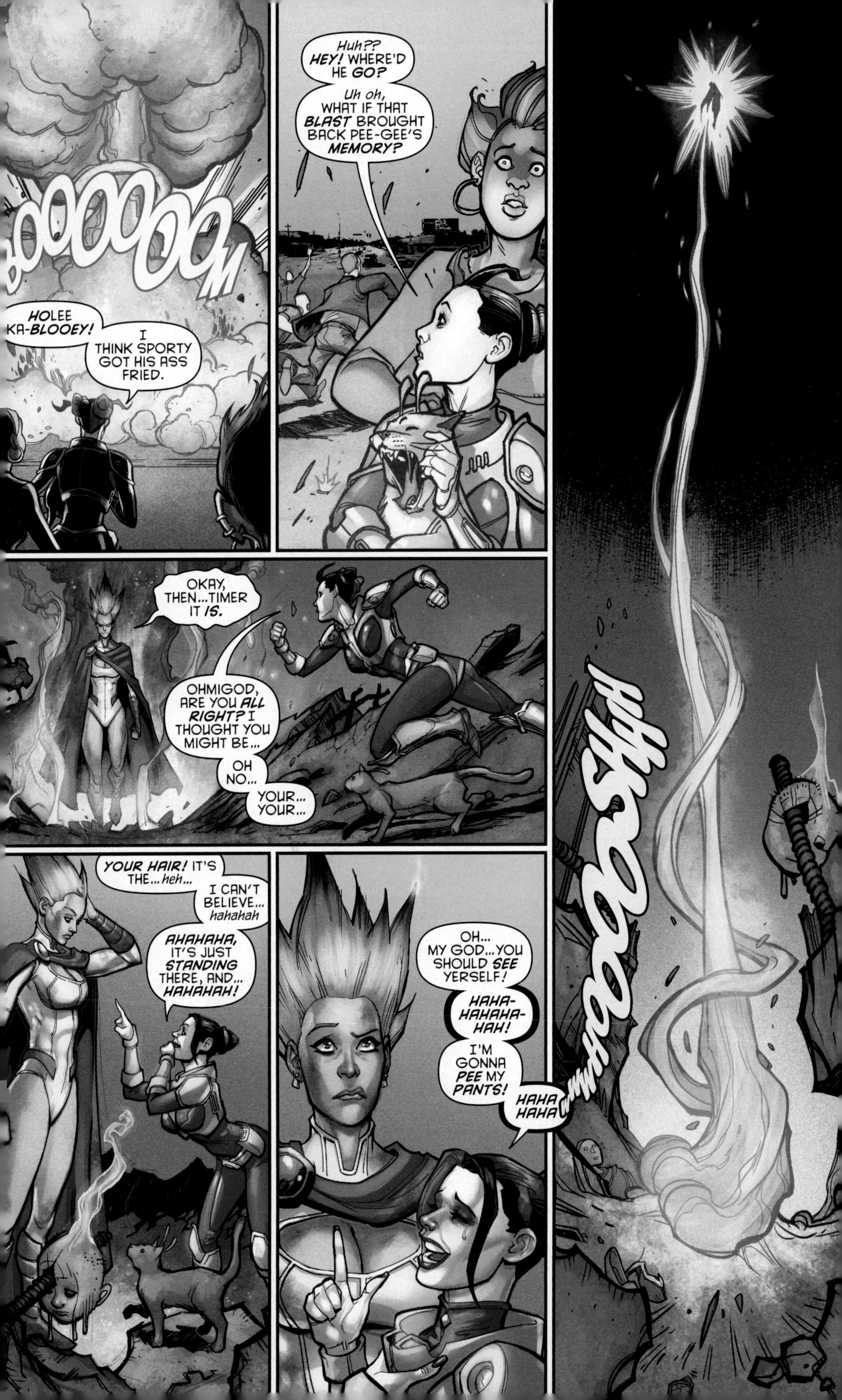
OOOOOOOM
HOLEE KA-BLOOEY!
I THINK SPORTY GOT HIS ASS FRIED.
Huh?? HEY! WHERE'D HE GO?
Uh oh, WHAT IF THAT BLAST BROUGHT BACK PEE-GEE'S MEMORY?
OKAY, THEN...TIMER IT IS.
OHMIGOD, ARE YOU ALL RIGHT? I THOUGHT YOU MIGHT BE...
OH NO...
YOUR... YOUR...
YOUR HAIR! IT'S THE...heh...
I CAN'T BELIEVE... hahahah
AHAHAHA, IT'S JUST STANDING THERE, AND... HAHAHAH!
OH... MY GOD...YOU SHOULD SEE YERSELF!
HAHA-HAHAHA-HAH!
I'M GONNA PEE MY PANTS!
HAHA HAHA

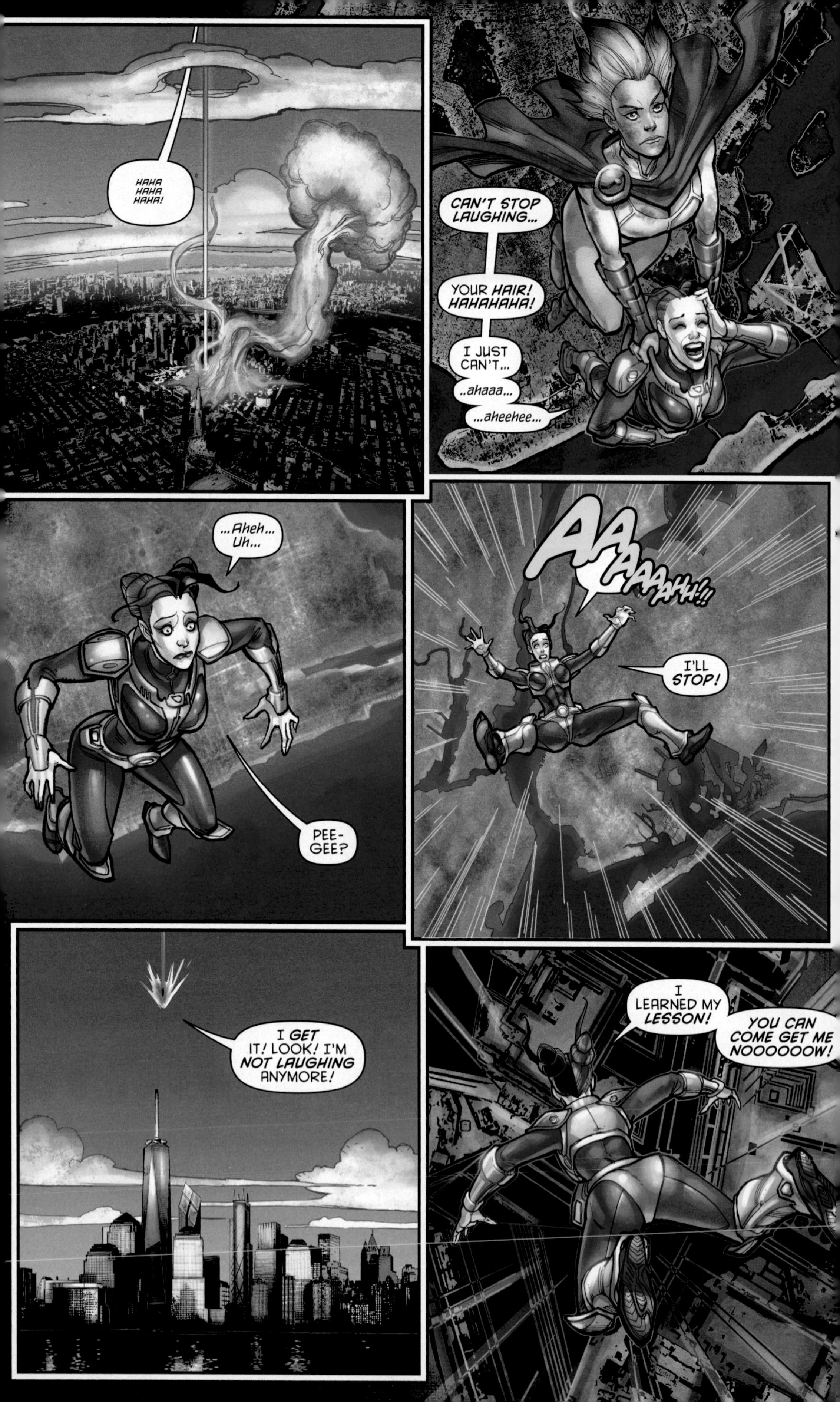
HAHA HAHA HAHA!
CAN'T STOP LAUGHING...
YOUR HAIR! HAHAHAHA!
I JUST CAN'T...
..ahaaa...
...aheehee...
...Aheh... Uh...
PEE-GEE?
AAAAAAHH!!!
I'LL STOP!
I GET IT! LOOK! I'M NOT LAUGHING ANYMORE!
I LEARNED MY LESSON!
YOU CAN COME GET ME NOOOOOOW!

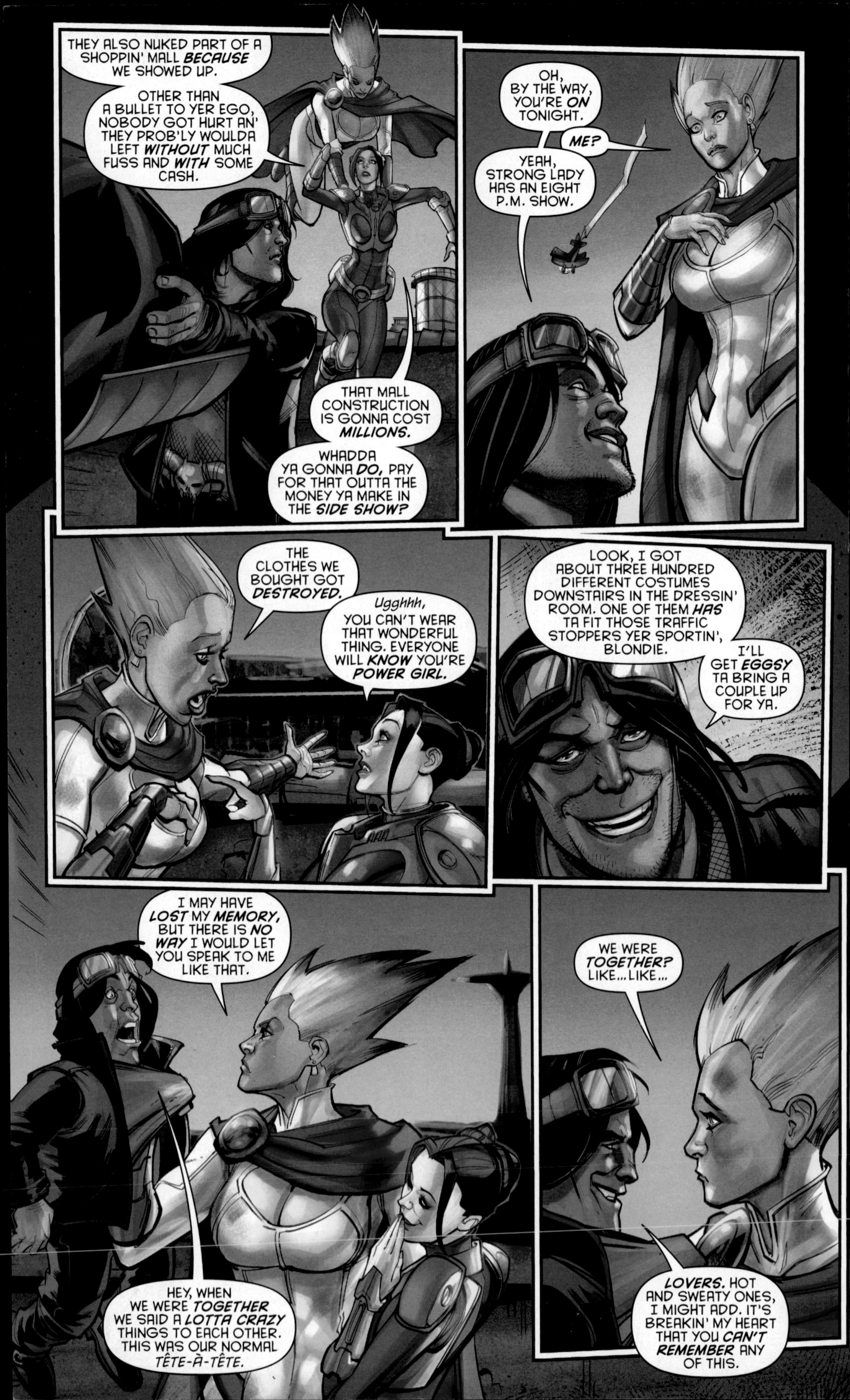

THEY ALSO NUKED PART OF A SHOPPIN' MALL *BECAUSE* WE SHOWED UP.
OTHER THAN A BULLET TO YER EGO, NOBODY GOT HURT AN' THEY PROB'LY WOULDA LEFT *WITHOUT* MUCH FUSS AND *WITH* SOME CASH.
THAT MALL CONSTRUCTION IS GONNA COST *MILLIONS.*
WHADDA YA GONNA *DO,* PAY FOR THAT OUTTA THE MONEY YA MAKE IN THE *SIDE SHOW?*
OH, BY THE WAY, YOU'RE *ON* TONIGHT.
ME?
YEAH, STRONG LADY HAS AN EIGHT P.M. SHOW.
THE CLOTHES WE BOUGHT GOT *DESTROYED.*
Ugghhh, YOU CAN'T WEAR THAT WONDERFUL THING. EVERYONE WILL *KNOW* YOU'RE *POWER GIRL.*
LOOK, I GOT ABOUT THREE HUNDRED DIFFERENT COSTUMES DOWNSTAIRS IN THE DRESSIN' ROOM. ONE OF THEM *HAS* TA FIT THOSE TRAFFIC STOPPERS YER SPORTIN', BLONDIE.
I'LL GET *EGGSY* TA BRING A COUPLE UP FOR YA.
I MAY HAVE *LOST* MY *MEMORY,* BUT THERE IS *NO WAY* I WOULD LET YOU SPEAK TO ME LIKE THAT.
HEY, WHEN WE WERE *TOGETHER* WE SAID A *LOTTA CRAZY* THINGS TO EACH OTHER. THIS WAS OUR NORMAL *TÊTE-À-TÊTE.*
WE WERE *TOGETHER?* LIKE...LIKE...
LOVERS. HOT AND SWEATY ONES, I MIGHT ADD. IT'S BREAKIN' MY HEART THAT YOU *CAN'T REMEMBER* ANY OF THIS.

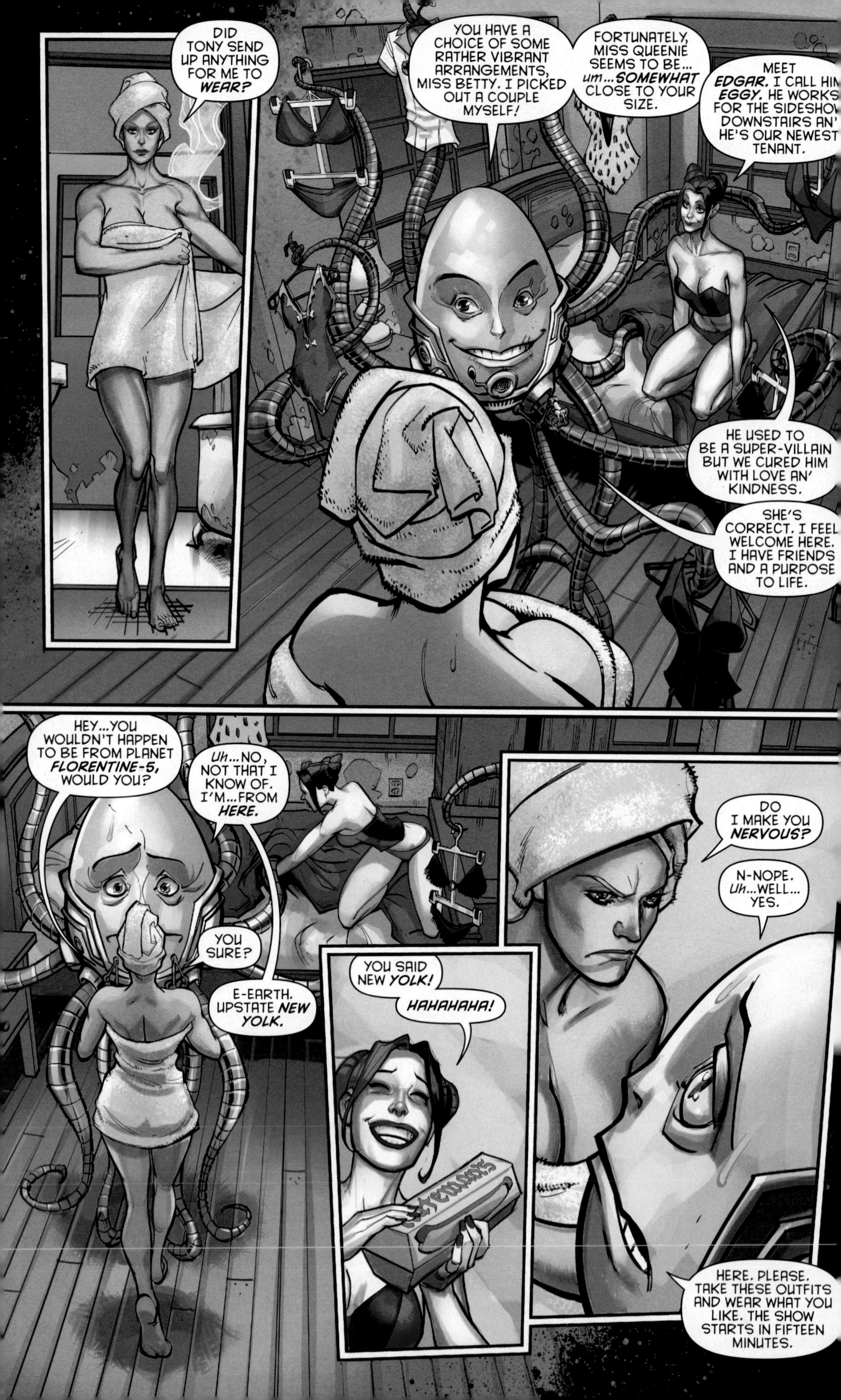
DID TONY SEND UP ANYTHING FOR ME TO *WEAR?*
YOU HAVE A CHOICE OF SOME RATHER VIBRANT ARRANGEMENTS, MISS BETTY. I PICKED OUT A COUPLE MYSELF!
FORTUNATELY, MISS QUEENIE SEEMS TO BE... *UM...SOMEWHAT* CLOSE TO YOUR SIZE.
MEET *EDGAR.* I CALL HIM *EGGY.* HE WORKS FOR THE SIDESHOW DOWNSTAIRS AN' HE'S OUR NEWEST TENANT.
HE USED TO BE A SUPER-VILLAIN BUT WE CURED HIM WITH LOVE AN' KINDNESS.
SHE'S CORRECT. I FEEL WELCOME HERE. I HAVE FRIENDS AND A PURPOSE TO LIFE.
HEY...YOU WOULDN'T HAPPEN TO BE FROM PLANET *FLORENTINE-5,* WOULD YOU?
*UH...*NO, NOT THAT I KNOW OF. I'M...FROM *HERE.*
YOU SURE?
E-EARTH. UPSTATE *NEW YOLK.*
YOU SAID NEW *YOLK!*
HAHAHAHA!
DO I MAKE YOU *NERVOUS?*
N-NOPE. *UH...*WELL... YES.
HERE. PLEASE. TAKE THESE OUTFITS AND WEAR WHAT YOU LIKE. THE SHOW STARTS IN FIFTEEN MINUTES.

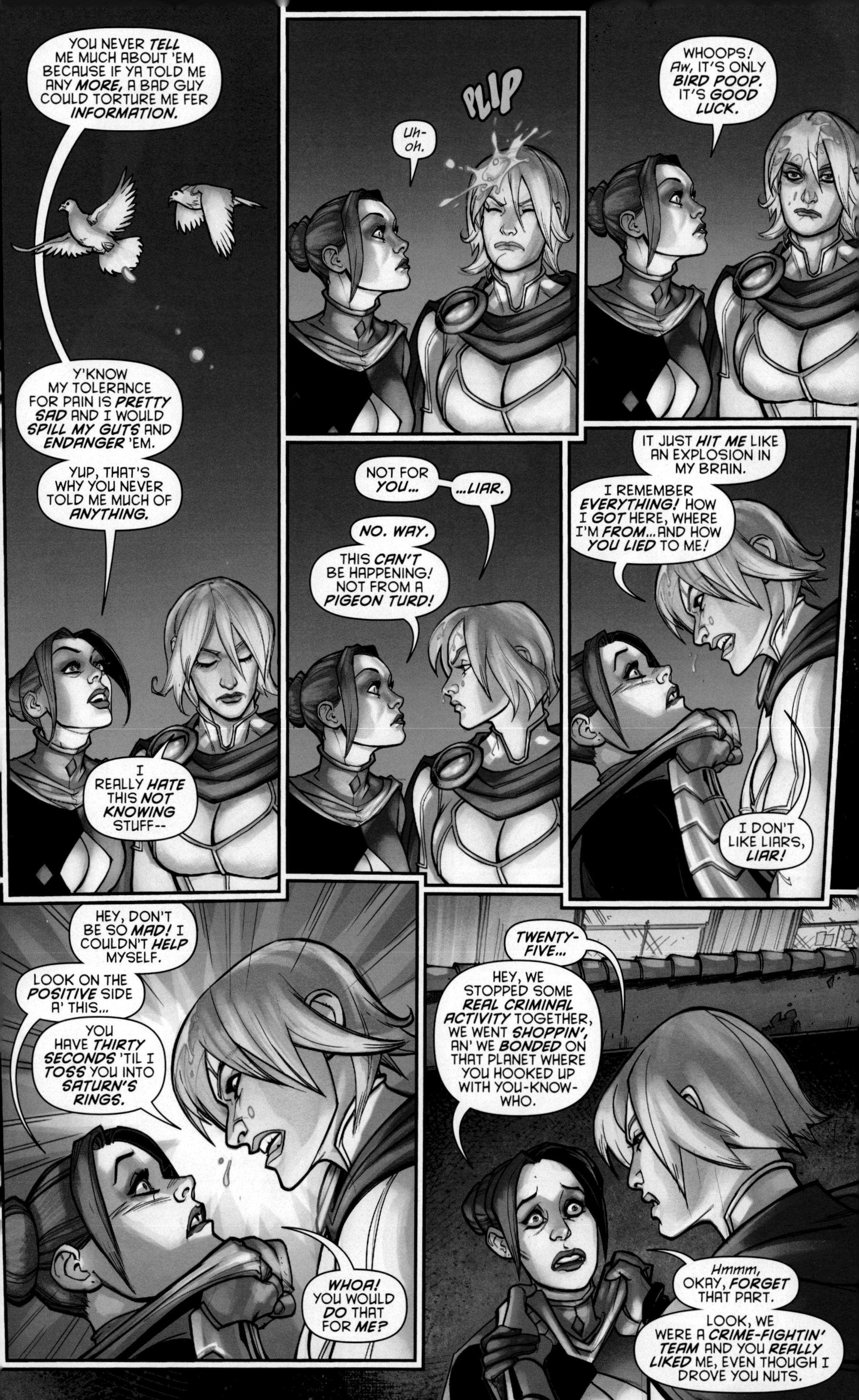
YOU NEVER TELL ME MUCH ABOUT 'EM BECAUSE IF YA TOLD ME ANY MORE, A BAD GUY COULD TORTURE ME FER INFORMATION.
Y'KNOW MY TOLERANCE FOR PAIN IS PRETTY SAD AND I WOULD SPILL MY GUTS AND ENDANGER 'EM.
YUP, THAT'S WHY YOU NEVER TOLD ME MUCH OF ANYTHING.
I REALLY HATE THIS NOT KNOWING STUFF--
PLIP
Uh-oh.
WHOOPS! Aw, IT'S ONLY BIRD POOP. IT'S GOOD LUCK.
NOT FOR YOU...
...LIAR.
NO. WAY.
THIS CAN'T BE HAPPENING! NOT FROM A PIGEON TURD!
IT JUST HIT ME LIKE AN EXPLOSION IN MY BRAIN.
I REMEMBER EVERYTHING! HOW I GOT HERE, WHERE I'M FROM...AND HOW YOU LIED TO ME!
I DON'T LIKE LIARS, LIAR!
HEY, DON'T BE SO MAD! I COULDN'T HELP MYSELF.
LOOK ON THE POSITIVE SIDE A' THIS...
YOU HAVE THIRTY SECONDS 'TIL I TOSS YOU INTO SATURN'S RINGS.
WHOA! YOU WOULD DO THAT FOR ME?
TWENTY-FIVE...
HEY, WE STOPPED SOME REAL CRIMINAL ACTIVITY TOGETHER, WE WENT SHOPPIN', AN' WE BONDED ON THAT PLANET WHERE YOU HOOKED UP WITH YOU-KNOW-WHO.
Hmmm, OKAY, FORGET THAT PART.
LOOK, WE WERE A CRIME-FIGHTIN' TEAM AND YOU REALLY LIKED ME, EVEN THOUGH I DROVE YOU NUTS.

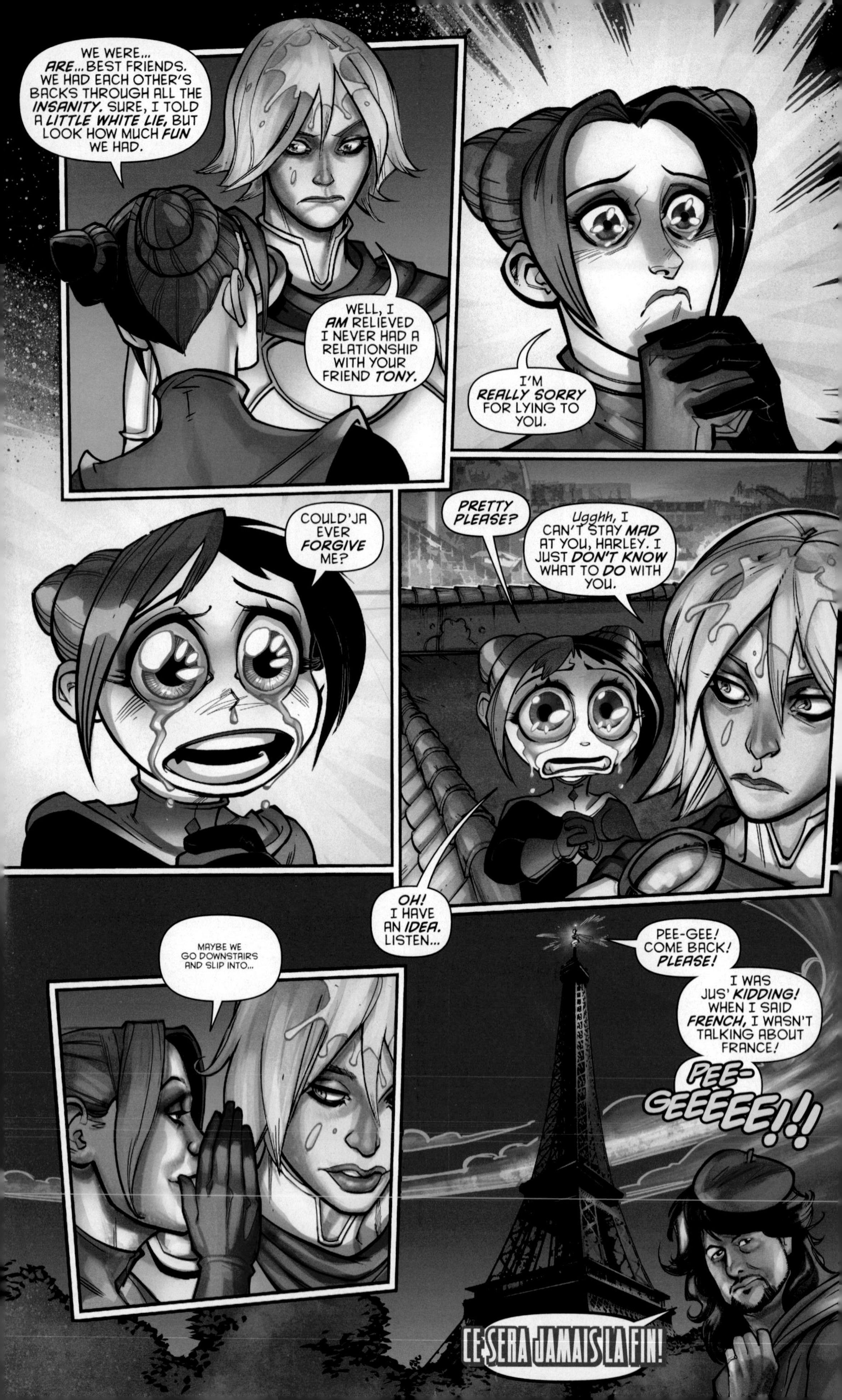
WE WERE... ARE... BEST FRIENDS. WE HAD EACH OTHER'S BACKS THROUGH ALL THE INSANITY. SURE, I TOLD A LITTLE WHITE LIE, BUT LOOK HOW MUCH FUN WE HAD.
WELL, I AM RELIEVED I NEVER HAD A RELATIONSHIP WITH YOUR FRIEND TONY.
I'M REALLY SORRY FOR LYING TO YOU.
COULD'JA EVER FORGIVE ME?
PRETTY PLEASE?
Ugghh, I CAN'T STAY MAD AT YOU, HARLEY. I JUST DON'T KNOW WHAT TO DO WITH YOU.
OH! I HAVE AN IDEA. LISTEN...
MAYBE WE GO DOWNSTAIRS AND SLIP INTO...
PEE-GEE! COME BACK! PLEASE!
I WAS JUS' KIDDING! WHEN I SAID FRENCH, I WASN'T TALKING ABOUT FRANCE!
PEE-GEEEEEE!!!
CE SERA JAMAIS LA FIN!

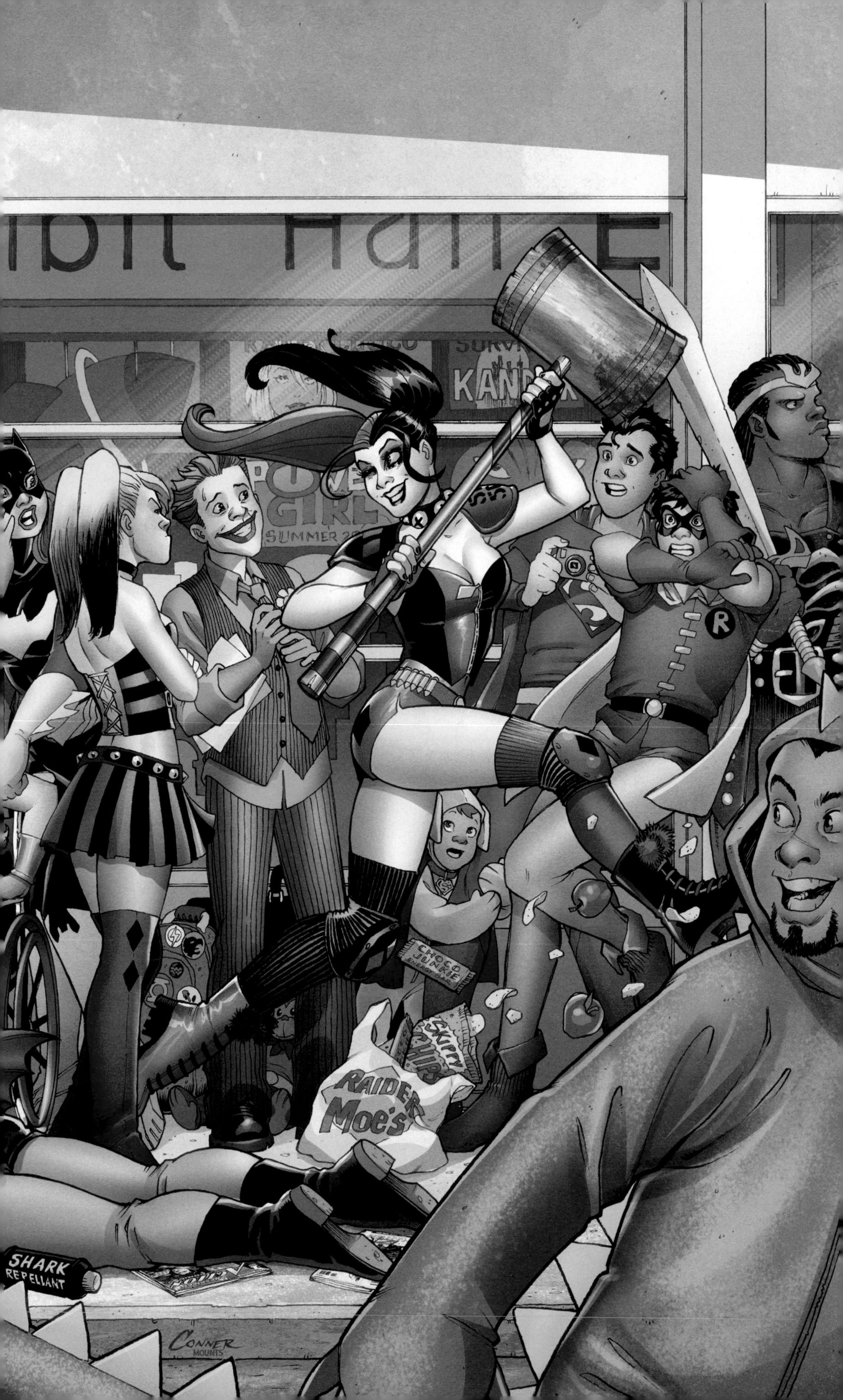
CHOCO JUNKIE
SKIPPY CHIPS
RAIDER Moe's
SHARK REPELLANT
CONNER
MOUNTS

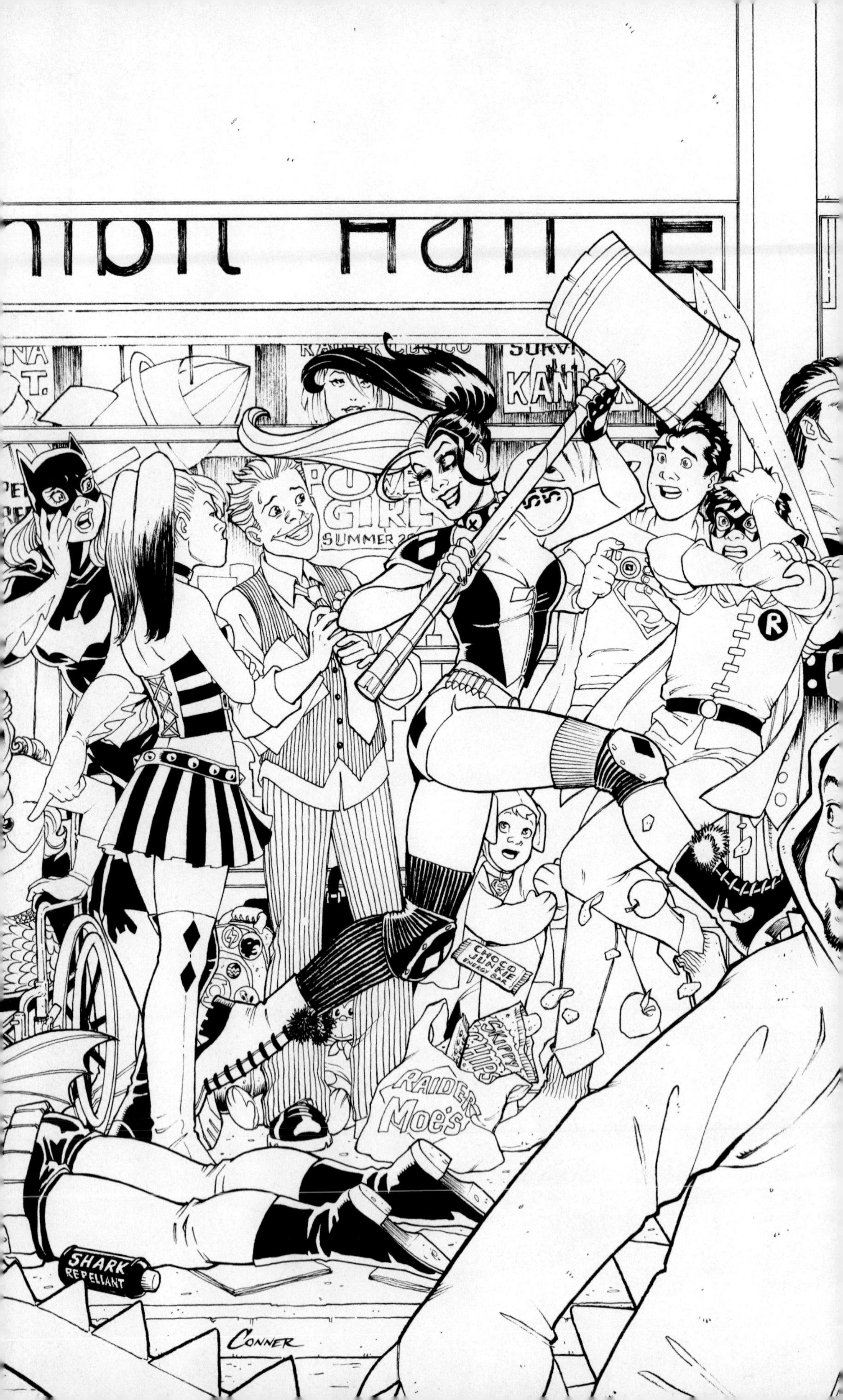
CHOCO JUNKIE
ENERGY BAR
SKIPPY CHIPS
RAIDER
Moe's
SHARK
REPELLANT
CONNER

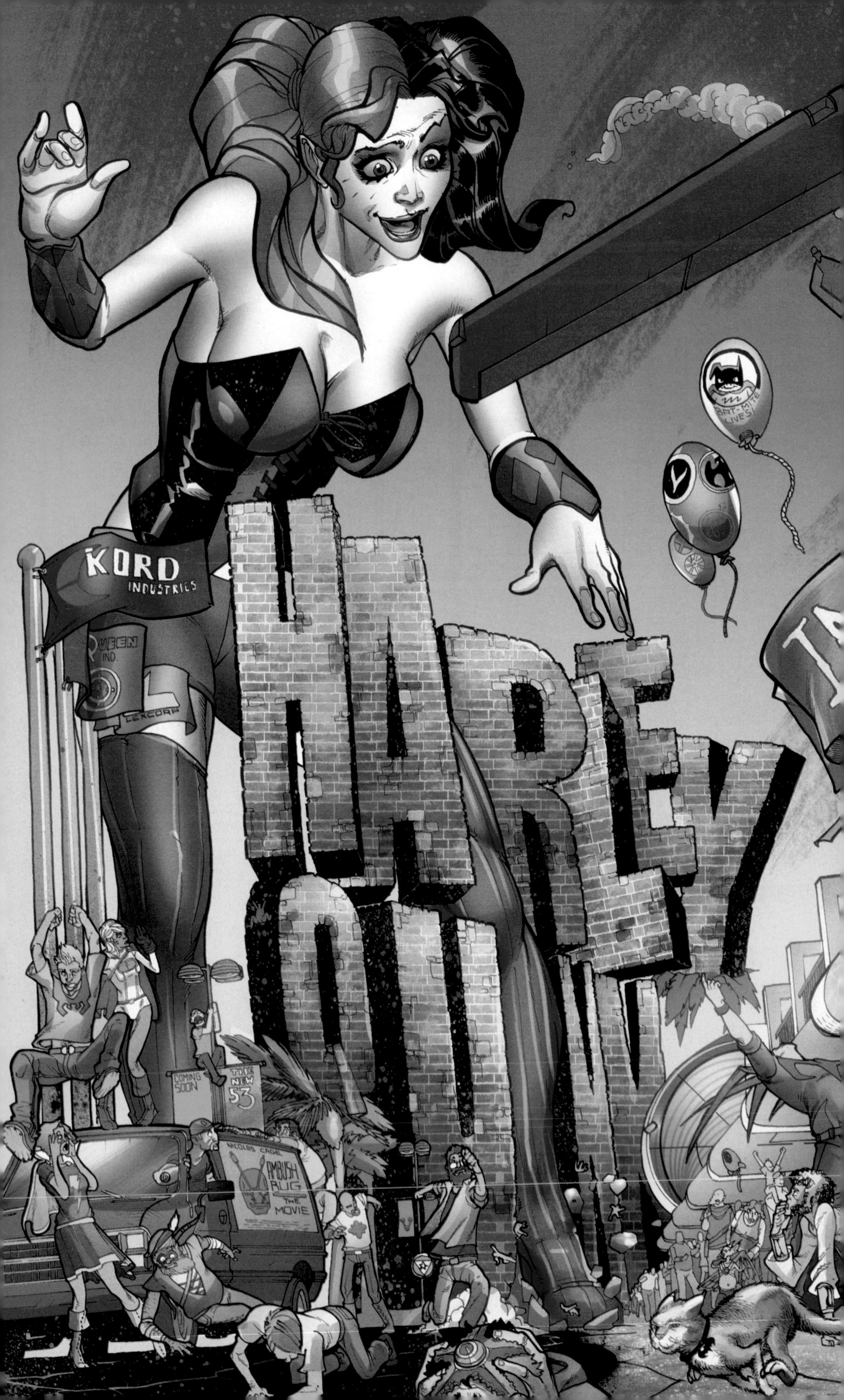

HARLEY QUINN
KORD INDUSTRIES
QUEEN IND.
LEXCORP
BAT-MITE LIVES!
COMING SOON
THE NEW 53
NICOLAS CAGE
AMBUSH BUG
THE MOVIE

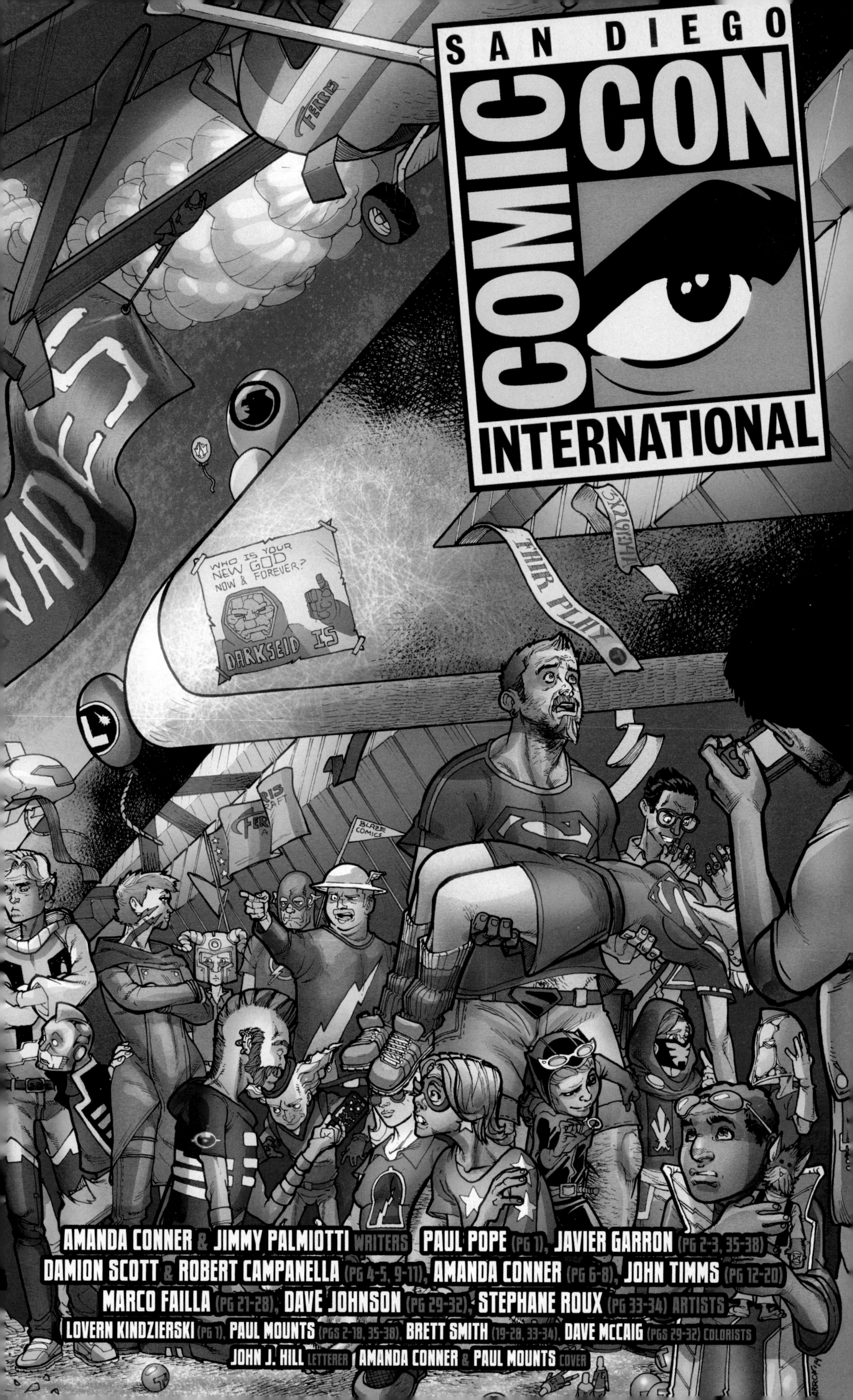
SAN DIEGO
COMIC CON
INTERNATIONAL
FERRIS
WHO IS YOUR NEW GOD NOW & FOREVER?
DARKSEID IS
FAIR PLAY
BLAZE COMICS

AMANDA CONNER & JIMMY PALMIOTTI WRITERS PAUL POPE (PG 1), JAVIER GARRON (PG 2-3, 35-38)
DAMION SCOTT & ROBERT CAMPANELLA (PG 4-5, 9-11), AMANDA CONNER (PG 6-8), JOHN TIMMS (PG 12-20)
MARCO FAILLA (PG 21-28), DAVE JOHNSON (PG 29-32), STEPHANE ROUX (PG 33-34) ARTISTS
LOVERN KINDZIERSKI (PG 1), PAUL MOUNTS (PGS 2-18, 35-38), BRETT SMITH (19-28, 33-34), DAVE McCAIG (PGS 29-32) COLORISTS
JOHN J. HILL LETTERER AMANDA CONNER & PAUL MOUNTS COVER

DAY ONE : TUESDAY.

OH MY GOD, I'M *REALLY HERE.* ALL I GOTTA DO IS FIND AN *EDITOR.*

HI, IS THERE AN EDITOR AROUND THAT I CAN SHOW MY *WORK* TO?

SINCE YOU GOT ALL DRESSED UP, WHY DON'T YOU GO TALK TO *BOB HARRAS* OVER THERE?

HE'S THE *EDITOR-IN-CHIEF.* IF HE LIKES YOUR WORK, YOU'RE AS GOOD AS IN.

HOW CAN I EVER *THANK YOU* KATIE?

ARE YOU GONNA BRING BACK *TALIA AL GHUL?*

WHEN IS *SCOTT SNYDER* SUPPOSED TO GET HERE?

WHY ISN'T GREEN LANTERN TRI-MONTHLY?

WHEN YOU ARE RICH AND FAMOUS, HIRE ME OUT OF THIS SOUL-SUCKING JOB.

DEAL.

YOU MISSED A PORTFOLIO REVIEW ABOUT AN HOUR AGO. WE'LL HAVE *ANOTHER* ONE *TOMORROW.*

Ugghh, TOMORROW?

Katie Kubert
DC Editor

IF I GET BATMAN TO LOOK *BAD* IN FRONT OF HIM, MISTAH HARRAS WON'T BELIEVE A WORD HE SAYS, AND THEN I CAN GET HIS ATTENTION AND SHOW HIM MY WORK.

Hmm.

DRATS! BATMAN! AND HE'S TALKING TO BOB HARRAS.

HE'S PROB'LY TELLING MR. HARRAS TO LOOK OUT FOR ME, OR SOMETHING.

WHAT AM I GONNA DO?

HOW DO I GET BATMAN TO *LOOK BAD,* THOUGH? THAT SUIT IS COOL ON *SO MANY LEVELS.*

I GOT IT!

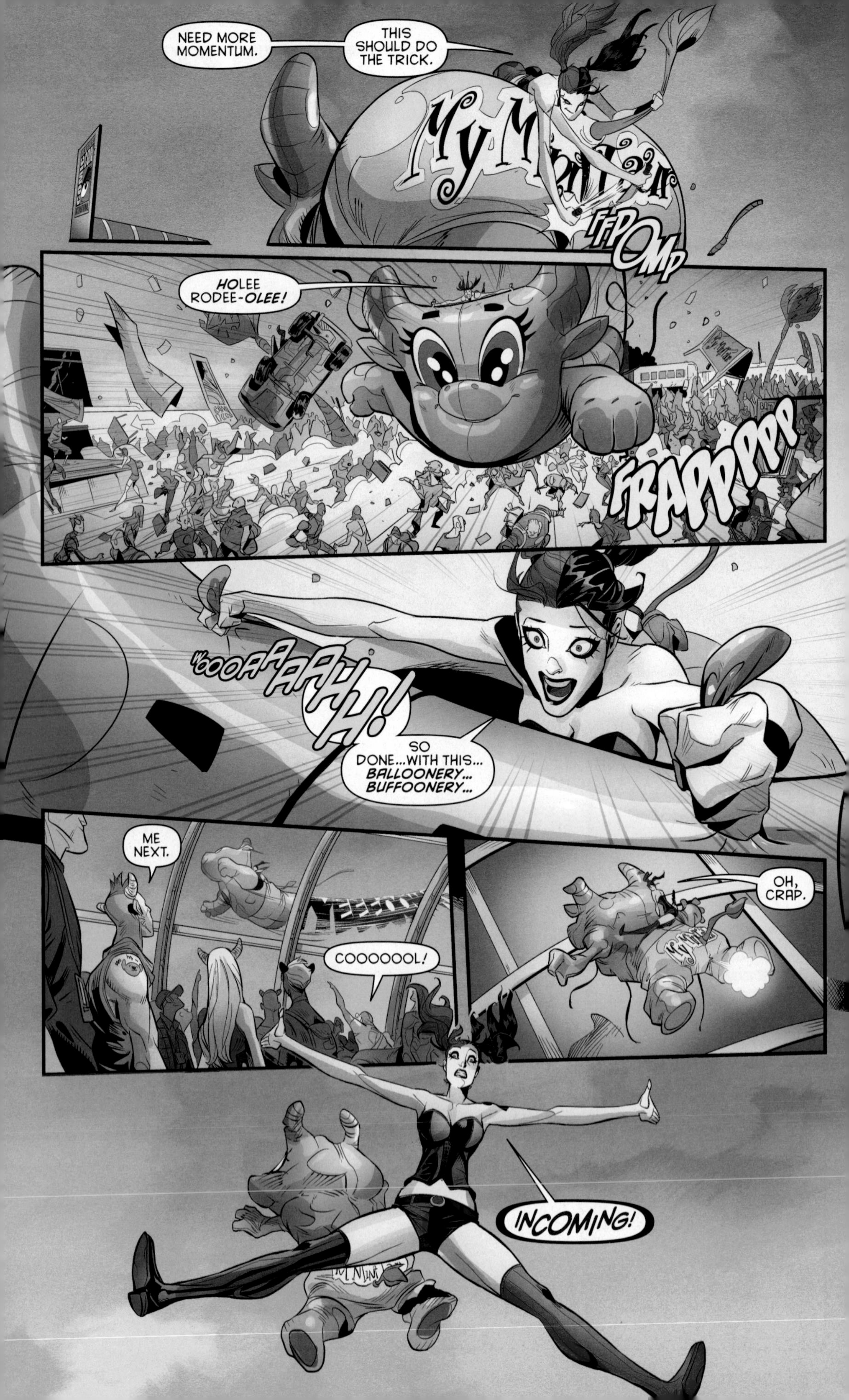
NEED MORE MOMENTUM.
THIS SHOULD DO THE TRICK.
My Mini Tour
FFPOMP
HOLEE RODEE-OLEE!
FRAPPPPP
WOOOAAAAHH!
SO DONE...WITH THIS... BALLOONERY... BUFFOONERY...
ME NEXT.
COOOOOOL!
OH, CRAP.
INCOMING!

DAY FOUR. FRIDAY. 4 A.M.

BACK AT THE CON, AT A MORE REASONABLE HOUR...

TONY, CAN I TAKE A BREAK FOR A BIT?

SURE, JUST DON'T GET YOUR-SELF *THROWN OUT* AGAIN, PLEASE. I NEED YOU BACK HERE.

DON'T WORRY. I WON'T LET THAT HAPPEN AGAIN.

HOLEE-CLUSTERFOLEE, IT'S A FRIGGIN' *ZOO* IN HERE!

...WITH THE NEW 52 SEPTEMBER EVENT WE HAVE COMING UP, EACH AND EVERY TITLE WILL COME WITH A SPECIAL *4-D COVER.* IT'S BASICALLY A 3-D COVER, AND THE EXTRA *"D"* IS FOR *"DIDIO"* AS I WILL BE FEATURED IN THE BACKGROUND OF EVERY BOOK.

THIS EXTRAORDINARY COVER IS MADE OF AN INDESTRUCTIBLE WEAVE OF PAPER WHICH IS GUARANTEED TO SURVIVE A *NUCLEAR ATTACK.*

TO PRODUCE THESE SPECIAL COVERS, WE HAD TO MINE ONE OF THE MOST REMOTE PLACES ON EARTH, AND TO DO SO, MELT PART OF THE *SOUTH POLE* IN THE PROCESS.

LET'S BE HONEST, IT WAS GONNA MELT EVENTUALLY, AM I *RIGHT?*

WIN! A PORTFOLIO REVIEW JIM LEE

ALSO, WE'LL BE LAUNCHING A *NEW* LINE OF BOOKS THAT DO NOT HAVE *ANY* EDITORIAL OVERSEEING THE CONTENT.

WE CALL THIS *D-C-YOU.* EACH CREATOR DOES WHATEVER THEY LIKE WITH THE CHARACTER OF THEIR CHOICE AND GOES *CRAZY.*

WE DON'T EXPECT THESE BOOKS TO SELL AT *ALL,* SO WE ARE SETTING THE PRINT RUN AT 1,000 COPIES EACH. THAT SOUNDS ABOUT RIGHT, NO?

CUT! WE GOT A PHOTO BOMBER IN THE SHOT.

SECURITY!

MISTAH DIDIO, IF I CAN HAVE A MINUTE TO SHOW YOU MY SAMPLES, I'M SURE YOU'LL WANNA ADD ME TO YOUR ROSTER OF TALENTED ARTISTS!

AT THIS POINT, YOU MIGHT AS WELL PLAY THE *LOTTERY* FOR A SPECIAL PORTFOLIO REVIEW BY *JIM LEE* ON SATURDAY, BUT FOR NOW, YOU ARE OFFICIALLY *BANNED* FROM THE BOOTH FOR THE REST OF THE DAY.

I HEAR THE COMPANY ACROSS THE WAY IS LOOKING FOR REALLY *CHEAP* ARTISTS.

I *TRIED* THEM. THEY AREN'T LOOKING FOR ANYTHING *NEW* OR ORIGINAL.

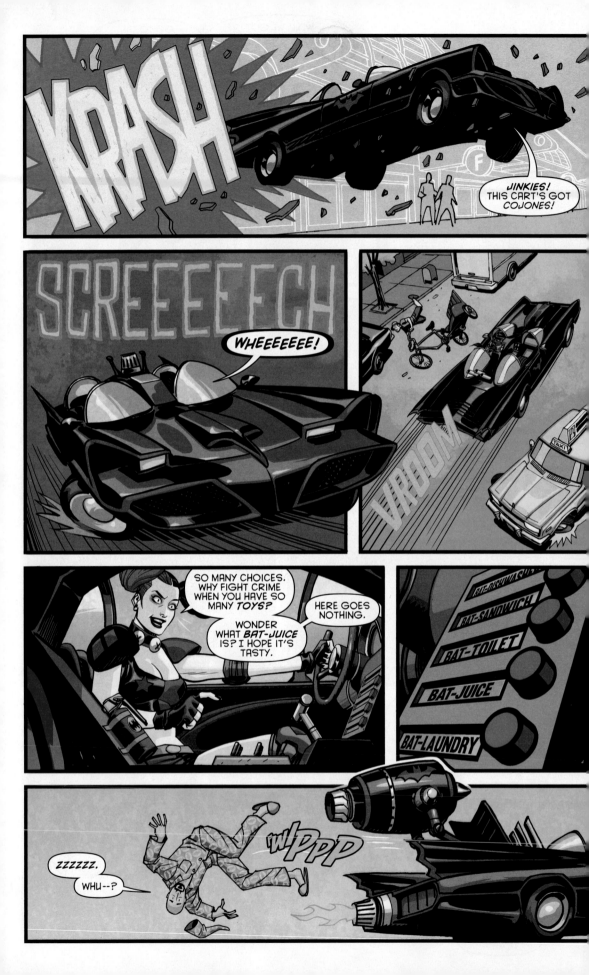

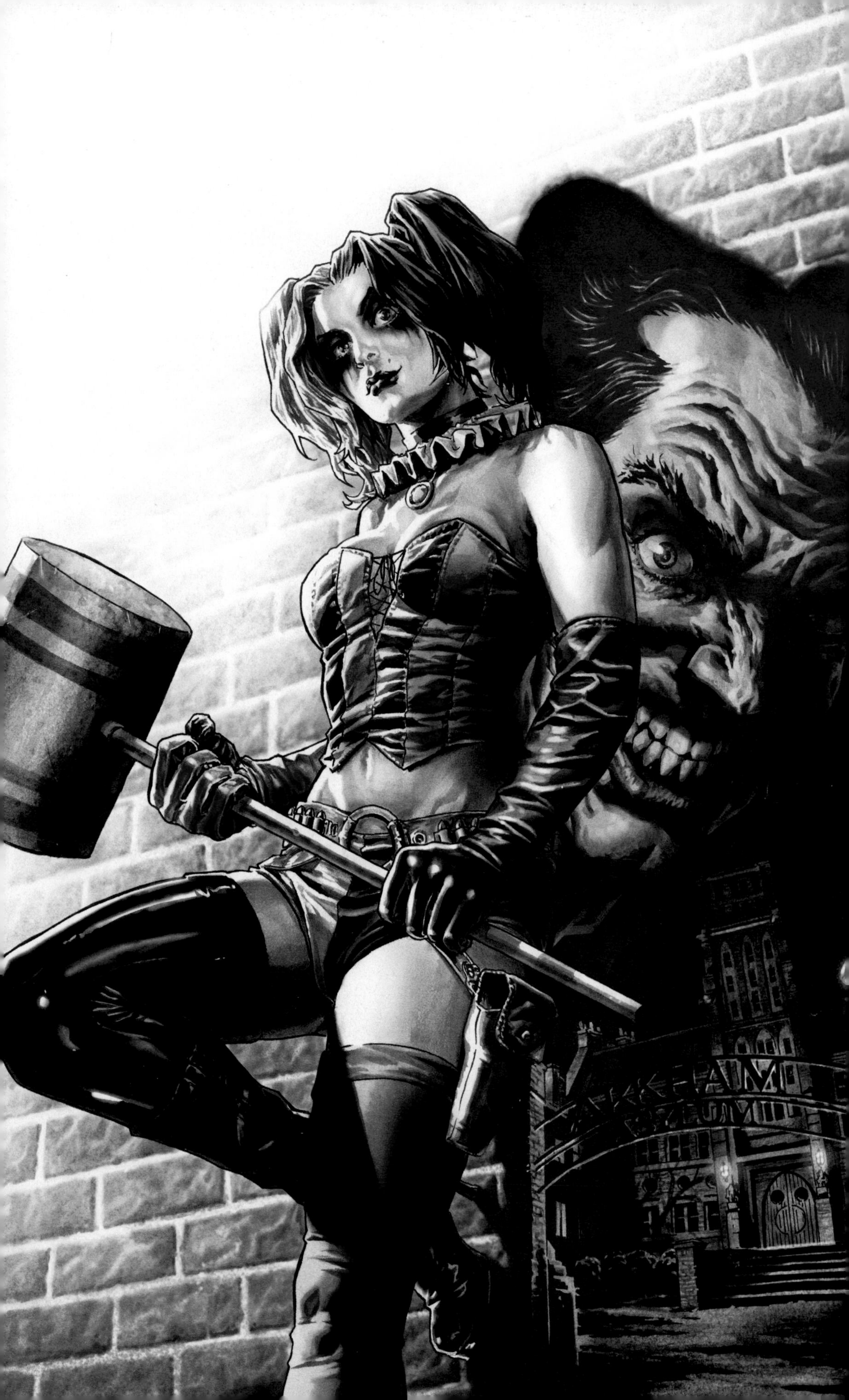

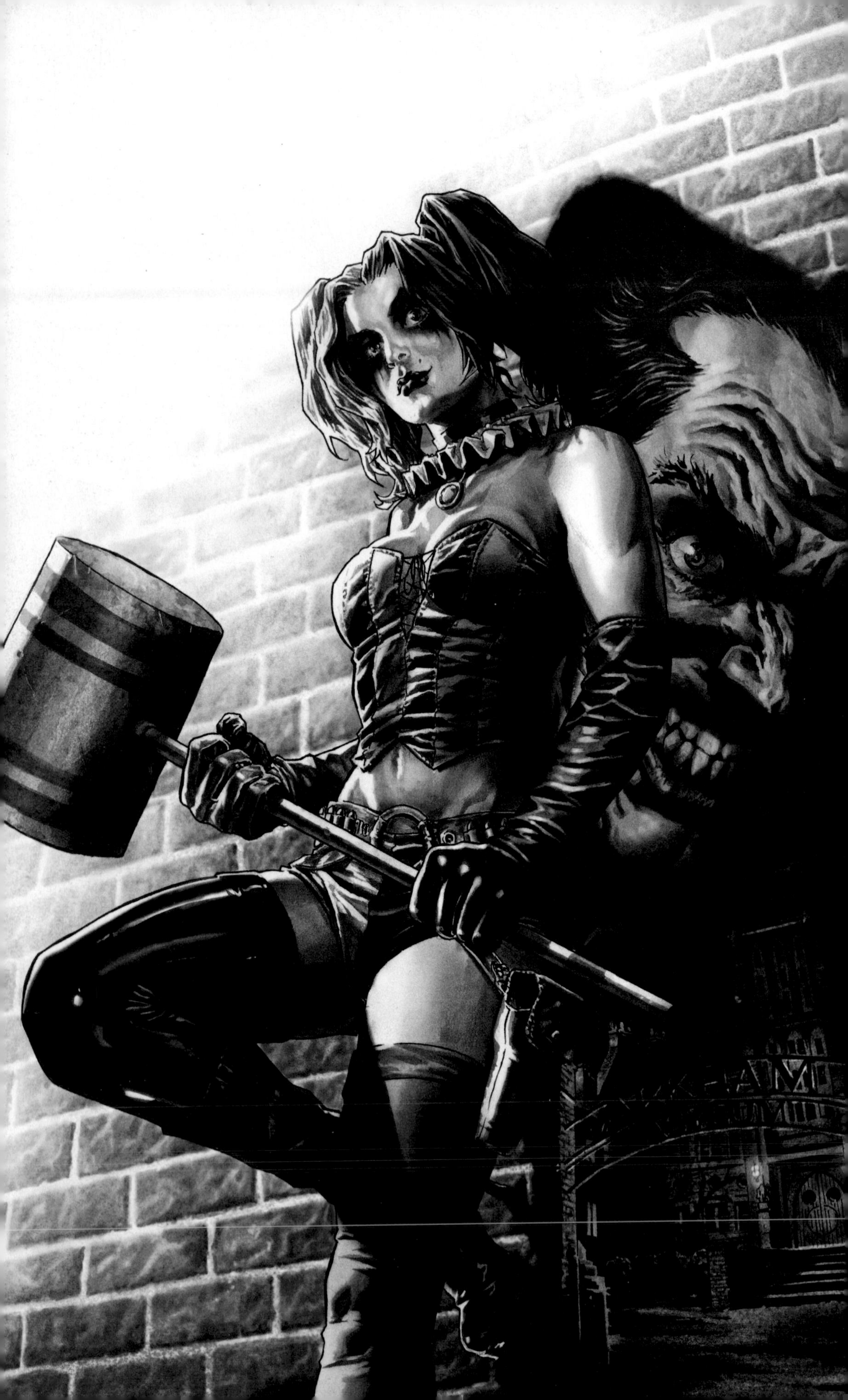

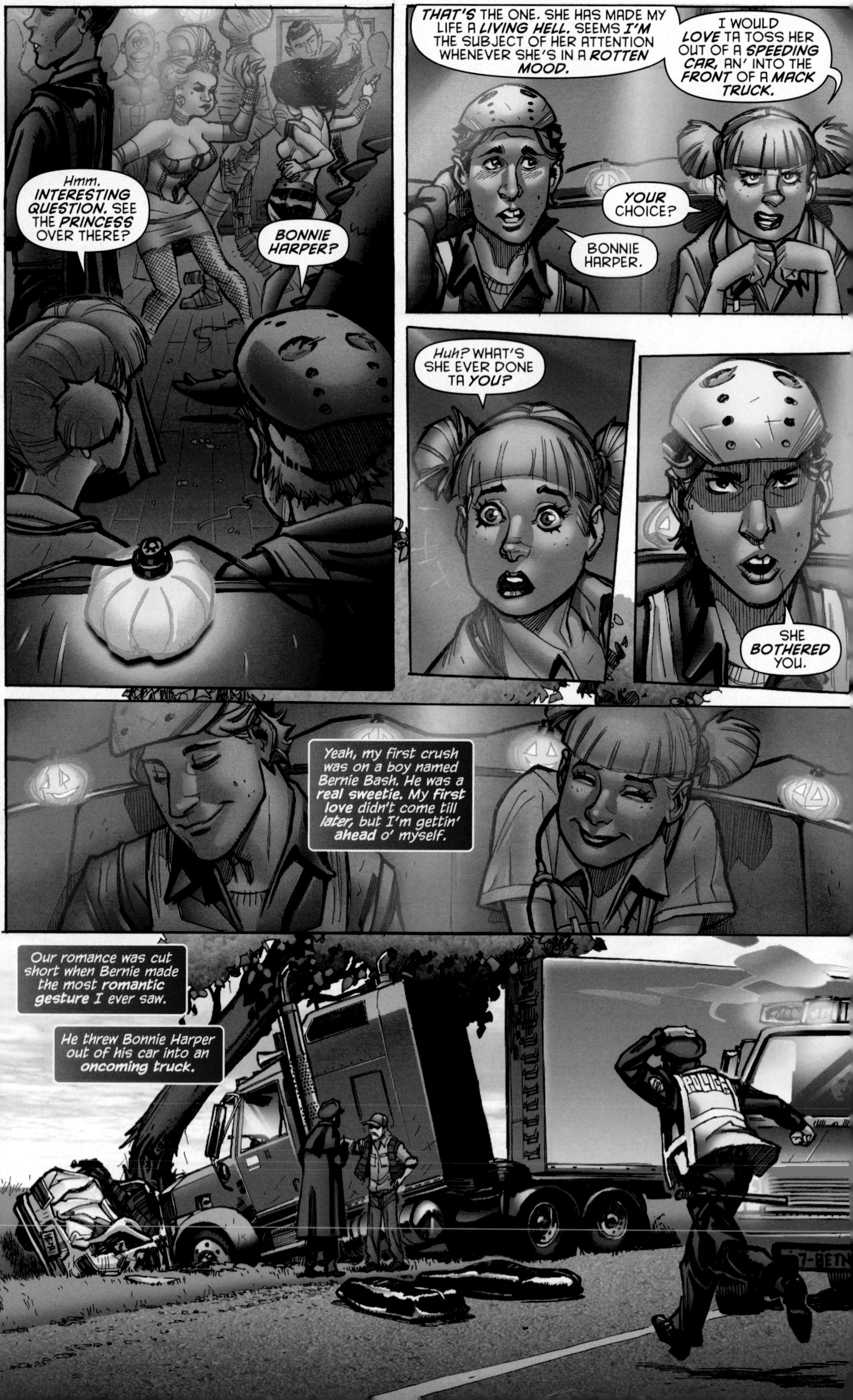
Hmm. INTERESTING QUESTION. SEE THE PRINCESS OVER THERE?
BONNIE HARPER?
THAT'S THE ONE. SHE HAS MADE MY LIFE A LIVING HELL. SEEMS I'M THE SUBJECT OF HER ATTENTION WHENEVER SHE'S IN A ROTTEN MOOD.
I WOULD LOVE TA TOSS HER OUT OF A SPEEDING CAR, AN' INTO THE FRONT OF A MACK TRUCK.
YOUR CHOICE?
BONNIE HARPER.
Huh? WHAT'S SHE EVER DONE TA YOU?
SHE BOTHERED YOU.
Yeah, my first crush was on a boy named Bernie Bash. He was a real sweetie. My first love didn't come till later, but I'm gettin' ahead o' myself.
Our romance was cut short when Bernie made the most romantic gesture I ever saw.
He threw Bonnie Harper out of his car into an oncoming truck.
POLICE

I cut school and got a good seat in court as I watched them take Bernie away. He was sent away to juvenile detention fer, like, ever.

Not only was he my first crush, but I think that was when I shed my first tear of heartbreak.

I prefer ta be happy, if you didn't know that about me already.

A few weeks later I broke into Bernie's parents' place while they were out. I wanted to find something I could remember him by.

The place looked like someone mounted an entire zoo on the wall.

Bein' the junior psychologist, this explained a few things.

I knew the minute I came into the room I had found the single item that would always remind me of Bernie.

Later on I found out Bernie was stabbed ta death over a side a' mashed potatoes a year later.

I've kept 'im ever since.

Well. That explained why the letters had stopped.

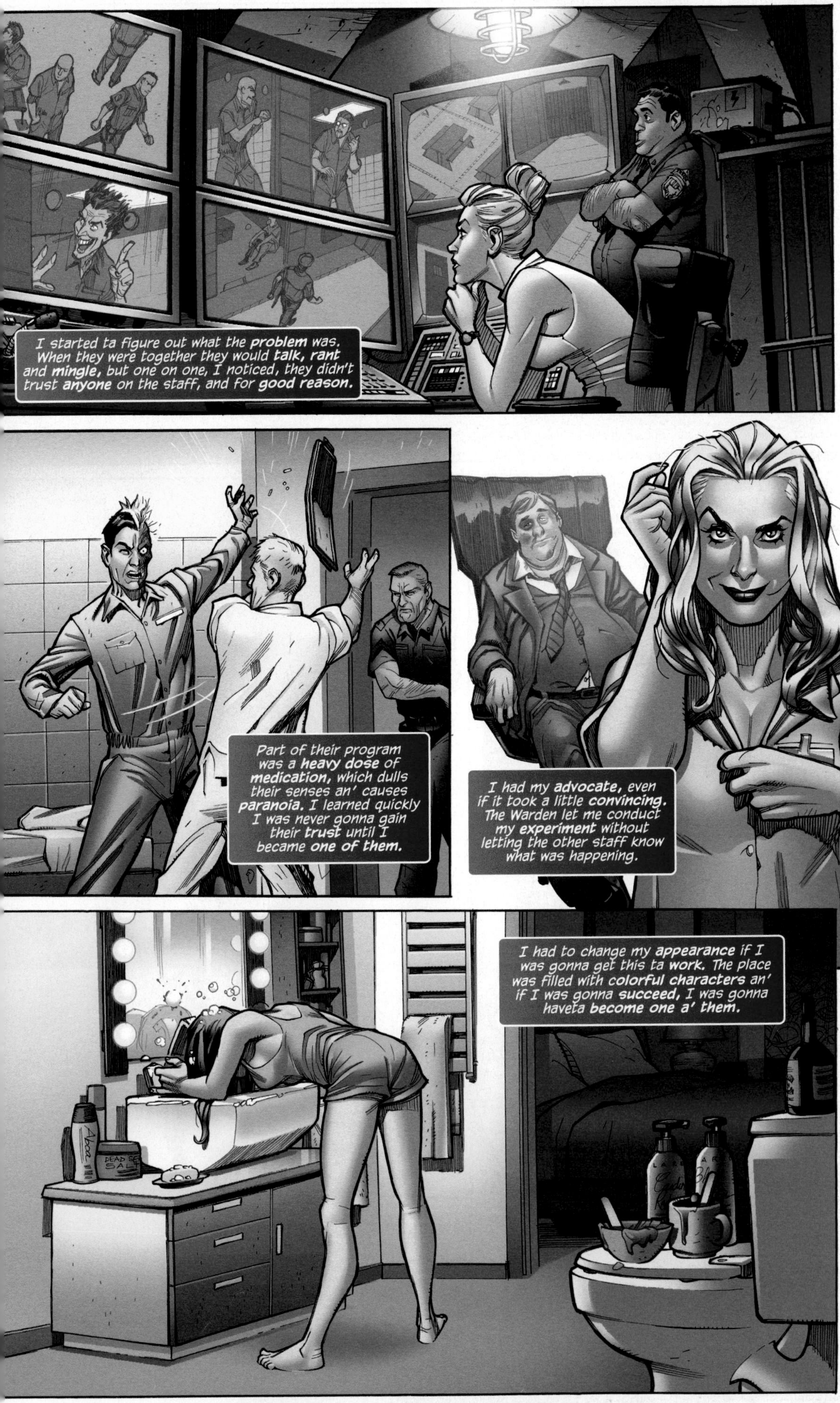
I started ta figure out what the problem was. When they were together they would talk, rant and mingle, but one on one, I noticed, they didn't trust anyone on the staff, and for good reason.
Part of their program was a heavy dose of medication, which dulls their senses an' causes paranoia. I learned quickly I was never gonna gain their trust until I became one of them.
I had my advocate, even if it took a little convincing. The Warden let me conduct my experiment without letting the other staff know what was happening.
I had to change my appearance if I was gonna get this ta work. The place was filled with colorful characters an' if I was gonna succeed, I was gonna haveta become one a' them.
DEAD SEA SALT

VARIANT COVER GALLERY

HARLEY QUINN #9
Selfie variant cover by Amanda Conner and Paul Mounts

HARLEY QUINN #10
Variant cover by Amanda Conner and Paul Mounts

HARLEY QUINN #11
Variant cover by Amanda Conner and Paul Mounts

HARLEY QUINN #11
Monster variant cover by Yanick Paquette and Nathan Fairbairn

HARLEY QUINN #12
Variant cover by Amanda Conner and Paul Mounts

HARLEY QUINN #12
LEGO variant cover

HARLEY QUINN #13
Variant cover by Amanda Conner and Alex Sinclair

HARLEY QUINN #13
Variant cover by Darwyn Cooke

HARLEY QUINN INVADES COMIC-CON INTERNATIONAL SAN DIEGO #1
Full wraparound cover by Amanda Conner and Paul Mounts

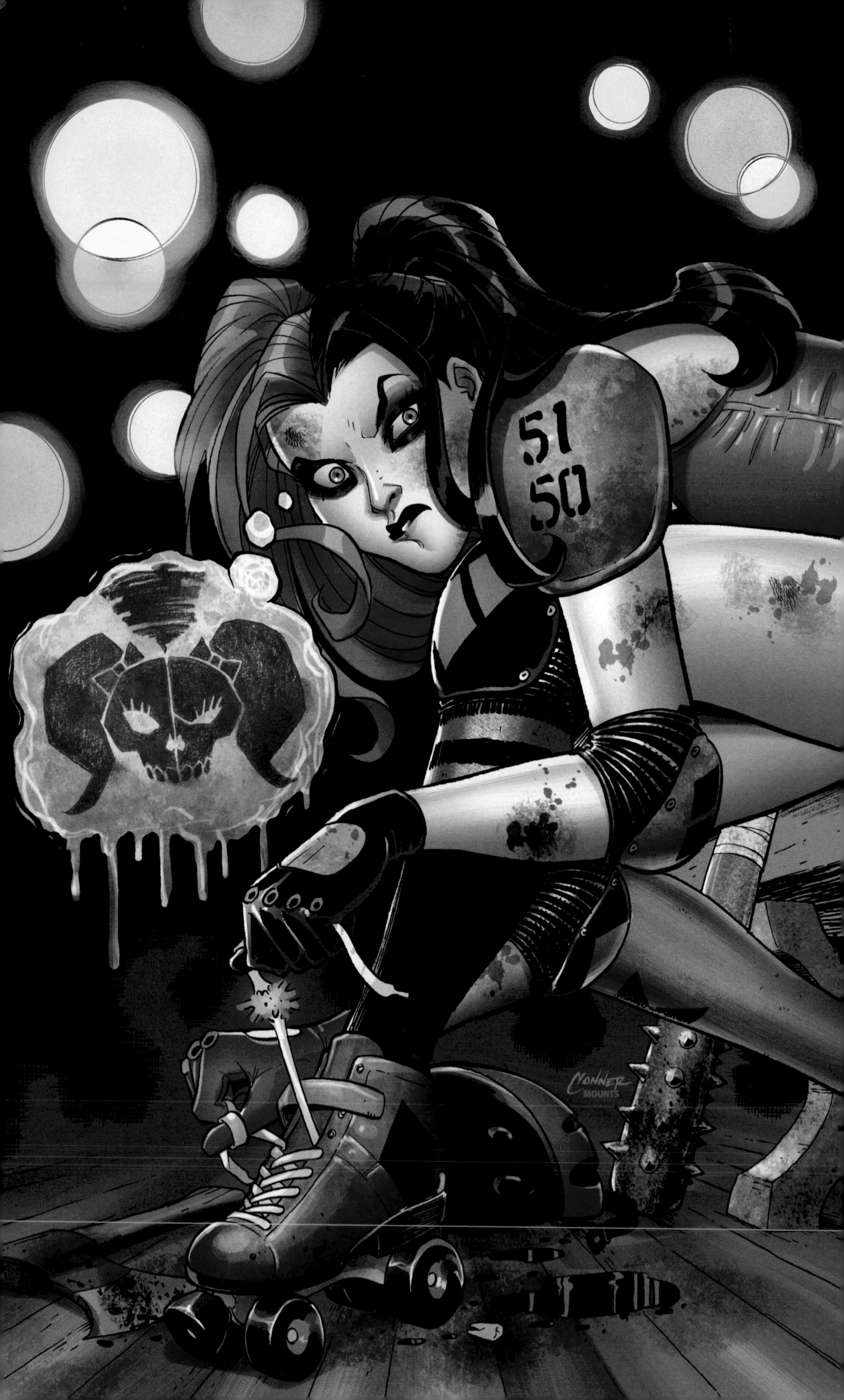
51
50
CONNER
MOUNTS

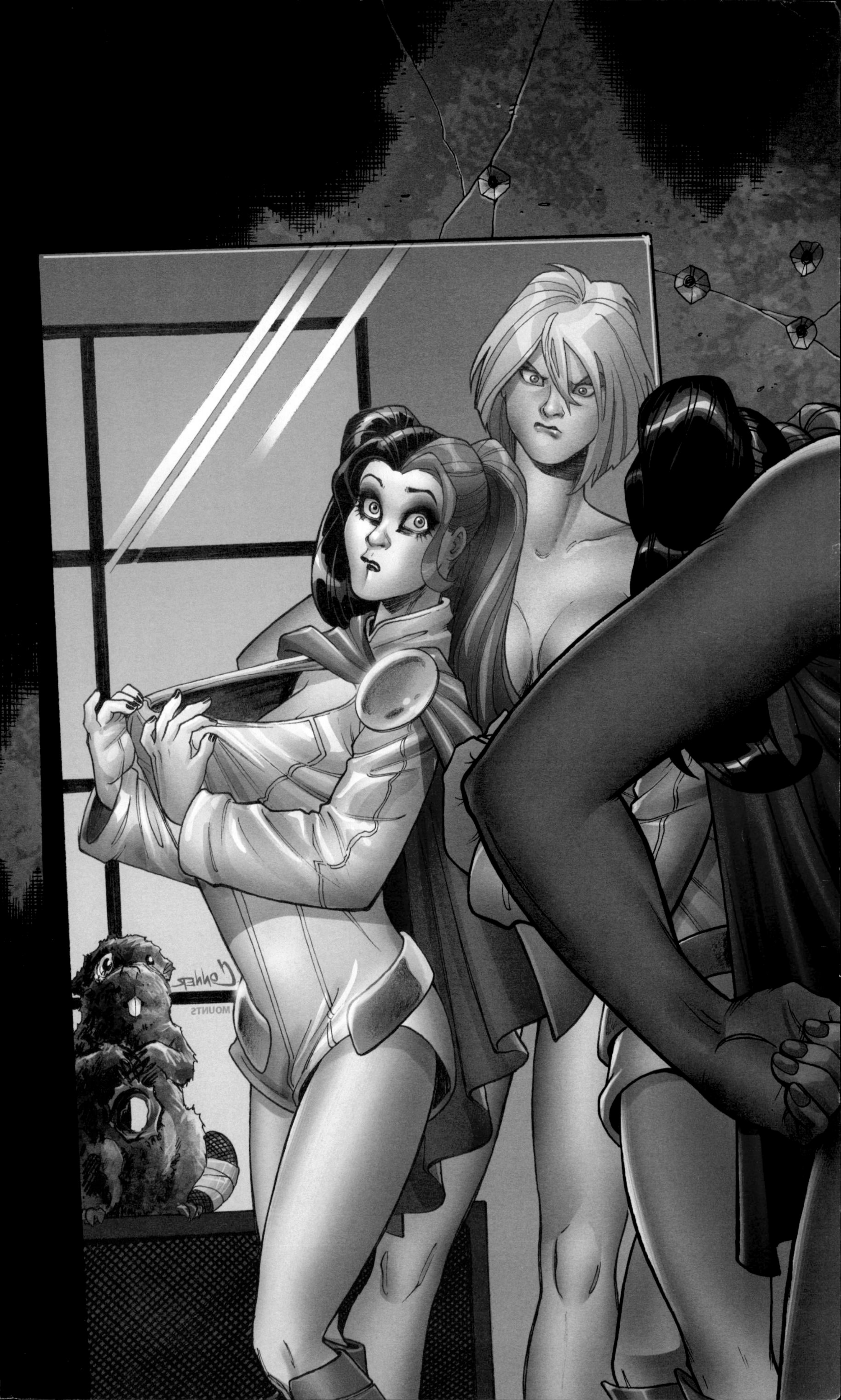

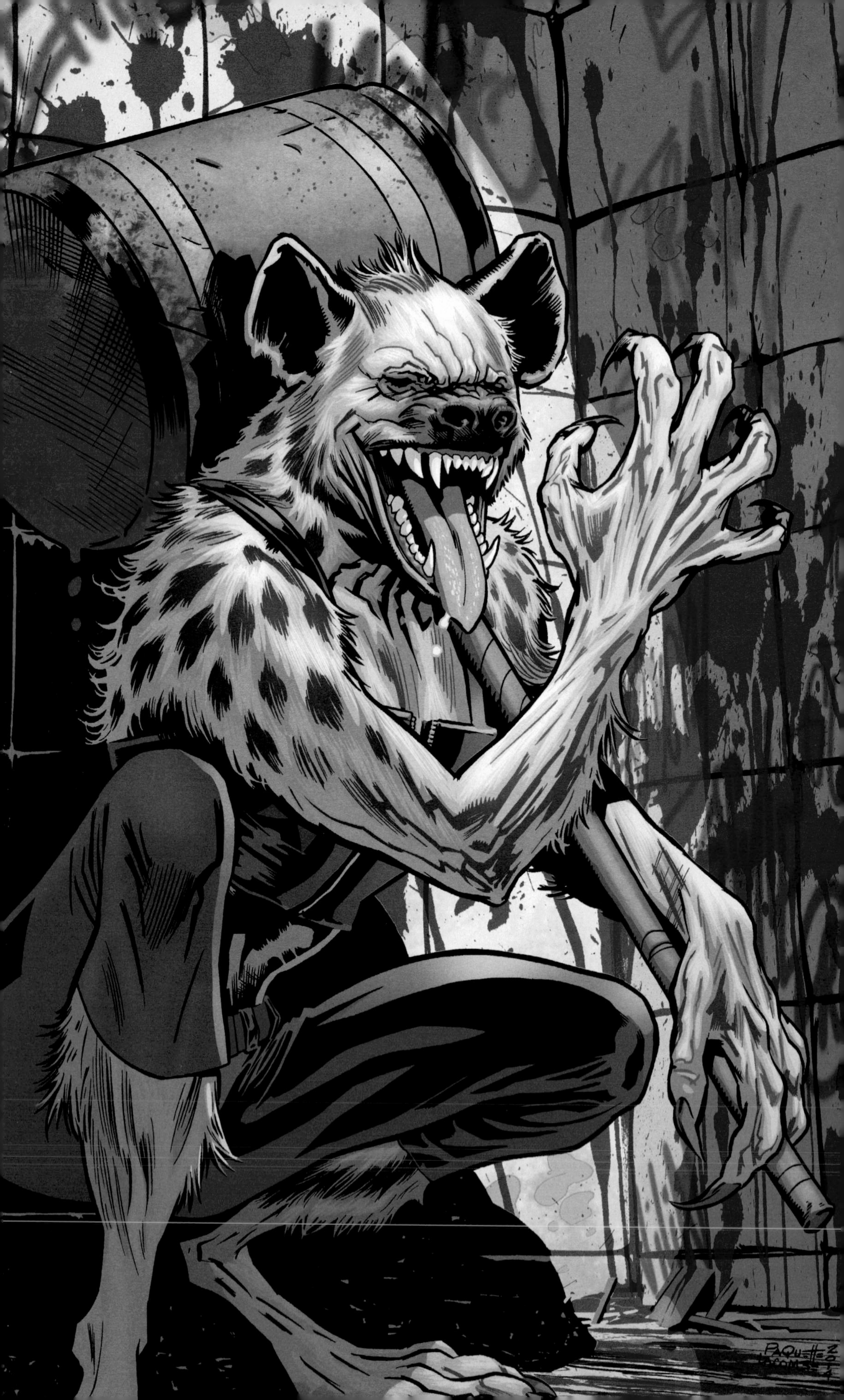
PAQUETTE 2014

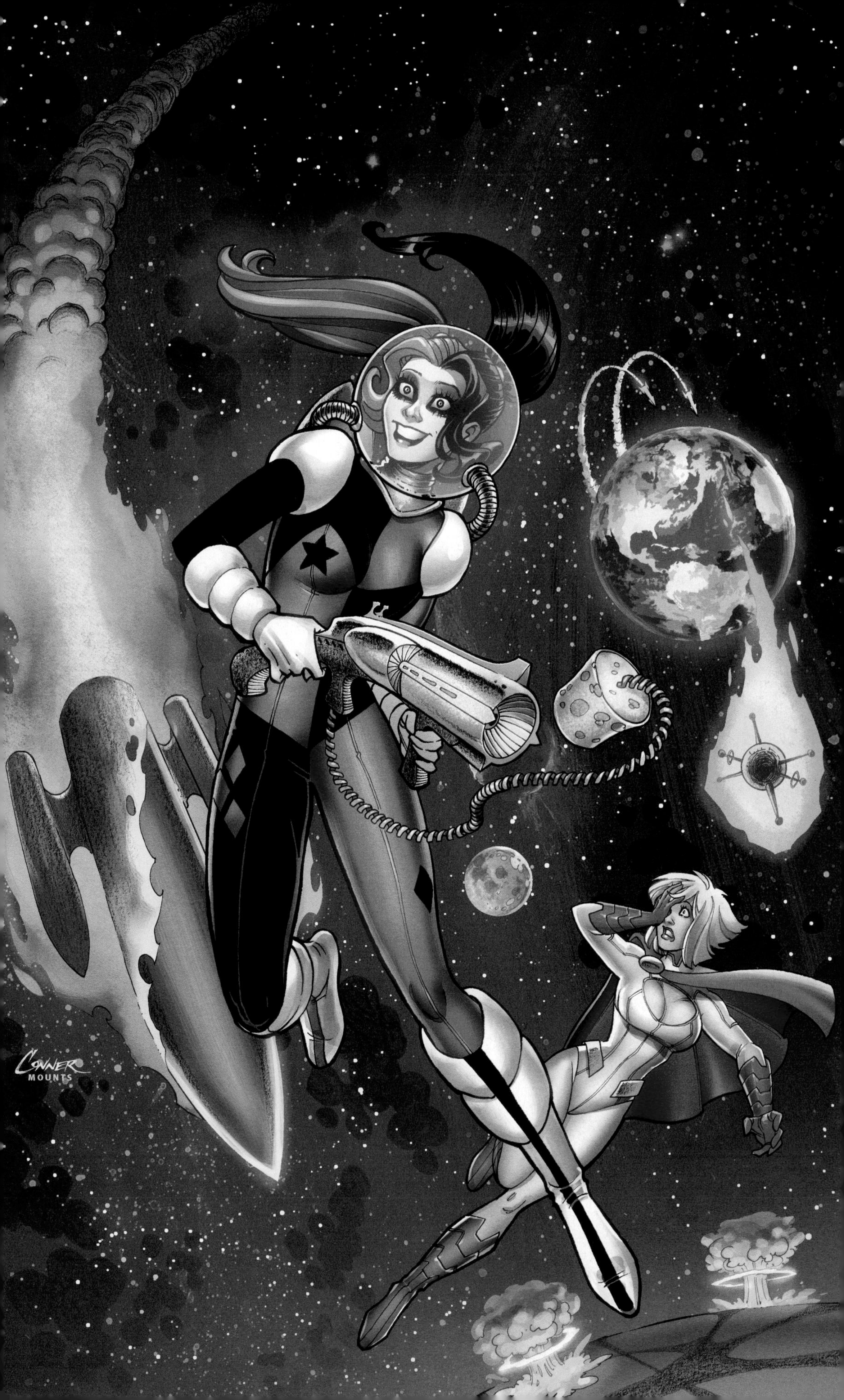
CONNER
MOUNTS

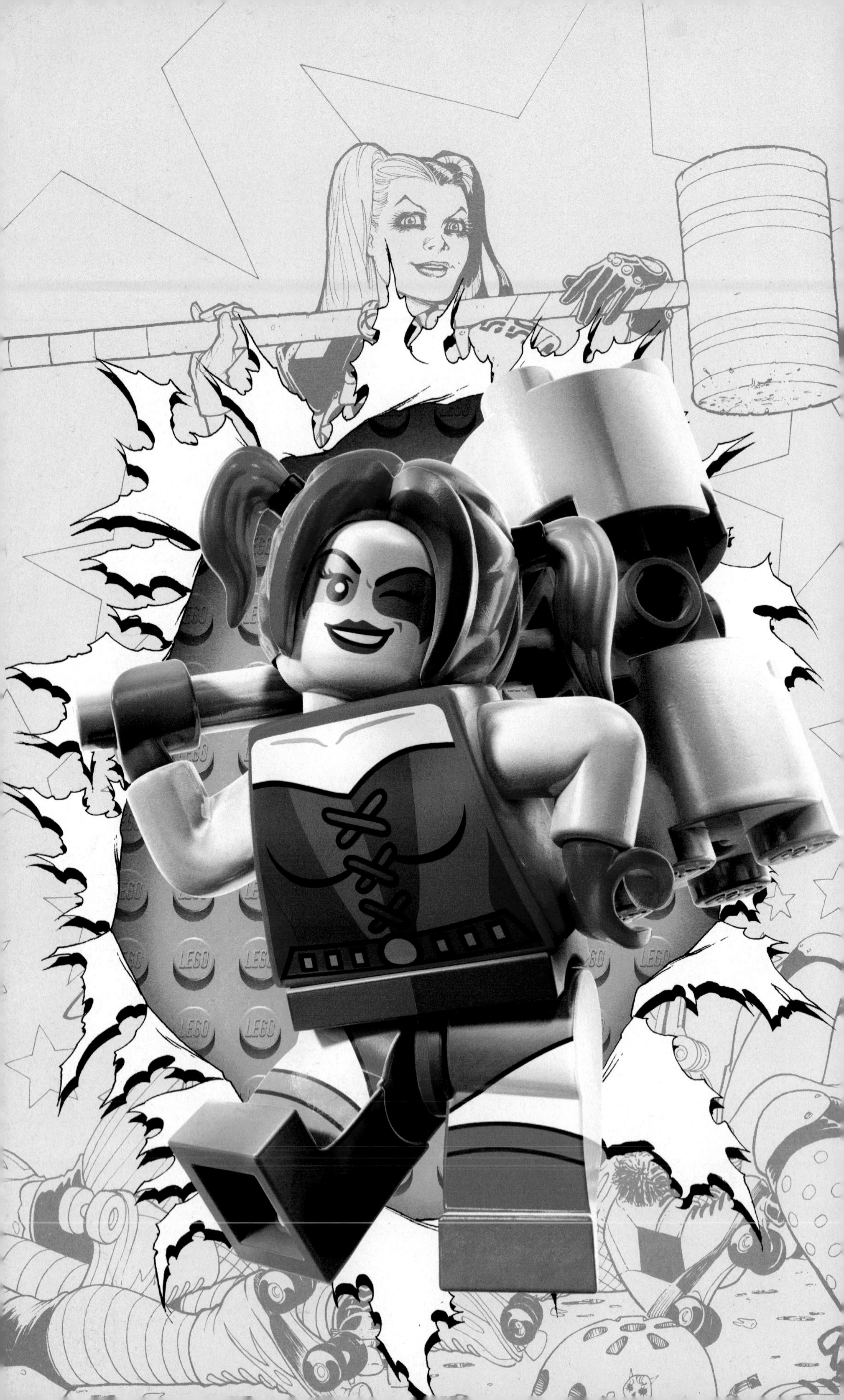

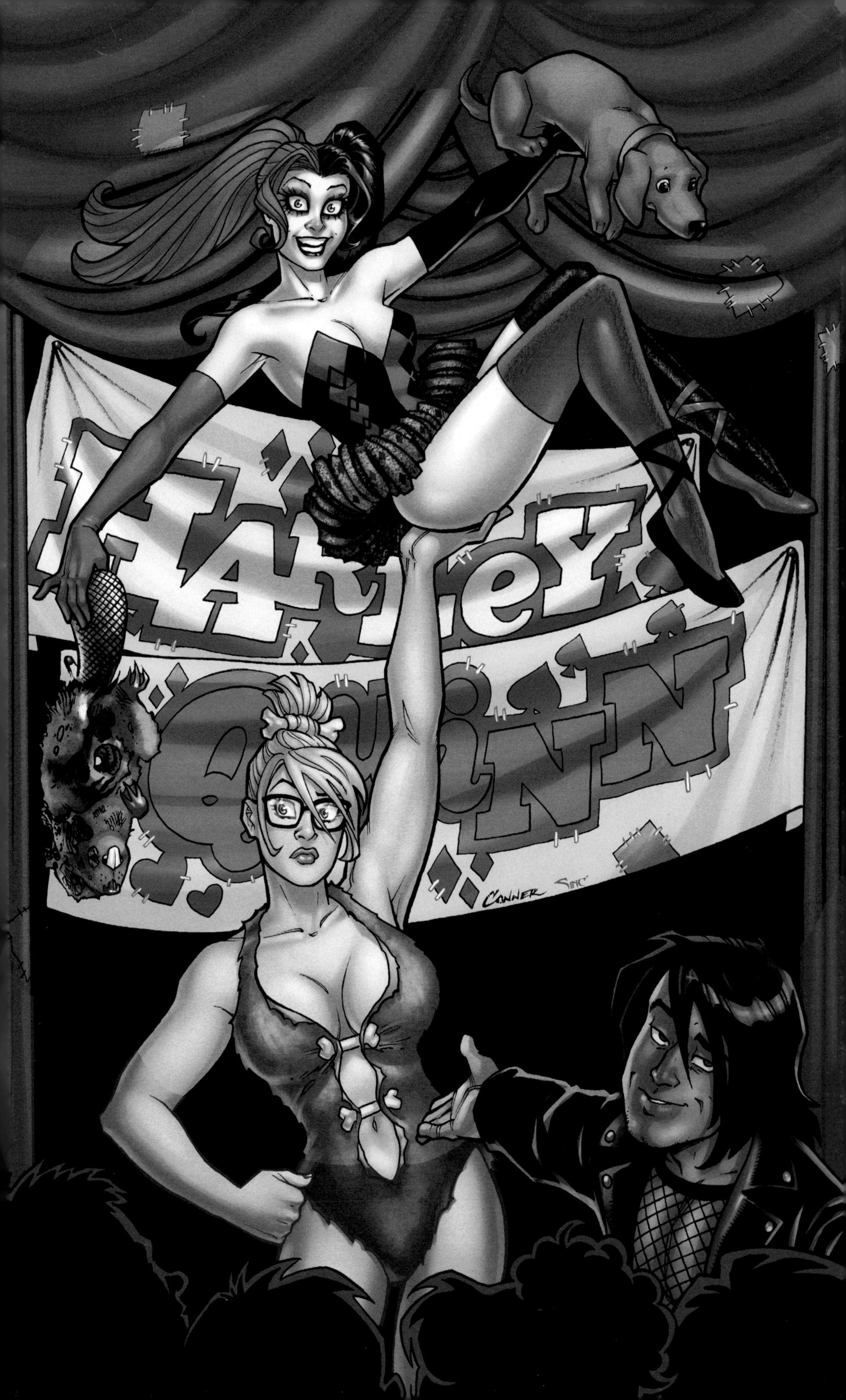
CONNER SINC

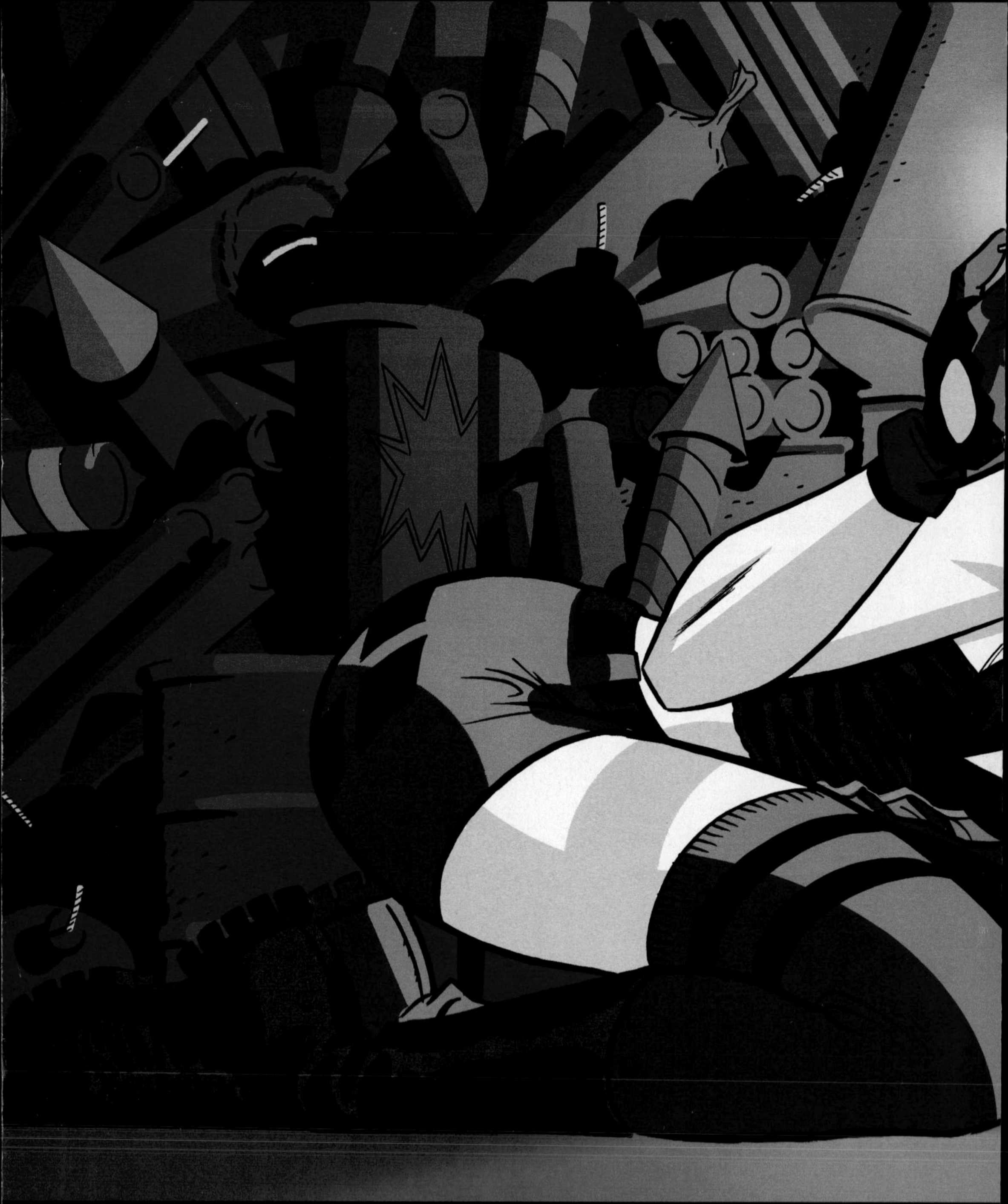

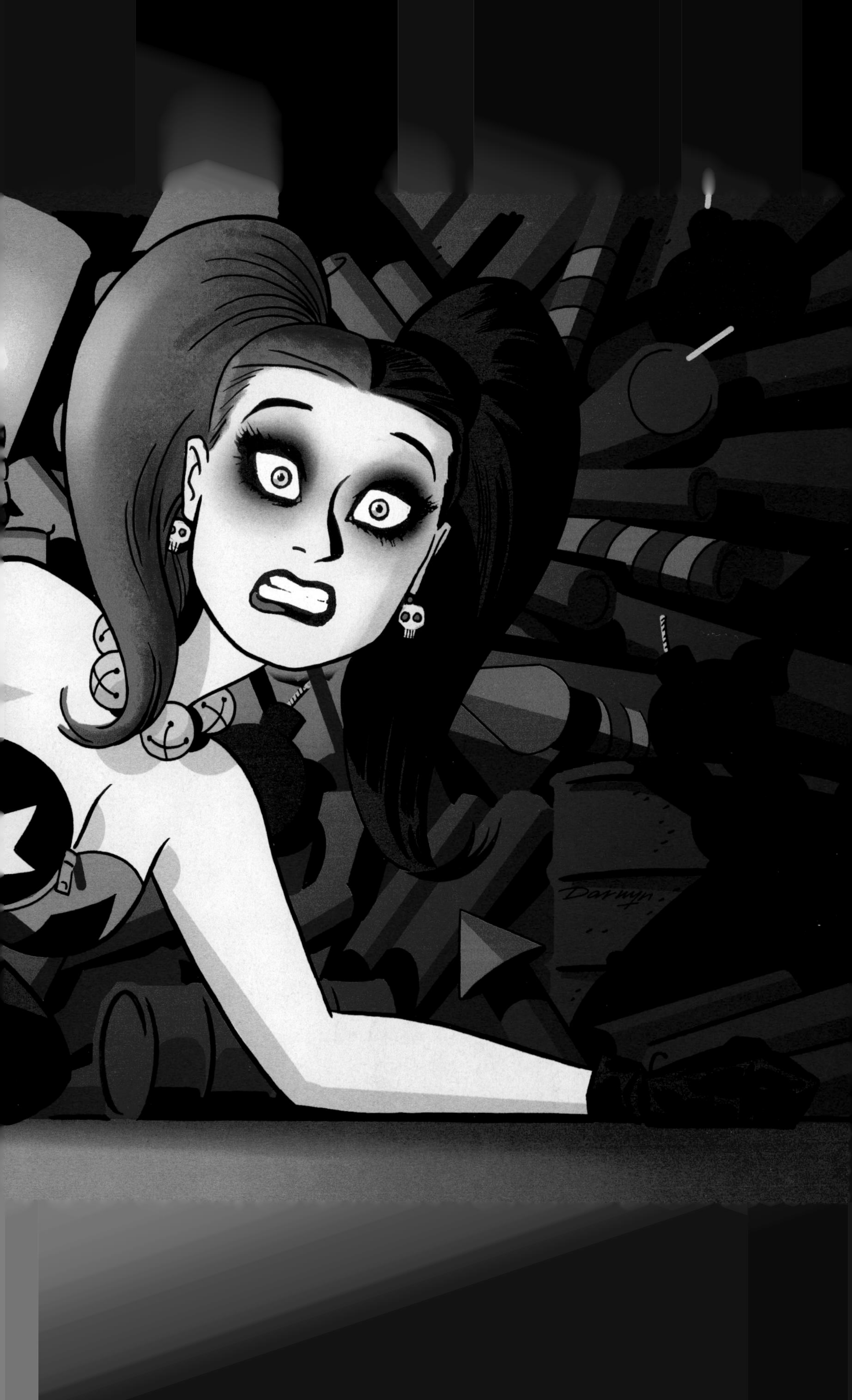

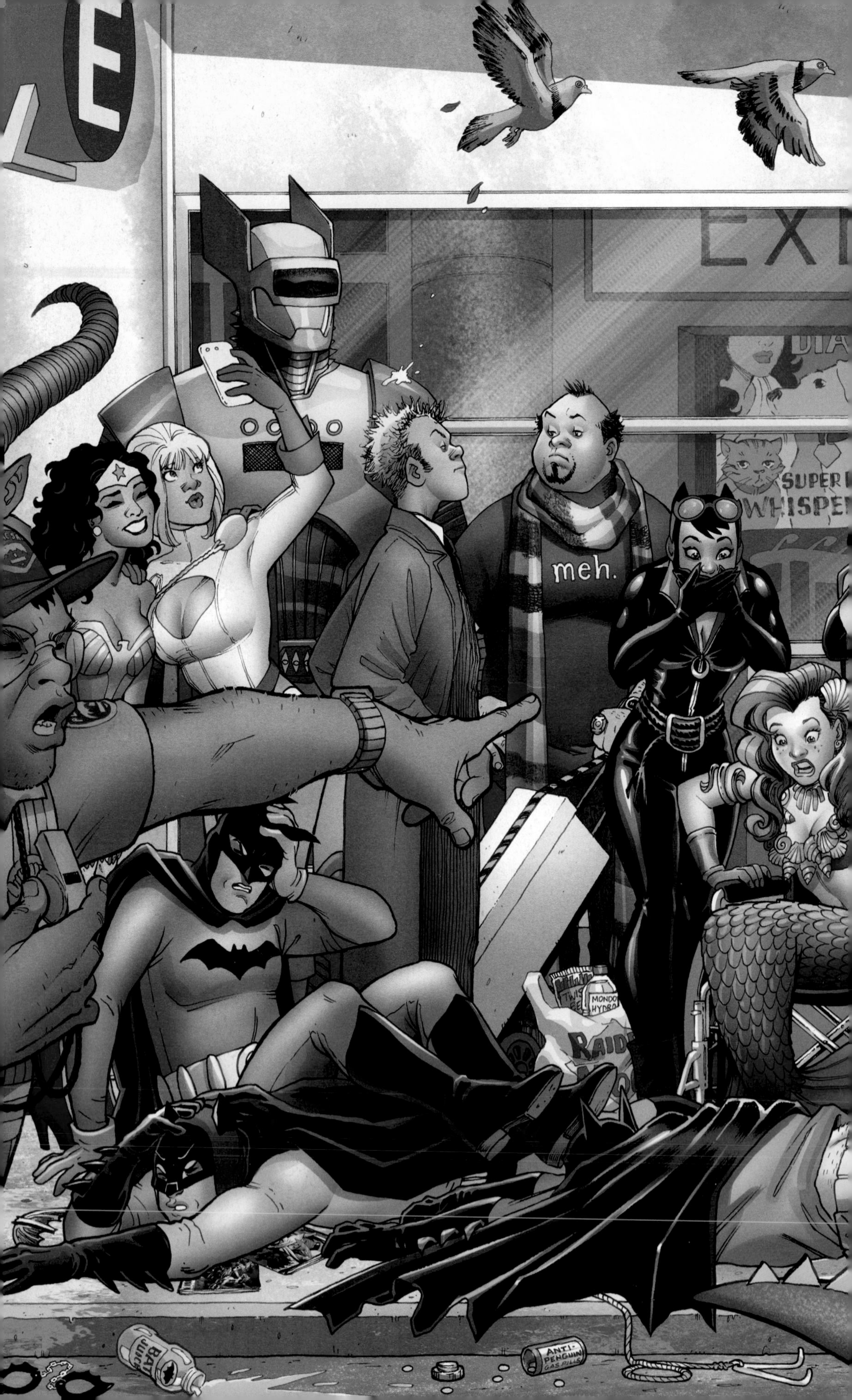
meh.
SUPER
ANTI-PENGUIN GAS PILLS
BAT

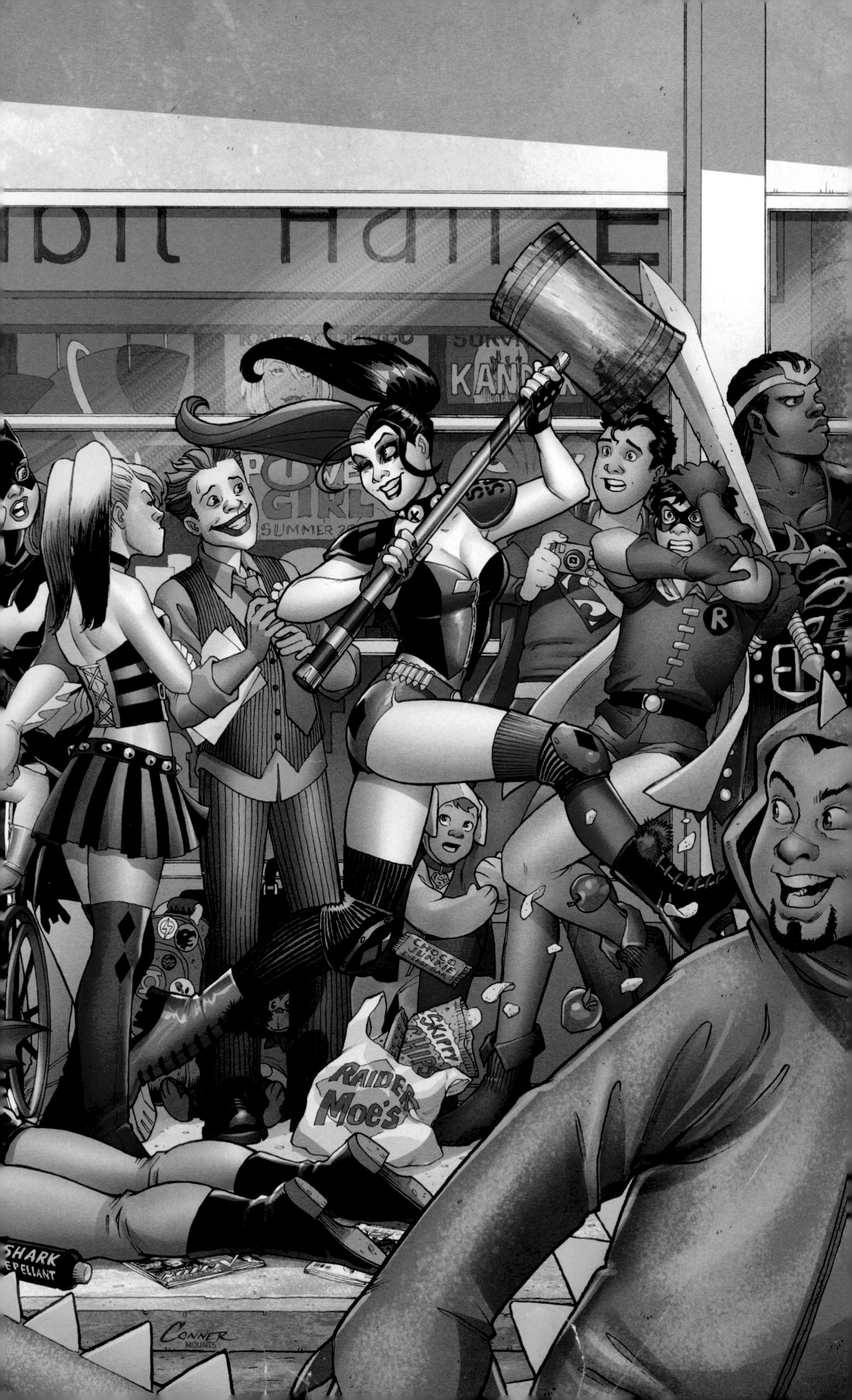
GIRL
CHOCO JUNKIE
ENERGY BAR
SKIPPY CHIPS
RAIDER Moe's
SHARK
CONNER
MOUNTS

Cover sketches by Amanda Conner

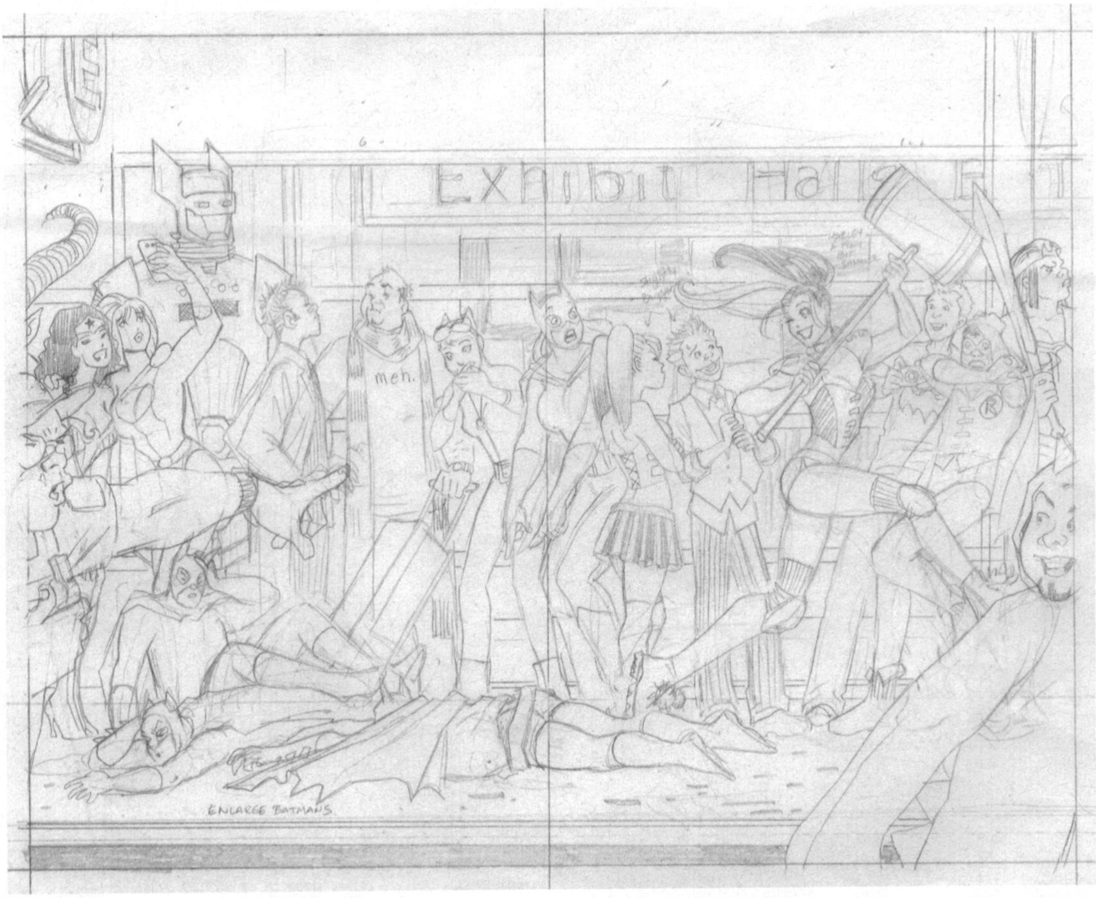

Exhibit
meh.
ENLARGE BATMANS

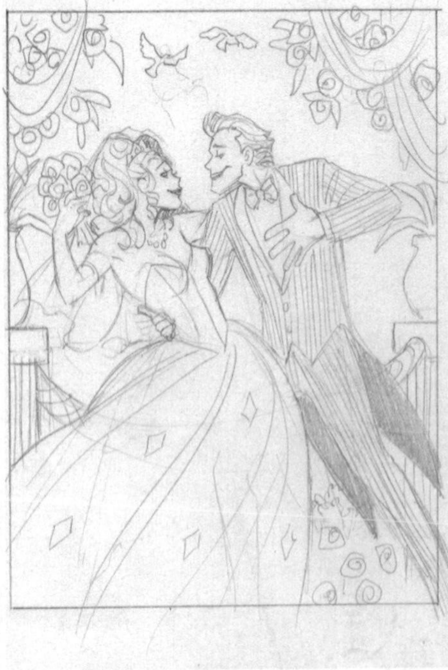

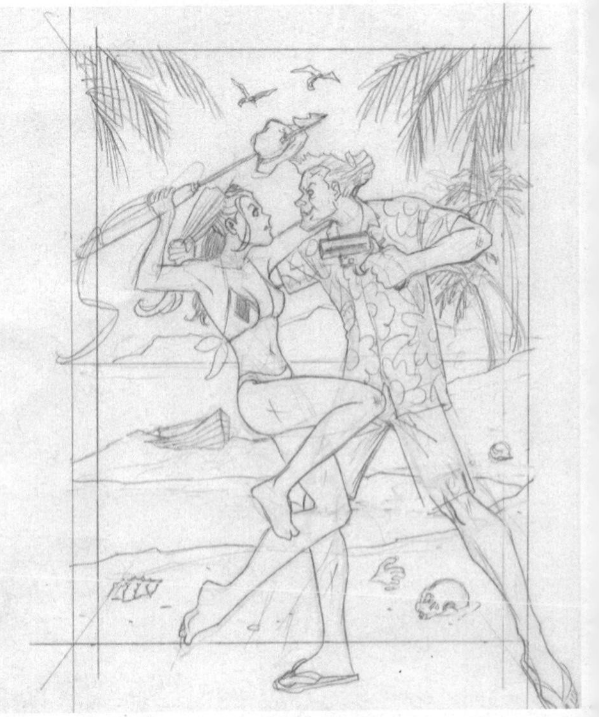

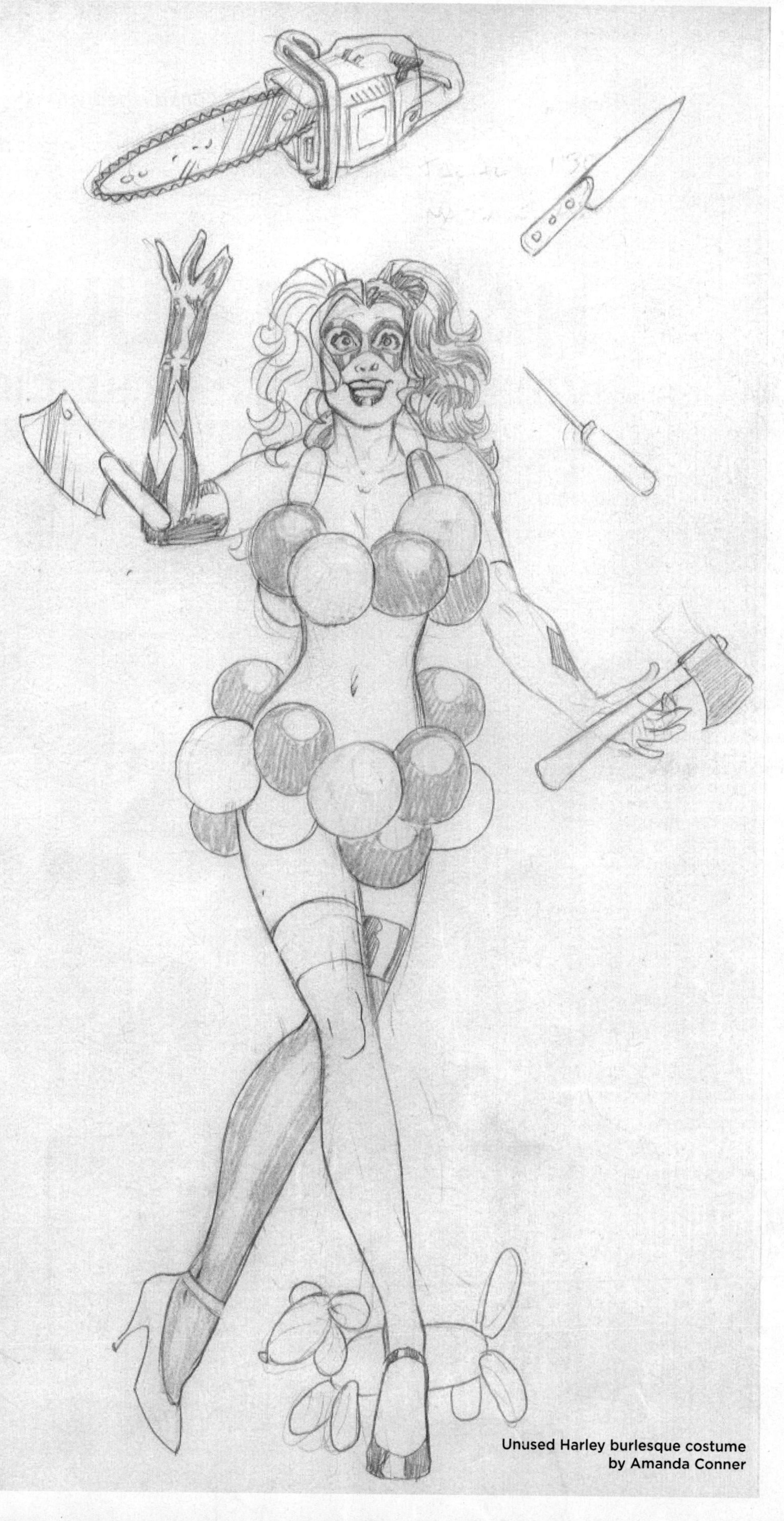

Unused Harley burlesque costume
by Amanda Conner

"Chaotic and unabashedly fun."—IGN

*"I'm enjoying HARLEY QUINN a great deal;
it's silly, it's funny, it's irreverent."*
—COMIC BOOK RESOURCES

HARLEY QUINN
VOLUME 1: HOT IN THE CITY

**SUICIDE SQUAD VOL. 1:
KICKED IN THE TEETH**

**with ADAM GLASS and
FEDERICO DALLOCCHIO**

**HARLEY QUINN:
PRELUDES AND
KNOCK-KNOCK JOKES**

**with KARL KESEL and
TERRY DODSON**

**BATMAN: MAD LOVE
AND OTHER STORIES**

**with PAUL DINI
and BRUCE TIMM**

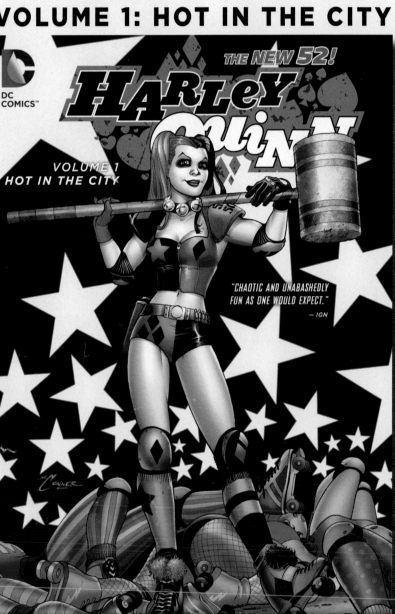